PILSNER

PILSNER

How the Beer of Kings
Changed the World

TOM ACITELLI

CHICAGO
REVIEW
PRESS

Published by Chicago Review Press Incorporated
814 North Franklin Street
Chicago, Illinois 60610
ISBN 978-1-64160-182-5

Library of Congress Cataloging-in-Publication Data
Names: Acitelli, Tom, author.
Title: Pilsner: how the beer of kings changed the world / Tom Acitelli.
Description: Chicago, Illinois: Chicago Review Press, 2020. | Includes
    bibliographical references and index. | Summary: "The remarkable story
    of the world's most popular style of beer, from its humble birth in a
    far corner of the Austrian Empire in 1842 to its present dominance
    worldwide. Shattering myths about the style's origins and immediate
    parentage, this book shows how pilsner influenced everything from
    modern-day advertising and marketing to today's craft beer movement"—
    Provided by publisher.
Identifiers: LCCN 2020007838 | ISBN 9781641601825 (trade paperback) |
    ISBN 9781641601832 (adobe pdf) | ISBN 9781641601856 (epub) |
    ISBN 9781641601849 (kindle edition)
Subjects: LCSH: Anheuser-Busch, Inc.—History. | Brewing industry—
    United States—History. | Busch family.
Classification: LCC HD9397.U54 A8226 2020 | DDC 338.7/663420973—dc23
LC record available at https://lccn.loc.gov/2020007838

Cover design: Jonathan Hahn
Cover image: iStock.com/naumoid
Typesetting: Nord Compo

Printed in the United States of America
5 4 3 2 1

To my brothers, Angelo and Mark

CONTENTS

Introduction

AT THE RIGHT PLACE AND TIME

Cambridge, Massachusetts

On October 10, 1913, Adolphus Busch, the world's largest brewer and one of its richest men, died while holidaying at his estate near the Rhine River in Hesse, Germany, at the age of seventy-four. Among the events that Busch's death triggered was the payment by his widow, Lilly, of nearly $1.4 million to Harvard University for the construction of America's first museum devoted to the art of German-speaking Europe. Adolphus Busch—a prolific philanthropist and fundraiser for causes that included the recovery efforts from the San Francisco earthquake of 1906 and myriad civic improvements in St. Louis, his adopted hometown and seat of his Anheuser-Busch brewery—had already given generously to the museum effort, which stretched back to the late 1890s.

In 1906, Busch, who then had no other connection to Harvard, had donated the equivalent of $50,000 in today's dollars to the effort, and had undertaken to raise even more funds from other wealthy German Americans. He soon despaired of the effort. "I am still working for the good cause, however without flattering prospects," Busch telegraphed Kuno Francke, a German literary scholar at Harvard who had first argued for the museum in 1897. "Most of our millionaires are not deserving their possessions. Providence made a mistake in bestowing wealth upon them." Busch, though, kept at it. He told relatives and associates how much such a museum at America's oldest university would mean to him and to other German Americans. They had, only a short few decades before, been the subject of nativist scorn as thousands, then hundreds of thousands, arrived in America following revolutions and counterrevolutions in their homelands. Nearly one million Germans—almost 5 percent of the US population at the time—had poured in during the 1850s alone. Busch was among that number, though he was better off than most: his parents ran a successful wholesale business in Hesse, selling winemaking and brewing supplies. But as the twenty-first of twenty-two children, Busch knew early on that he could not expect much in the way of inheritance. With three of his brothers, he decamped in 1857 for St. Louis, which was already a popular destination for Germans, who drove an eightfold increase in the city's population from 1840 to 1860.

Such popularity among Germans also meant that St. Louis was a fertile ground for breweries, for the two inevitably went hand in hand—a fact not lost on nativists nervous about the immigrant influx. "Breweries have multiplied, and beer barrels and beer bottles are all around us," Daniel Dorchester, a Mayflower descendant and influential New England politician and clergyman would write in a survey of American drinking habits in the 1800s. In it, Dorchester zeroed in on how the popularity of beer had risen alongside the arrival of "certain elements," as Dorchester described Germans such as Adolphus Busch. In particular, the Germans brought a taste for lighter, crisper lager beer to America, and its popularity spread wherever they put down roots. And the precise style of lager beer that German immigrants and other Americans were gravitating toward "in immense quantities . . . everywhere," according to English chronicler D. W. Mitchell, was pilsner.

While born in 1842 in the city of Pilsen in Bohemia in what was then the Austrian Empire and what is now Czechia, pilsner is at its heart a Bavarian beer, a German creation. Its inventor, an acerbic brewmaster named Josef Groll, was born and raised in Bavaria, and he worked with other Bavarians and Bavarian techniques to develop pilsner. The style's original all-important yeast, the microorganisms that convert the sugary starch of the grains to intoxicating ethanol, came from Bavaria. Bavarian Germans made and popularized its stylistic predecessors, other lighter-looking and lighter-tasting lagers from which pilsner evolved. And it would be mostly Germans who whisked pilsner to America to commence its rocket-ship rise to world ubiquity.

Almost in recognition of the limitations of its geographical marker, pilsner-style beer would end up going by many other names, including "Bohemian lager," "American lager," "continental lager," "adjunct lager," and "light lager"—the last sometimes a catchall for the types of beer that immediately preceded pilsner as well as for the style itself, which would represent the apotheosis of the brewer's art. Brewers of the twenty-first century sometimes describe pilsner as "naked," for like no other style before it, its effervescent clarity offers nowhere for a flaw to hide. The style became the standard of popular beer. Commercially, wherever it went, which was at first usually wherever Germans went, pilsner found a gracious welcome.

Adolphus Busch realized the potential for this brightest and bubbliest of beer styles quicker than most, and he would use pilsner to build his brewing empire, beginning in the 1860s. Its flagship by the 1870s was Budweiser, a Bohemian lager that shared all the hallmarks of pilsner: light-tasting and gold-colored; crisp, even bubbly in mouthfeel; and relatively low in alcohol. Drinkers could knock back pilsners in those "immense quantities" and not feel the same deleterious effects of whiskey and fruit-based alcoholic beverages, the two tipples that pilsner was edging out as the nation's most popular alcoholic beverage. "A dozen years ago," Mitchell noted in 1862, "brandy and whiskey were the popular drinks; now they have, in a great measure, given place to this lager bier, with its three per cent of alcohol."

This popularity unnerved temperance advocates, of which Daniel Dorchester was one. He saw the prohibition of alcohol as "our next emancipation," comparing it to the abolition of slavery in 1865 and the ban on polygamy in 1876. Zealots like Dorchester came tantalizingly close to achieving it: four states—Maine, Vermont, Kansas, and Iowa—had largely banned alcohol production and consumption by 1884, the year of Dorchester's treatise, as had hundreds of counties and municipalities nationwide. But then came the Germans with their pilsner, threatening to gum up the works. (Dorchester titled his chapter on the rise of beer "The Beer Invasion.") Perhaps because it was so much lower in alcohol than whiskey and brandy—and even hard cider, the tipple of choice for so many of Dorchester's fellow New Englanders—beer, especially lighter lagers such as pilsner, seemed a dangerous third way in alcohol consumption. "Specious pleadings have been made for beer, as promotive of health, constitutional development, and even of temperance," Dorchester wrote, "and the example of Germany, as a land of temperance fostered by beer, has been falsely and deceptively advocated."

Still, the "example of Germany" was increasingly hard to avoid in America's cities by the end of the nineteenth century. Conviviality and joviality were the hallmarks of their beer gardens and pubs, their get-togethers and formal festivals. "A German festival is always full of life, spirit, and fun," as one St. Louis newspaper editor put it. An observer in Richmond, Virginia, was so taken with German-infused beer culture that he pronounced it as signaling a turn toward a "new and pleasant phase" for American society in general. Never mind that Germans quickly became celebrated for their industriousness and ambition, living proof that alcohol did not automatically lead to skid row as so many temperance advocates preached.

Of course, Dorchester and his fellow "drys" would win in the end, with Prohibition enacted in 1919 and in force for thirteen years after. It would prove the nadir for pilsner in the United States. After Repeal in 1933, however, pilsner would sweep all before it to become not only the bestselling alcoholic beverage in the United States—a distinction it likely held at the turn of the nineteenth century—but the bestselling beer style in the world, a status it has yet to relinquish and one bestowed despite countless twists on the original. "Imitation pilsners today account for 95 percent of global beer volume— although most of these beers bear little of the character of the original," as *The Oxford Companion to Beer* put it well after the start of the twenty-first century. Pilsner—maker of fortunes like that of Adolphus Busch, scourge of temperance advocates such as Daniel Dorchester, and reshaper of American social life and drinking habits—would achieve a status within a century of its birth that few foodstuffs have ever attained. It was the first truly global alcoholic beverage, its myriad iterations from multiple breweries reproduced to exact specifications and yet on a grand scale that drinks like whiskey, wine, and brandy—with their longer aging times and their mercurial, easily spoiled ingredients—could never mimic. A Budweiser made in St. Louis or a Miller made in Milwaukee tasted and looked the same in Mexico City or Chicago or Pretoria or Peking as it did in its hometown.

To achieve this homogeneity on such a scale, breweries such as Anheuser-Busch, Pabst, Heineken, and Miller had to bend industrialization to their will. They bought distributorships, ice producers, even railroad lines. The mass production and vertical integration of these pilsner producers inspired changes in business that industries as disparate as automobiles and computers picked up on. And it did not stop with the nuts and bolts of pilsner production. Anheuser-Busch and Miller, in particular, led a revolution in marketing and advertising beginning in the late twentieth century that seeped into popular culture and the practices of Madison Avenue and Silicon Valley.

Along the way, this pilsner, this drink of the people, had a way of intersecting with major world events. These intersections began even before its birth in 1842. They continued through the end of the nineteenth century with the rise of imperialism and colonization, and through the two world wars of the twentieth century. It was that first conflagration, which began a year after Adolphus Busch's death in 1913, that stalled his dream of a Germanic art museum at Harvard. Rising anti-German feeling in the United States after the outbreak of the Great War gave university officials pause. They could not possibly sanction a building that included artwork that Kaiser

Wilhelm II, supreme warlord of the German armed forces, had donated. Harvard delayed the opening of the museum in what it called Adolphus Busch Hall until 1921, three years after the war's end. The official reason was "lack of coal."

I live in Cambridge, Massachusetts, around the corner from Adolphus Busch Hall, which was modeled after the castle in Hesse where Busch vacationed and where he eventually died. A mix of medieval and Renaissance design, the building's most striking feature is a capacious main hall inspired by the naves of churches from the Middle Ages, complete with a barrel ceiling and large pillars around arched windows. It's a sanctuary for many of the original donations for the Germanic museum, including plaster casts of German works from the kaiser, though the bulk of the collection moved on to other Harvard buildings in the early 1990s. Adolphus Busch Hall is also one of the many tangible signs of the influence of pilsner throughout the past two centuries and a reminder of the surprisingly small group of characters who shaped its rise.

The world had never seen a beer as bright and bubbly as pilsner. To be sure, there had been pale beers and beers with exceptional clarity, particularly from the part of the world from which pilsner came, but never one golden like the pilsner first produced in 1842, nor one quite as effervescent. What's more, it was born during a creative supernova in Europe that also produced marvels such as the railroad, the transatlantic steamer, the telegraph, the penny post (which revolutionized mail and communications), and photography. Never mind that the same mid-nineteenth-century period saw the rise of tectonic political, economic, and artistic ideas, including Marxism, Romanticism, and nationalism—the last turning out to be integral to the spread of pilsner beyond its Bohemian nest. Its home continent's rapid industrialization, and therefore its pivot away from a primarily agrarian way of life, played right into pilsner's rise, too. "It was a time of endings and beginnings, of changes of great magnitude in science, social structure, communications, politics, political and economic thought, and literature," the Princeton historian Jerome Blum would write. "These changes led to revolutionary transformations in the way that men for long centuries had lived and thought."

It's no surprise that this most transformative of moments in brewing occurred smack-dab in the middle of such a transformative epoch. Pilsner was a product of its time and place, feeding off both as the yeast feeds off sugar during fermentation. For pilsner might have remained a curiosity of central European food and drink well into the twentieth, if not twenty-first, century, as had so many beer styles, were it not for the age's scientific advancements and industrial scramble. For one thing, given that it was the color of gold (or sunshine) when the next lightest beer styles were reddish or amber, pilsner looked particularly appealing and unique in bottles and glasses, which came along en masse just when the style needed them to in order to spread. Were it not for the political tumult, pilsner likely never would have made it to America, where it mutated and grew to conquer palates and production lines worldwide. Pilsner picked the best time to be born, and the best time to leave home.

In the end, it became one of the most ubiquitous features of food and drink in the modern era, an omnipresence in the business world and in national cultures. When the offshoot of the company that Adolphus Busch cofounded with his father-in-law Eberhard Anheuser acquired its biggest rival in 2016, it was the biggest consumer business deal ever by dollar volume—not just in brewing, but *ever*. When commentators in Manhattan or Washington, DC, sought ways to describe the typical Donald Trump voter in the wake of the 2016 presidential election, they reached for some reference to beer drinking—and the most popular beer style in the United States remains pilsner. So thoroughly does pilsner dominate the international beer market that large chunks of its history read like a history of the brewing industry itself, particularly in the United States, where the style really took off.

In fact, it's almost too popular, a victim of its own stunning success. "Today, for most beer drinkers, pilsner is simply synonymous with lager," the British beer critic Pete Brown explained in 2012. Much of it is homogenous, interchangeable, the only real differences the labels and the slogans. That ubiquity and homogeneity spurred a backlash beginning in the late 1970s that saw styles such as India pale ale and porter—which the rise of pilsner had nearly killed off—return in popularity, particularly with younger consumers. Only since the late 1990s has pilsner begun to enjoy a voguish return stylistically, whatever its sales. It has turned a corner in taste as smaller breweries tackle the challenge of this most naked of beers and consumers embrace the results in assessments as probing as those they usually reserve for IPA, the most popular style among the craft beer set. This attention has infused pilsner with fresh commercial lifeblood and likely ensured its health for decades to come.

This book tells the story of the rise of pilsner in all its tentacular glory to every corner of the globe. In doing so, it shows how it survived and thrived, while other paler, lighter styles stalled—Neanderthals to pilsner's modern human. This book also debunks myths about pilsner's creation and rise—not least the myth of Pilsner as a Czech rather than a Bavarian glory—a rise that Adolphus Busch summed up neatly very early on. When he was trying to come up with a slogan for his newly bottled Budweiser pilsner in the 1890s, Busch inverted the old Bohemian slogan for pilsner: "the beer of kings."

PART I

1

A DIVINE PLAN

Circa 820–1516 | St. Gall, Switzerland

The Plan of St. Gall is the only surviving full architectural drawing from the seven centuries between the western Roman Empire's fall in the late 400s and the second century of the Middle Ages in the 1200s. It details how monks in the tradition of St. Benedict, the patron saint of Europe who died in 547, planned to enlarge a nearly century-old self-sustaining community in a mountainous area near Lake Constance in present-day Switzerland beginning around 820. As monks were among the few peoples who wrote much down in Europe in those centuries, the Plan of St. Gall is a particularly attractive document for historians and others wanting to know what was considered necessary and important at that time. It survived only because an unknown monk who saw it in the late twelfth century had the foresight to fold it just so and preserve it within the abbey's library, where it remains, as one historian put it, "a very detailed sketch of the 'ideal monastery' . . . where the whole world is reordered to the service of God."

Beer was apparently an important part of that divine order, right up there with the salvation to be found in the churches planned for the site, the knowledge to be gleaned from a proposed library, and the sustenance to be found via the animals of the stables. The Plan of St. Gall includes what are essentially blueprints for three separate breweries. It appears the monks never got these breweries up and running simultaneously, but their designs remain the oldest on record for larger-scale brewing in Europe, proof of beer's prominence on the Continent and a foreshadowing of what was to come a thousand years later.

One of the breweries planned for St. Gall was for guests, one for monks, and one for the religious pilgrims and the poor. The Rule of St. Benedict, upon which this and other monasteries were built, required the monks to welcome the stranger, however indigent. Beer was the prime beverage offered to these and other arrivals, especially in areas of northern and central Europe where grain was more plentiful than grapes for wine—and primarily because it was not water. Water could be brackish, dangerous, difficult to deliver clean, and often unpleasant to drink. Beer was different—purer and, then as now, often delicious. It was the boiling that rendered it purer. The boiling destroyed bacteria that the monks could not see or understand, much like they could not see or understand the yeast or its role in fermentation. They just knew that beer invariably ended up a healthier, tastier alternative than water, and they needed it for their many guests. It was integral to monasteries. Monks throughout Europe became the most proficient brewers and were likely the first to pivot toward producing beer on a larger scale.

The beer the monks would have made—that anyone would have made, all the way back to the earliest brewers in the mountains of present-day Iran, four millennia before the common era—was dark, rich, and sometimes chunky, with the consistency of watery oatmeal. Filtration was nonexistent and malting, or roasting, of grains invariably produced dark varieties, which in turn produced dark beer. What's more, the whole thing was poorly defined. Much of what brewers produced for millennia was ale because its yeast fermented at the top of the brewing vat rather than the bottom, producing a foamy, creamy layer during fermentation. The word *ale* to describe this subset of beer, though, did not come into vogue until the 1800s and even later in some parts of the world. *Beer* generally sufficed.

Beer was and is understood to be fermented grain, whatever the grain might be, plus seasoning. That seasoning before modern times might have been as varied as tree bark, plant roots, and herbs such as rosemary and thyme. Hops, a crisply bitter flower, became standard only in the fifteenth century. Before then, hops would have been known mostly as a medicine, a reputation that continued even after their integration into beer. Lord Sidmouth, a British prime minister under George III, was said to have recommended a pillow full of hops to aid his sovereign's sleep. Because of the lack of filtration and the conditions under which beer fermented—usually in open vessels—bits of these herbs, barks, roots, and hops showed up floating in the finished product, rendering it that much darker, that much less clear. Yeast's role in converting the sugars of the grains into intoxicating ethanol wasn't fully understood yet, but the detritus from that top-fermenting yeast would often show up too—slinky, slippery little gobs that looked not unlike mold spores.

For thousands upon thousands of years, this was beer, even as the monks' largish ad hoc operations gave way to standardization and to the first hints of commercial brewing, by which designated brewers made beer for profit under this or that government license—and some did quite well given their preindustrial limitations. In 1610 in Munich, capital of the brewing juggernaut that was then the independent dukedom of Bavaria, nearly one in five commercial brewers belonged to the highest level of taxpayers. All thirty-two of Antwerp's commercial breweries by the late 1660s belonged to that Dutch city's wealthiest 5 percent. The beers they produced did gradually shed some of the herbs and barks, etcetera, settling on malted barley, water, and hops as the main ingredients—again, yeast was largely a mystery—and styles began to take shape, though all beer remained more or less inky and thick ales.

What's more, ale seeped into culture, both popular and highbrow, becoming that much more synonymous with beer. Ale in central and northern Europe was a drink for both the commoner and the lord of the manor, a reassuringly everyday accoutrement to existences that were often nasty, brutish, and short. "Would I were in an alehouse in London! I would give all my fame for a pot of ale and safety," Shakespeare would have a character declare in act 3 of *Henry V*, written in the late 1590s. "It is better to think of church in the alehouse than to think of the alehouse in church," went a quotation attributed to Protestant reformer Martin Luther, such a big imbiber that his friends nicknamed him "the king of hops." Even if Shakespeare, who died in 1611, and Luther, who died in 1546, had somehow lived all the way into the early 1800s, they would still have been familiar with any beer they might have encountered in their native lands, for it changed little in the intervening two centuries. Then it changed a lot, and fast.

2

LAGER AND ITS RIVALS

1516–1818 | Ingolstadt, Bavaria

Wilhelm Wittelsbach was twenty-three when he ascended to the throne of the duchy of Bavaria in March 1508 upon the death of his father. A later print showed a stout man with a square jaw covered in a wiry brown beard. He looked intense and burdened. Maybe so, for Wilhelm's family had controlled the statelet of Bavaria—which by the time of his ascension covered much of what would become southern Germany, including bits of the Tyrolean Alps in present-day Italy—since the late 1100s. Agriculture was the major industry, and hops were among the major crops. Not inconsequently, beer was a major part of the Bavarian economy and the duchy's culture. But as beer made that transition from monastic by-product to commercial staple in the late Middle Ages, its quality had degraded. Brewers, even in beer-crazy Bavaria, were still tossing in herbs, roots, even soot to both pad out their recipes and hide defects as they hustled to meet demand. Duke Wilhelm IV, as he styled himself, sought to put a stop to such practices. He also wanted to prevent brewers from using wheat as a grain in beer—better to have that for bread to feed his subjects—and to stop what had become wild and wide fluctuations in the price of beer. Wilhelm also knew that narrowing what went into beer could help him in collecting taxes on the beverage and its ingredients.

So on April 23, 1516, before a gathering of noblemen and other gentry in the courtyard of Ingolstadt's New Castle (so named because the castle dated only from the previous century) on the banks of the Danube River, Wilhelm decreed that all beers made in Bavaria would be made only from water, hops, and barley (he, like everyone else, did not understand, much less fully comprehend, the role of yeast). What came to be called the Reinheitsgebot was the world's first known food purity law, a landmark of autocratic legislation whose influence would fan out from Ingolstadt to the rest of the Germanic states in the coming four centuries—and then to the world. It would especially ride the rise of lager.

Lager, the other big subset of beer besides ale, was born of a hybrid yeast strain, part of which might have been born and raised in South America—for yeast is a living organism—before decamping for Europe aboard one or more boats plying the Atlantic. The yeast ferments on the bottom of the kettle rather than on the top as with ales, leaving behind a cleaner, clearer beer generally lighter in taste and lower in alcoholic kick. Lager also tends to crackle with carbonation more than ales, which develop deeper, thicker, stiller heads when poured, while lagers' might be wispily thin and shorter lived. Lager only hit its stride in the nineteenth century. Until then, beer usually became a lager or an ale by accident. Ale yeast grows faster than lager yeast and can ferment at warmer temperatures. The slower-growing lager yeast can only really ferment at a sustained cooler temperature. So a mash of grains and hops left out tended to ferment into an ale because invariably the temperature around it was warmer—and, besides, the ale yeast got to the sugars in the grains more quickly.

But brewers in central and northern Europe, in present-day Bavaria, in particular, eventually discovered that storing mashes in cooler caves and caverns fostered the growth of the yeast that produced lagers. The practice was common by the start of the nineteenth century—*lager* comes from the German *lagern*, meaning "to store"—even if the yeasts themselves had yet to be isolated for easy replication and despite the length of time and the amount of labor it took to store the beer for fermentation and aging. Ale's relatively fast fermentation and its resiliency at nearly all temperatures had aided its march out of the Middle East millennia before and had sustained its dominance before the dawn of mechanical refrigeration in the late nineteenth century. But lager was a presence by the early 1800s, especially in what became southern Germany. Part of this had to do with geography. There were copious caverns and caves to choose from in the Alps. Another part was Duke Wilhelm's decree, which had the almost immediate effect of slamming the brakes on any innovation in beer style in southern Germany.

The Reinheitsgebot shoehorned brewers in Bavaria into using only certain ingredients and proportions of those ingredients. While the beers they produced became some of the most popular and imitated in central and northern Europe, they were more remarkable for their uniformity than for their individuality. It was beer streamlined, boiled down—literally and figuratively—to its basics. But that was fine for Wilhelm and his subjects. The most popular type of Bavarian beer post–purity decree was a relatively simple lager called *dunkel*. "For many years [it] was the everyday beer of Bavaria," according to the brewmaster and critic Garrett Oliver. "When the Reinheitsgebot first came into force in 1516," he explained, "most of the beer made in Bavaria was an early form of dunkel."

It only grew in reach after the purity law. Dunkel was dark in color (hence the name, from the German for "dark"), mildly heavy in mouthfeel, lower in alcohol than most ales, and easy to drink one after the other—perfect for a society in which beer was an ordinary foodstuff and the year revolved around the procession of Catholic feast days. In fact, that original decree from Wilhelm referenced brewing from St. Michael's Day on September 29 to St. George's Day on April 23—in other words, the coolest days of the Bavarian calendar, and therefore the choicest months for brewing lagers that depended on cooler temperatures. Wilhelm's son—Albrecht V, an avid beer fan like his father and one of the world's great coin collectors, to boot—went on to ban brewing altogether during the warmer months between these saintly feast days. It was another way to ensure quality in beer. It worked. It enhanced the reputation of southern Germany's beers for clarity and uniformity and that of its brewers for their technical prowess for making it so. Yet, taken together, the dukes' decrees ensured that southern Germany would not be an incubator of change in brewing, which in these centuries of ignorance of yeast strains and bacteria nonetheless remained more of an art than a science anyway.

Change instead would fall to brewers farther north—in particular, the United Kingdom and what became Belgium. In these places, multiple styles flourished that had little in common with the Bavarians' clean, smooth dunkel. The United Kingdom, which then included Ireland, became especially well known for two ales that were pretty much opaque in appearance, with a richness that bordered on creaminess in taste. Porter was a brownish- to black-colored style dating from the 1700s and born in England of the darker malt roasts so common in the era. For a time, it was probably the world's bestselling beer, given the ballooning reach of the British Empire and its business allies, such as the East India Company, which would come to control a sizable chunk of the Indian subcontinent. A September 1759 request to a London merchant from a country squire in the English colony of Virginia read, "1 Hogshead best Porter." George Washington's request was one of several times the future Founding Father would order, or simply praise, porter. Stout, an equally brownish-black though sweeter cousin of porter, also came into its own in the eighteenth century, not least behind the growth of St. James's Gate Brewery (home of Guinness), which started in Dublin the same year Washington requested his hogshead, or sixty-four-gallon cask.

Meanwhile, in what became Belgium in 1830, brewers experimented with fruit in beer, crafting styles such as the cherry-infused *kriek* or the raspberry-flavored *framboise*, both of which were versions of a sour wheat-based beer subset called *lambic*. Then there were the more esoteric Germanic styles beyond Bavaria, including *gose* out of the town of Goslar. It had a salty taste via the water from the Gose River and a sourness that some found pleasing but that virtually assured its anonymity beyond northern Europe until American craft beer fans discovered it. There was *Berliner weisse*, too, a lower-alcohol beer from the North Sea port of Hamburg that was also sour as well as bubbly and that became a particular favorite of Napoleon's invading French soldiers, who likened it to champagne. None of these would enjoy the popularity of porter or stout, the leading ales of the day by the 1800s, and none would enjoy even the localized popularity of dunkel in Bavaria, probably the most referenced lager of the day, if for nothing more than its clarity and uniformity.

But none of these, in turn, would prove as popular or as influential as a style that arose in the United Kingdom during the same period. It caused a sensation, particularly among brewers in Germanic lands such as Austria and Bavaria because it was unlike anything anyone had seen in beer's long, long history. So . . . pale.

3

THIEVES ABROAD

1818–1833 | Burton-upon-Trent, England; Schwechat, Austrian Empire; Munich

The young Austrian visitor casually dipped his specially designed walking stick into the fermenting beer in the English brewery, waited a few seconds, and then removed it just as casually. Anton Dreher had gotten what he wanted: some of that internationally famous English pale ale in the making to take back to his lodgings and analyze.

Dreher was twenty-three years old in 1833, and three years away from taking over the Schwechat brewery that his father had acquired near Vienna in 1796 after emigrating from the Lake Constance area bordering Bavaria, Switzerland, and the Austrian Empire. A lithograph of the younger Dreher thirty years later would show a tall, pear-shaped man with a thin, drooping mustache and a similarly lean spool of brown hair above a high forehead, large ears, and a particularly prominent, beaked nose. His eyes were sharp and vacant, as if Dreher were staring off into a distance few others could see. As it was, he was in England as part of a long fact-finding mission on behalf of his father's brewery. He and his companions had visited breweries in Munich (then the capital of an independent Bavarian kingdom), Scotland, and London—and the English countryside. This was how research in brewing was done then, with sometimes surreptitious visits to competitors that often involved months on the road.

In particular, Dreher and company had made their way in sailboats, carriages, and on foot to Burton-upon-Trent, then and now one of the most famous brewing locales in the beer-quaffing world. It was there that Dreher's specially designed walking sticks got their true workout. The sticks were born of the necessity for samples, samples that could not be had because Dreher and his traveling companions from central Europe were never left unsupervised around the fermenting beer they saw. By the time they got to Burton-upon-Trent, Dreher and company realized that the flasks they had originally brought were simply not going to cut it. The flasks were too obvious. "Our art of stealing, which we became especially masterly in, furnished us already with an almost complete fermentation," a companion of Dreher's wrote in a letter home. The companion went on, "Nevertheless, I feel daily a shiver running down my spine when we enter the brewery and I count myself fortunate to come out of it without getting a beating. In order to avoid it in the future, we are now having walking sticks made of steel, lacquered, with a valve at the lower end, so that when the stick is dipped, it fills. When taken out, the valve closes and we have the beer in the stick and that way we can steal more safely."

And so it went. When Dreher's party arrived in Burton-upon-Trent in 1833, the town was just on the cusp of a phenomenal late-nineteenth-century growth spurt that would see its population grow from around seven thousand to more than thirty thousand by 1900. Much of that growth would be thanks to twin revolutions in transportation—in particular the railroad, but also improvements in England's already-vaunted canal system—and in industrialization, which brought workers and their families in from the country to toil in manufacturing plants. Some of Burton-upon-Trent's most robust manufacturers were its breweries. Prominent names such as Bass and Allsopp had been churning out ales since the late 1700s, employing first dozens and then thousands, and exporting their wares to the far corners of the United Kingdom and even to the Continent. This was no small feat in an age when goods moved at the speed of wind or horses and ale in general did not travel well, bacteria a specific—and then anonymous—menace as the drink sloshed along in barrels. Ale was best drunk nearest its source. But the successful exportation of the Burton-upon-Trent brews meant that all the way over in central Austria Dreher had come upon the beer and had hatched his reconnaissance mission.

Burton-upon-Trent was the high point of that mission. Brewing in the enclave dated from at least the eleventh century, when monks built a Benedictine abbey beside the River Trent in the then-lush forestland about halfway between Birmingham and Nottingham. By the end of the century, the abbey's beer had obtained at least a little dash of fame. Verse said to be from 1295 by an unknown poet went:

> The Abbot of Burton brewed good ale,
> On Fridays when they fasted.
> But the Abbot of Burton never tasted his own
> As long as his neighbor's lasted.

An inventory of rental properties in the town of eighteen hundred a quarter century later found no brewers among the tradespeople—only the abbey produced any sort of beer for wider consumption. That reality held for at least another 220 years or so, changing only in 1540, when Henry VIII in establishing the Church of England dissolved Catholic monasteries. The abbey at Burton-upon-Trent ceased to exist, its land and resources appropriated. Smaller brewers gradually took over its brewing trade, and by the early eighteenth century the renown of the beers of Burton-upon-Trent stretched all the way to London more than two days' travel south. "At Lichfield, the ale is incomparable, as it is all over this county of Stafford," Daniel Defoe, a writer most famous for the novel *Robinson Crusoe*, noted at the time. "Burton is the most famous town for it," he claimed, going on to remark that "the best character you can give to ale in London is calling it Burton Ale, and that they brew, in London, some that goes by that denomination."

It was probably initially the water supply that made Burton's beers so sought after. Wells provided water particularly high in calcium and magnesium sulfates. Such "hard water," then as now, was freakishly ideal for brewing ales. By the time Anton Dreher rolled in a century and a half after Defoe wrote, a technical innovation had enhanced not only the taste of Burton beers from places such as Bass and Allsopp but, crucially for the future of food and drink worldwide, the appearance, too. Breweries in Burton, most famously Bass, were using a wood-barrel, gravity-powered fermentation system that clumsily yet steadily separated out the yeast. That separation left behind unusually pellucid beer, the best example yet of what came to be called pale ale.

The style name said it all: it was the clearest, most detritus-free beer anyone had ever seen, even though it still looked reddish, or like amber at its lightest. Breweries in northern Europe and the United Kingdom had been producing pale ale since the 1700s, primarily through roasting malts to a lighter color. That practice took a giant leap forward in 1818, when an English engineer named Daniel Wheeler patented an invention for more uniformly roasting the malts used in brewing. Before, brewers generally spread the malt on a perforated floor and lit a fire underneath from wood, coal, or coke. The result was not only an unevenness in the roasting—with some malts roasted faster and more deeply than others—but a general darkness and smokiness. Some would get scorched, in fact. The resulting beer could be unappetizingly smoky-tasting and opaque. Wheeler's invention replaced the floor kiln with a revolving metal drum that never exposed the grain directly to the fire. Now, for the first time, brewers could easily adjust the darkness or lightness of their malts. Paler ales—and pale ale—became that much more common in the United Kingdom.

It was the rudimentary filtration system, however—the gravity powered contraptions that cleared out much of the yeast and left behind a clearer beer—that made Burton brews the finest examples yet of pale ale. What's more, Burton's brewing triumph was a great example of how a regional beer style could spread from its hometown to well beyond. Not every style could or would. Taste held some back. Some just weren't the sort of beer one drank one after the other. The inability to reproduce for audiences farther from the brewery stymied the spread of others. Then there were those styles such as porter and stout in the United Kingdom that leaped upon a larger commercial stage only because of the growing fortunes of their home countries. For instance, by 1833, the year Anton Dreher visited Burton-upon-Trent, Guinness was shipping its stout as far afield as South Carolina, West Africa, and Barbados—each in the political and/or the commercial orbits of the United Kingdom.

One of Dreher's traveling companions—the one who wrote home about his gratitude over not getting beaten for stealing samples—would have known or have learned about all this, for he was steeped in brewing as much as Dreher, if not more so. Blond-haired, with a blond mustache below a low, prominent nose, Gabriel Sedlmayr was barely past his twentieth birthday when he journeyed from Munich to England and elsewhere with his older colleague Dreher. Like Dreher, Sedlmayr was on a bit of a reconnaissance mission for his father. In Sedlmayr's case, his father, also named Gabriel Sedlmayr, owned the Spaten brewery, which was the third largest in Munich. The elder Sedlmayr had purchased it through a brewmaster at the Bavarian royal court in 1807, four years before the birth of his firstborn son and namesake. It already had had quite a history by then, having started life as a brewpub—a brewery that made and sold its wares on the same site—in 1397, adapting to centuries of evolution in beer and brewing as the beverage wended its way from monastic mainstay to commercial juggernaut in central Europe. By the time the Späth family acquired the brewery in 1622—and named it after itself, Spaten, which means "spade" in German—it was best known for turning out those deceptively simple yet popular lagers called dunkel for a Bavarian market that expected consistency.

The more than three-hundred-year-old Reinheitsgebot had shoehorned the brewers into using but a handful of ingredients, but there was nothing that said that brewers could not play within those constraints. Government imposition and that tradition—long tradition—demanded only that certain ingredients be used to make beer in Bavaria and other southern German states. Neither dictated much about techniques. And were not brewers in England using techniques to craft beers that no one alive had seen or tasted before? Now it was the Germans' turn.

4

OVER THE HORIZON

1838–1848 | New York City; Munich; Schwechat, Austria

The stars shone upon New York City on a crystal clear night as the crowds gathered at the Battery wharf in Lower Manhattan. It was April 22, 1838, a Sunday, the only day of the week that most laborers and civil servants had off. All day and for several days prior, news had been rippling through New York about the impending arrival of two ships over the horizon: the *Sirius* and the *Great Western*. Each had left the United Kingdom at least a couple of weeks before—the newspapers said different things—with the 703-ton *Sirius* leaving from Cork on Ireland's southern shore and the 1,320-ton *Great Western* via England's River Severn. They were racing to New York.

Both the *Sirius* and the *Great Western* were top-of-the-line steamships. This was important. For as long as anyone alive could remember, crossing the Atlantic involved sailing, and sailing ships took anywhere from a few weeks to nearly three months to traverse the Atlantic, with speed and even navigation hostage to the weather. The first steamships had begun plying the ocean between the Old and New Worlds in 1819, cutting the crossing time first by days and then by weeks. But none until the *Sirius* and the *Great Western* had really been designed to make the crossing at a particularly brisk pace. Nor were potential customers quite sold on steamships traveling that fast on the open waters. Disastrous steamship explosions were depressingly common. The gawkers at Manhattan's Battery on April 22 almost certainly did not know yet, but the day before a collapsed flue caused the explosion of a steamship on the Mississippi River, killing more than one hundred people. The private backers and designers behind the *Sirius* and the *Great Western* were trying to prove a point then, one that aviators would find themselves having to prove a hundred years later—that their vessels could quickly (and safely) cross the Atlantic.

The *Sirius* came into sight that Sunday night a little after ten, dropping anchor at the Battery amid cheers from a crowd acutely aware that they had just witnessed something historic. The ship had made the journey from Cork in nineteen days with forty passengers, plus crew. It had run out of fuel just as the crew spied Sandy Hook, New Jersey. The captain risked a mutiny in refusing to raise the sails the last leg into New York Harbor, instead ordering the firemen to break off the spars on the unused mast and feed those into the furnace. It worked, and the *Sirius* beat the *Great Western* by a few hours—though the much larger vessel made the crossing in a mere fifteen days. THE BEGINNING OF THE NEW AGE IN STEAM POWER, went the headline in the *New York Herald* on April 23 above a glowing article that declared the ships' arrivals as "thus solving the problem of possibility" regarding quick and safe transatlantic travel. Soon after, a Canadian named Samuel Cunard and some investors launched a venture that would lead to the first regular steamship service between the United Kingdom and North America. The maiden voyage for that venture was in March 1840. Perhaps as a nod to the uniqueness of such travel in the annals of humankind, the ship for that first voyage was called the *Unicorn*.

The people on Manhattan's Battery would have found this revolution in travel inconceivable at the start of the 1830s, such speed seemingly the stuff of the penny dreadfuls that flooded the reading public that decade in England. The dramatic change was one of many revolutions of the time. Most of these were far from thunderclaps of unexpected activity, but as in the case of the race between the *Sirius* and the *Great Western*, the culminations of years of planning and pursuit. However labored their journeys, these insurgencies invariably arrived in shocking fashion. They shredded norms and upended the ways of doing things—and usually quite quickly in both cases.

Europe was halfway through the 1820s when the world's first steam-powered railway rolled out along twenty-seven miles through the English cities of Stockton and Darlington. Within fifteen years of that 1825 debut, steam railroads were rolling out across Europe, Canada, and the United States, and—with speeds of up to thirty-six miles per hour, never mind the greater capacity and relative comfort—they quickly "made coaches obsolete." They also made trading in goods that much easier, especially for previously more isolated businesses, including breweries. "In Bavaria, small-time brewers were barely making ends meet until opportunities for export arrived with railroads and steamers," one historian notes. Around the same time, another form of conveyance—this one for news and information—arose that would intersect with the rise of the railroads. Until the 1840s, news and information traveled as fast as a horse, a boat, or a human could carry it. In 1843, Samuel Morse, a painter and an art professor at New York University in Manhattan, obtained a congressional subsidy of $30,000 to run a telegraph line thirty-seven miles from Baltimore to Washington, DC. Morse had been tinkering with electrical communication for years, adjusting his rudimentary telecommunications device and gathering investors for the effort. It paid off in 1844 with the opening of that Baltimore-Washington line via Morse's immortal first phrase, "What hath God wrought." Telegraph lines spread after 1844 faster than railroad lines. In Britain there were thirteen miles in 1838. Fifteen years later, there were four thousand, such astonishing growth driven in part by the need to coordinate railroad schedules.

In a two-week span in 1839, just as railroads and telegraphs began unspooling at great distances on two continents, a French painter named Louis-Jacques-Mandé Daguerre and an English aristocrat named William Henry Fox Talbot announced separate discoveries concerning the reproduction of images. Daguerre could fix an image on a silvered sheet of copper, while Talbot could produce a negative image on a sheet of sensitized paper. Both methods—developed independently—gave birth to modern photography. By the end of the 1840s, the mass production of photography was possible and the chronicling of human experience would never quite be the same.

There were all sorts of smaller revolutions in all sorts of fields during this same period in the nineteenth century, so much so that it is difficult to overstate the pace of innovation. In 1840 the United Kingdom introduced the penny post, the first uniformly standard, one-size-fits-all method for paying for the mailing of a letter. It launched a revolution in mail, once the provenance of those wealthy enough to pay someone—usually a servant who had other tasks as well—to deliver a letter or a card. In 1846 William T. G. Morton became the first surgeon to successfully use ether for surgery, in this case removing part of a neck tumor from a patient at Massachusetts General Hospital in Boston. In 1850 Isaac Singer invented the fastest sewing machine anyone had seen, helping revolutionize the production of clothing in an era when most humans could only hope to possess but one or two changes of clothes during an entire lifetime. There were other revolutionaries waiting in the wings. Eight years before Singer's invention, Louis Pasteur earned his baccalaureate degree and started on a path of scientific research that would become an insurrection in itself. And eight years before *that*, Charles Darwin was starting to keep detailed notes about animals he encountered during his time traveling aboard the HMS *Beagle*.

There were several reasons for this pace of change then—from the late 1830s through the 1850s—and not earlier. One factor was the proliferation of steamships and steam trains. Even people of limited means could now travel to faraway places. Another factor was the revolution in communications, with knowledge of this or that advancement moving at the speed of the telegraph—or the railroad car carrying letters—rather than literal word of mouth. And this acceleration, both in travel and in communications, furthered trade between nations and societies in ways inconceivable a couple of generations before.

The world was getting smaller, and nowhere more so than in Europe and the United States, where emerging middle classes were engaging with commercial marketplaces well beyond their own geographic spheres. The Industrial Revolution, which had begun to sweep out of the United Kingdom in the late 1700s, was making it possible for the first time in history to turn out relatively large quantities of the same goods in short periods of time. Those goods could then be shipped farther and wider than ever before. Industrialization was also altering the relationship to work for millions, shifting droves of people from the farm to the city and from the small merchant or manufacturing shop to large production factories and industrial yards. Indeed, the populations of many Western cities boomed in the early nineteenth century—London, already the world's largest city by 1815, tripled in population by 1860 to well over three million, and New York City went from sixty thousand to roughly eight times that over a similar period. But to be sure, much of the economies of the nations of Europe and of the United States still remained based on smaller-scale manufacturing and the growing and selling of crops. In the United Kingdom, where it all started, most manufacturing firms employed fifty or fewer workers by midcentury. Giant factory floors and clanging assembly lines were still many years off. In the United States, the most valuable single commodity remained human beings themselves. The nation's four million enslaved African Americans were worth more than the invested value of America's railroads, factories, and banks combined, probably the single biggest reason for southern aristocrats' tenacious defense of the heinous institution.

Still, the revolutions in so many fields gave the 1830s and the 1840s a feeling of inevitability. The world was tipping in many ways, and many things would never be the same. "To improve the means of communication, then, is to promote a real, positive, and practical liberty; it is to extend to all the members of the human family the power of traversing and turning to account the globe, which has been given to them as their patrimony," wrote the French engineer Michel Chevalier, who toured the United States in the 1830s. He went on to explain that "the effect of the most perfect system of transportation is to reduce the distance not only between different places, but different classes." It was an era in which people dreamed big and realized instantly the opportunities that changes afforded them.

Brewing was a part of this transformation. Perhaps the revolution in brewing was not as consequential as those in communications or in transportation—or in surgical procedures—but it was a big deal nonetheless, and those in the thick of it realized it.

Gabriel Sedlmayr and Anton Dreher, those thieving visitors to major British breweries in the early 1830s, were the leading revolutionaries in brewing at the time. Their research and techniques, born largely of that UK reconnaissance, led to two new and lasting styles in the early 1840s.

Sedlmayr's contribution came to be called *märzen*, after the German word for the month of March. There had been such beers for at least decades before Sedlmayr's Spaten brewery introduced one in 1841. Brewers made these beers in March, just before it got too hot in an era before mechanical refrigeration, and then stored them through the spring and summer, releasing them in fall—thus märzen became synonymous in some places with Oktoberfest, a grand seasonal celebration of everything Bavarian. Spaten's märzen was revolutionary for Bavaria because Sedlmayr's brewery used the indirect kilning technique that its boss had seen firsthand in England. This technique produced what came to be called Munich malt, which in turn produced a Spaten märzen that was less dark than the brewery's usual dunkels. For its time and place, Spaten's creation was an unusually light-colored lager.

Dreher's contribution a few hundred miles to the east near Vienna was similar. He used the same indirect kilning technique and produced a lighter, more uniform malt called—not surprisingly—Vienna malt. It, too, produced an amber-hued lager with a lighter body and mouthfeel than most Austrians were used to seeing and tasting in their beers. This so-called Vienna lager from Dreher's Schwechat brewery also debuted in 1841.

Dreher's Vienna lager and Sedlmayr's märzen were rightfully seen together as a high-water mark for Continental brewing up to that point in the nineteenth century. They were very much the product of the revolutions in science, communication, and transportation transpiring then. The 1833 reconnaissance to English breweries (such as Bass) might have been in those arduous pre-railroad days, but it was the railroad that helped along the subsequent correspondence between Dreher and Sedlmayr as they discussed experimenting with techniques and the changing science of brewing.

This tinkering with what in central Europe were age-old approaches to making the area's most popular beverage was very much in the spirit of the age. And, while märzen and Vienna lager helped to make Spaten and

Schwechat the largest breweries in their respective nations, the most reso-
nating effect that both had was in inspiring the creation of a significantly
different style in the Slavic fringe of the sprawling Austrian Empire. This
style was much lighter-colored and lighter-tasting than both, and lighter even
than pale ale, with an effervescence none could hope to match. The tectonic
shifts of the age would aid this new style as well, hastening it on its way to
becoming the most popular of them all.

5

"WE MUST HAVE GOOD AND CHEAP BEER"

1838–1839 | Pilsen, Austrian Empire

Located near the confluence of four rivers in the region of Bohemia, in present-day western Czechia, the city of Pilsen by the 1830s was typical of other midsize cities in the vast Austrian Empire, which stretched from the Adriatic Sea through present-day Poland and from the Swiss Alps in the west to the Carpathian Mountains in the east. It was a vast patchwork of nearly fifty million people from myriad ethnic and religious backgrounds, with at least ten languages spoken in the empire—German being the official language at the royal court in Vienna, the capital. The empire encompassed much of present-day central Europe, with other primarily German-speaking states such as Prussia, Bavaria, and Saxony to the northwest, the larger Ottoman Empire to the south, the still larger Russian Empire to the east, and Switzerland and a bevy of Italian states, many under Austrian domination, to the west.

The Cathedral of Saint Bartholomew dominated Pilsen's main square, as it does today. It had been there since around the time of Pilsen's founding in the late thirteenth century and featured a spire stretching to nearly 190 feet. The square had shops and carts and served as a kind of supermarket-cum-mall for the surrounding town of low-rise stone and wooden buildings. And, like other midsized and smaller cities in the demographically diverse empire (and unlike the larger, teeming metropolises such as Vienna), Pilsen had one dominant group and then everyone else. The vast majority of residents—perhaps as many as four in five—were ethnically Czech, with a sizable German minority rounding out the rest of the populace.

Consequently, Czech was the most commonly spoken language, too. The town's mayor, Martin Kopecký, made Czech-language attractions such as plays and concerts a priority during his twenty-two-year government, which ended in 1850, no small feat as the region's reigning German nobility "had little interest in Czech culture." That Germanic hegemony helped explain why the local dominance of the Czech language and culture did not necessarily ensure economic dominance. Much of Pilsen's population, like much of surrounding Bohemia and other parts of the empire, fell under a kind of semifeudalism. The imperial aristocracy (which although predominantly German could also include fellow Czechs) demanded that many residents work a certain number of grueling days annually for them and hand over a certain amount of livestock and crops. This aristocracy tightly controlled vast tracts of land and passed property down through the generations, narrowing opportunity for advancement for the majority of Czechs in Bohemia since at that time land ownership usually meant economic independence. This was a recipe for mass discontent and surely contributed to the need for a stable and reliable supply of beer, a staple in both Czech and German life for as long as anyone alive in the late 1830s could recall.

At the same time, this pocket of Czech identity—like so much of the Austrian Empire beyond its major cities such as Vienna, Budapest, and Trieste—was also isolated geographically. Travel was only as fast as a horse or a human could move. Austrian emperor Francis I abhorred technological innovations and had blocked attempts to lay down railroad tracks in his domain. It was not until 1839, four years after Francis died, that the first steam-powered railroad would open in the Austrian Empire. It ran from Vienna to Brünn in the Moravia region to the east of Pilsen's Bohemia.

So work and trade for Pilsen's residents was a local affair. The town relied on crops and animals grown and raised in the surrounding region for Czech standards such as goulash and dumplings, with potatoes perhaps the most used ingredient. The residents also relied on local artisans and craftsmen, mostly fellow Czechs, to provide goods and services, including beer, though every now and then something made it in from the outside and took hold. Consumption and production records for beer in Bohemia are spotty or nonexistent for much of the region's history, but by the start of the 1800s, Bohemia had several breweries. The number would grow steadily during the century to more than one hundred. That growth came from demand, but also from the reality that beer tasted best fresh and could spoil easily in an age before widespread refrigeration. Wine aged well most of the time; beer did not. Most Bohemian brewers made those rich, thick ales that only had a hint of bitterness. These mid-nineteenth-century concoctions would have been familiar in texture and taste to drinkers of ales in centuries past.

There was one notable exception, and it came from well outside Pilsen— from outside Bohemia, in fact. That probably explains why accounts of it survive. What Pilsen residents called "Bavarian beer"—even though much of it might have been made beyond that German statelet—had been around for decades by the time it raised red flags among city leaders invested in the local brewing trade. One of those city leaders was Václav Mirwald, the owner of a pub and hotel called the Golden Eagle. Mirwald was also one of Pilsen's several dozen burghers, local aristocrats relatively rich in property and influence. He was also one of the 289 burghers who had a right to collect profits from the city's brewing trade, though he, like other burghers, might not necessarily brew himself. Mirwald did collect money from beer sales at his inn, giving him a double financial incentive to stand athwart the influx of Bavarian beer. In the late 1830s Mirwald began hosting regular meetings of his fellow burghers at the Golden Eagle to discuss what to do about this foreign beer, which the burghers' customers seemed to greatly prefer over local drink. Mirwald would invariably end these meetings with a simple exhortation: "We must have good and cheap beer."

What set this so-called Bavarian beer apart was its texture, appearance, and taste. It was so unlike the ale everyone knew about. The Bavarian imports looked lighter. They also tasted lighter and had a lighter mouthfeel. Light beer—it was a novelty to the Bohemians. However, contrary to myths that would arise in the coming decades, it was not totally unfamiliar. There had been a beer called *samec*, brewed in the Bohemian town of Žatec—Saaz in German—about sixty miles north of Pilsen in an area particularly suited for the growing of hops. It was a beer of such note it warranted a mention in a sixteenth-century Latin text on brewing by the court physician of the Holy Roman emperor, who claimed at least nominal dominion over much of Europe. There was also a beer out of Rakovník, fifty miles north, which was said to have been brewed with barley left over from more desirable beers. Whatever their quality, these beers shared characteristics with the so-called Bavarian stuff. They were less opaque than ales and crisper, with thinner mouthfeels, and they tended to be much lower in alcohol, though still rather tasty. These beers and the Germanic ones that came later must have seemed to Pilsen residents rather unique, if not freakishly so, compared with much of the beer they were used to seeing and drinking.

The residents of Pilsen were discovering lagers.

It was not just that these lagers finding their ways into Pilsen were lighter, they were also uniformly better than what local brewers produced, according to surviving accounts. "Everywhere else they were adapting to the new way of brewing beer, by which they were accommodating the requests of the citizenry," went one account translated from Czech to English. "Only in Pilsen did everything remain in the old manner. This circumstance, which was joined by the worsening quality of many Pilsen brewers, caused foreign beers to be imported into Pilsen."

What's worse, this outside beer was cheaper than the beer made in Pilsen. It was a vicious cycle, at least as burghers such as Václav Mirwald saw it: the deteriorating quality of the more expensive Pilsen beer versus the less expensive, higher-quality outside beer meant more of that already sorry Pilsen beer remained unsold; and since beer can quickly degrade once tapped, that Pilsen beer only became that much more unpalatable. Investors were losing money, and the citizenry was losing patience. It all came to a head one bitterly cold February day in 1838, in an event that was probably a blip on history's radar then but that became a major turning point in food and drink worldwide: the disgruntled citizenry of Pilsen cheered as thirty-six barrels of beer were dumped in front of the town hall near the grand Gothic cathedral "as detrimental to the health and unsuitable for consumption."

By that point, the burghers who underwrote local brewing had been meeting regularly to discuss the situation, including at Mirwald's Golden Eagle hotel and pub. The burghers, some of whose powers stretched back to familial sinecures in the Middle Ages, had the most to lose through the current situation, and were already losing. Much of what survives of Mirwald's history stems from his role in the brewing controversy in Pilsen as the 1830s bled into the 1840s. The fact that these details survive speaks volumes about how important beer was to the Czechs. It was social lubricant, celebratory offering, and respite from often backbreaking toil all in one. And it was supposed to be relatively cheap and tasty—not expensive and iffy. It was easy to understand, then, why "the formerly thriving brewing business in Pilsen was deteriorating," went an account, and why the burghers' income from brewing was declining. A "bitter dissatisfaction rose among the burghers with brewing rights," who concluded that something had to be done before their income was "damaged for entire decades, or perhaps even forever."

And so the burghers decided to right the wrongs through a new brewery. On January 2, 1839, they issued a manifesto explaining themselves. This decision by the burghers of Pilsen has since taken on the aura of legend given the influence it would have on brewing and on food in general during the next nearly two centuries. At the time, though, it was more akin to a press release announcing a new venture or a legal brief on a proposed change released in one of the sleepier corners of one of the lesser European powers. Written in German, the governing language of the empire, it was not translated into English until the writer and critic Evan Rail did so in 2012, only adding to the aura for those who could not understand its context, much less its literal

meaning. Despite the choice to write in German, the audience for the burghers' statement was local: the largely Czech-speaking artisans, shopkeepers,
day laborers, farmers, and others who composed Pilsen's population.

Under the cumbersome title "Request of the Burghers with Brewing
Rights for the Construction of Their Own Malt- and Brew-House," the manifesto began with a rundown of how things had reached this point in January
1839. The burghers blamed unscrupulous brewers and maltsters—those who
prepared the grains essential to beer—for cheap, higher-quality beer flood-
ing the market and undermining the value of the burghers' rights as well as
disrespecting "the tradition of our ancestors in the city of Pilsen"—that is,
brewing itself. According to the manifesto, "The burghers of the time felt
this pressure from the brewers quite bitterly. Partly because of their excessive goodness, partly because they did not feel strong enough in themselves,
they refrained from undertaking anything against these harmful influences,
although the means to do so were not unknown to them."

The burghers then noted that they could continue to tolerate the dodgy
quality and relatively higher prices for Pilsen-made beer but for "a much
greater danger" that had arrived at the city gates in recent years. "Neighboring
dominions are attempting to establish storehouses in Pilsen of the very best
beer, samples of which have already been officially submitted and which by the
current price of barley and malt is being offered [much more cheaply] than
the price of our local beer." If something wasn't done, and fast, the burghers
noted, then the local brewing industry would not necessarily be wiped out
but rather disrupted to the point of making their brewing rights worthless.
Perhaps a bit hyperbolically, for news did not travel that far or wide in those
days, the burghers wrote that a similar fate "has already befallen the majority
of Czech cities in the same manner."

Having stated their challenge—to "provide better and cheaper beer to
the public"—the burghers moved quickly to a proposed solution. Again,
they hinted that it was something that other Czech towns and cities in the
empire had tried. The situation "can only be rectified if the burghers—as
has often happened in other towns—construct their own brewery and their
own malthouse." Such a move would save money on renting malthouses and
brewhouses, would slash overproduction and thus the spoilage of Pilsen beer
that was then so widespread, would keep more of the town's brewing profits
in the town itself, and, perhaps most important, "improve the quality of the
beer by proceeding to produce bottom-fermented beers and lagers, and in
so doing the market for Pilsner beer could be gained even outside the territory of Pilsen."

Pilsen's burghers were taking direct aim at Bavarian competitors on the other side of the imperial frontier. Contrary to some of the mythmaking that would pop up later surrounding the burghers' decision, theirs was a plan to brew on a large scale for the region from the get-go and to openly imitate these relatively newfangled bottom-fermenting lagers. It was going to be out with the old (ales) and in with the new (lagers), as the burghers saw it. They and those whom they hired would adopt the latest technologies to make lighter-colored and lighter-tasting beer. They would spend money to make money.

And they would brook no dissent. Perhaps led by Václav Mirwald, whose Golden Eagle hosted so many meetings about the dwindling quality of Pilsen's beers and the outside threats, the burghers closed their January 1839 manifesto almost daring anyone to disagree. "If some individuals, out of selfishness or unreason, let themselves be seduced into opposition against such a boon, it is to be reminded that such an effort of theirs will be in vain, for a way has been found to accomplish this plan conclusively."

The future was here and the burghers of Pilsen intended to seize it. What transpired between the manifesto in January 1839 and the debut of the beer it led to in November 1842 constituted nothing short of a revolution in food and drink, the acme of the ongoing quest to brew clearer, lighter beer. It would take the world a while to notice, though.

6

"THE RUDEST MAN IN BAVARIA" AND HIS ENABLERS

1839–1842 | Pilsen

The monk hid the vial of yeast in his cloak and made his way as gingerly as possible to the Bavarian-Austrian frontier. In a Europe of intense dynastic rivalries and frequent wars—there would be a major conflict roughly every seven years on the Continent in the nineteenth century—passage between international borders could be fraught for those flouting conventions or the law. The monk was flouting both with his contraband.

It was lager yeast from one of the many breweries in Bavaria, and it was meant for the brewery under construction in Pilsen on the western edge of the Austrian Empire. Given the lucrative trade that Bavarian brewers then enjoyed within their own kingdom, never mind with surrounding states such as Austria, the yeast was incredibly valuable. Without it, lager beer was not possible. Whatever mash the brewery in Pilsen could make, however skilled its maltsters were and pure its ingredients, the inevitable result would be a thicker, heavier ale that the people clearly did not want. They had made that much clear with the dumping of the thirty-six kegs on that frosty February day in 1838. Now it was nearly four years later, the brewery was ready, and the yeast was the last piece of the puzzle to stem the tide against the ocean of Bavarian lager washing through Pilsen. It fell to the monk to get the precious cargo to the brewery.

Surely no customs agent or soldier would hassle a monk, not in this most Catholic part of central Europe. The reigning dynasties—the Wittelsbachs in Bavaria and the Hapsburgs in Austria—were themselves devout defenders of the faith. Surely their devotion would trickle down to the rank and file who kept watch over their realms' borderlands. A monk would be shown deference, waved through without much fuss. The burghers of Pilsen were counting on it. The monk was counting on it. He made his way northeast-ward from Munich . . .

. . . And into legend. The story of a monk smuggling lager yeast to the brewery in Pilsen from one in Bavaria became one of many tall tales and misconceptions to arise about the Bohemian operation in the decades after its 1842 launch. For there was no monk, and there was no fraught journey across international frontiers. Instead, the development of the Pilsen brewery and its beer came down to three individuals, none men of the cloth. Rather, each practiced trades that would have seemed mundane, albeit eminently neces-sary, to their compatriots in 1840s Europe. Martin Stelzer was an architect. František Filaus was a builder. And Josef Groll was a brewer.

Martin Stelzer was born in 1815 just to the southwest of Pilsen. He would become well known for his Romanesque Revival design of the old synagogue in Pilsen and of a theater in the city as well, but those works were years away for Stelzer, who sported a bushy mustache across a long and slender face. Instead, it appears that the architect's first major commission in the region was the Burghers' Brewery, a commission that Stelzer landed around his twentieth-fifth birthday—and likely at least in part because he was one of those burghers with brewing rights. Architecture then was a self-taught field, and it would seem Stelzer was no different from others in his profession. He studied buildings and other structures that had already arisen and familiarized himself with the great styles from which they came. Nineteenth-century architecture, especially in Europe and the United States, was all about imitating these great styles. For the Burghers' Brewery, Stelzer leaned on Romanesque architecture. The style, which featured arched windows, tall towers, thick walls, and severe symmetry, grew up after the fall of the Roman Empire and before the Middle Ages. Romanesque would have had its heyday before the founding of Pilsen in 1295, and its lingering influence, along with the slightly younger Gothic style, would come to define a lot of major buildings in Bohemia.

As for the actual composition and layout of the Burghers' Brewery in Pilsen, Stelzer did not have to reach back through time. He had to travel. That he did less than a year after the burghers' January 1839 manifesto. Stel-zer's exact route remains unknown, but it did include stops in and around Munich in neighboring Bavaria. How could it not? It was the local sales of those bottom-fermenting lagers from Bavaria that the burghers were hop-ing to undercut with their new operation. What's more, Bavaria was prob-ably the leading brewing nation on the Continent. Those purity laws from the sixteenth century had had their intended effects. Bavarian brewers had cleaned up their acts and were justly famous for turning out uniformly clean and appetizing dark lagers with only a handful of ingredients and methods. Much of that beer was consumed within the kingdom itself—usually during religious festivals and nearly always from casks or kegs into dark vessels of wood or clay, and sometimes glass—but some of it was exported, as the Czechs in Bohemia knew all too well. To brewers, lager in Bavaria was a triumph of careful engineering, the clearest, cleanest brew on the Continent. To drinkers, it was an increasingly omnipresent foodstuff.

Stelzer, of course, was interested in the former. He wanted to know how Bavarian brewers turned out such consistently clear, clean beers, with little to no detritus floating about and with a lighter mouthfeel (and belly feel). It is unclear if he talked with Gabriel Sedlmayr during his trip, though perhaps he did. The Spaten brewery that Sedlmayr's father had acquired in 1807 was on its way to becoming the largest in Munich by output. The younger Gabriel Sedlmayr and his brother Josef had inherited Spaten after their father died in 1839, the same year that Stelzer would have visited.

Aside from being able to show the Czech architect the capaciousness of what was then a modern Continental brewery—one that ran on gravity as the ingredients came together higher up and the beer wended its way to cellars for the all-important lagering—Sedlmayr the younger would have been able to tell Stelzer of the latest malting and filtration techniques in England. Sedlmayr would have surely mentioned the 1833 trip to Burton-upon-Trent—perhaps with a mischievous grin as he recalled stealing the samples via that tricked-out walking stick—and the gravity-powered contraptions at breweries such as Bass that separated out the spent yeast and other detritus to leave behind remarkably unclouded beer. He might, too, have noted how British brewers were able to get just the right malt—or close to it—using newer kilning techniques, in particular, Daniel Wheeler's revolving metal drum.

In his conversation with Stelzer, Sedlmayr, as great an innovator and curious mind as the Continental brewing scene would produce in the nineteenth century, might have also reached way back to the late 1700s, when an English chemist, William Nicholson, developed the first easy-to-read saccharometer, a syringe-like device—bulbous on one end and narrowing sharply toward the other—that quickly became a staple in breweries in the United Kingdom and beyond. Nicholson's saccharometer, also called a hydrometer, measured the density of beer, including in its unfermented form, called wort. That density could tell a brewer the potential a beer had for alcohol production. The saccharometer also told brewers for the first time that paler malts produce more sugar per pound than darker malts—and therefore could produce not only clearer-looking beers but stronger ones, too. Gabriel Sedlmayr had bought a hydrometer during his English sojourn in the 1830s, and his Spaten was thought to be the first Continental brewery to use one, with momentous results. "The introduction of the saccharometer via the British represents the beginning of the scientific brewing in Germany," stated one researcher. Sedlmayr had set off to discover the latest in brewing technology in person and to relay it back to southern German brewers who lagged their British neighbor in such skill but were catching up fast. Or at least they hoped to—no purity laws bridled British brewers like they did in Bavaria.

Still, the purity laws did not prevent Sedlmayr from marrying these British techniques for ales to the brewing of lager in Bavaria. Anton Dreher, Sedlmayr's traveling companion during those brewery visits in the UK in 1833, also joined the techniques with lager brewing at his family brewery in Schwechat near Vienna. There is no evidence that Martin Stelzer visited Dreher, but it is entirely possible, given that they both lived in Austria and that Dreher's operation was fast becoming the biggest brewing concern in the Hapsburgs' empire. And, although both Sedlmayr and Dreher would use that hard-earned British know-how to introduce lighter-colored lager styles within a couple of years of Stelzer's reconnaissance, the beer their visitor would have seen made and would have tasted in late 1839 and early 1840 would have been those darker lagers called dunkels—made with some of those British innovations, including indirect kilning, but darker nonetheless.

Stelzer returned to Pilsen in early 1840 and shared his information with František Filaus. Unlike Stelzer, Filaus had a bit of a reputation by the time the burghers called on him to help design and develop their brewery. He was perhaps the most prominent developer in Pilsen at a time when the city—under the leadership of its longtime mayor, Martin Kopecký—was pivoting away from buildings mimicking its medieval roots and toward more modern designs. The most famous property Filaus built in Pilsen before the brewery was probably the theater, which opened in November 1832—ten years and one day before the tapping of that golden-hued beer that itself would be a nod to modernity. Some of the burghers with brewing rights, in fact, would fund the theater's construction at Kopecký's direction.

The theater, which would endure as Pilsen's most prominent until it was torn down in 1902, was a grand affair, with a more than twenty-two-foot-long brick proscenium arch running nearly thirty feet above the stage and several boxes for city bigwigs such as the burghers themselves. Kopecký and other leaders wanted to move their city into the modern age and away from the past. They also wanted to assert their Czech heritage. Most of the plays in the new theater, as in theaters throughout Austria, were in the empire's lingua franca of German. But now and then Kopecký and the local powers introduced Czech-language productions. None other than Austrian emperor Francis I took in one local play, complete with amateur actors from Pilsen, in 1833, a year after František Filaus completed the theater.

His work on the Burghers' Brewery would take about the same amount of time it took to build the theater: roughly two years, with the roof in place as early as fall 1840. Filaus and others selected a nearly one-and-a-quarter-acre site just to the east of the main part of Pilsen in an area that was popular with pedestrians and diners during the warmer months. The site was also ideal because the soft sandstone there was easy to excavate in order to create the caverns necessary to lager the brewery's finished product. What's more, it was near the Radbuza River, whose subterranean water table would provide a steady supply of water low in mineral deposits. While that "soft water" would prove key for the finished product, the site's biggest draw was likely its openness. The burghers intended their new brewery to be large for its time and place. Given the revolution that the brewery in Pilsen spawned, many later on would ascribe an artisanal vibe to Stelzer, Filaus, and others behind the brewery's design and development, fitting them into a twentieth- and twenty-first-century narrative about the evolution of food and drink. All indications are, though, that the capacious Romanesque contraption, which relied initially on gravity, water, and animals to power its brewing, was a routine affair in line with other brewery developments of the mid-to-late nineteenth century. Stelzer himself would go on to design other breweries in Austria, never mind hundreds of other buildings, his experience with the Pilsen brewery during his midtwenties clearly a boost for his career.

Still, the Burghers' Brewery was Pilsen's first modern production facility, an apparently clean mechanical break with the past. An eyewitness to its construction and start-up, the archivist Martin Hruška, rhapsodized about it. "The spacious building in a plain, yet graceful style has excellent cellars, mostly hewn in rock, which can accommodate some twelve thousand tubs, it has beautifully equipped copper rooms, two extremely large vats from which soaked barley grain falls onto a magnificent germinating floor." Hruška went on to note the pumping system that brought water to every room—except the granary—and the fact that "the brewery boasts all that belongs to such a huge brewing plant." That included "the English kiln heated by heat transferred from the boiling room, and the iron crusher made to an American design. It is linked to a water-lifting tackle . . . and propelled by a horse mill." Perhaps not remarkable by Bavarian or English standards, but this was heady stuff for Bohemia at the turn of the 1840s.

As for the beer that the new brewery would produce, that would also take on an almost supernatural aura as the decades marched on. Witness the legend of the monk smuggling yeast from Bavaria into Austria. Something grander than the local aristocracy's desire to undercut the Bavarian competition had to explain this revolutionary result in Pilsen. Yet when it came to hiring the most important figure in the brewery's initial triumvirate—the brewer—the Czech burghers of Pilsen did exactly what was most practical: they hired a German brewer from Bavaria who was adept at brewing lagers in a Bavarian tradition.

His name was Josef Groll. A bronze bust in his native town today shows a fleshy man with sleepy eyes and matted hair. Photographs of Groll later in life show much the same thing: a dourness, even fatigue, amid the beefy chin and the pronounced frown. There seems to have been a little mirth in the eyes, but Josef Groll by all accounts was likely not the jolly sort. When he arrived in Pilsen in either the spring or the summer of 1842—via either an offer the burghers sent through Stelzer or one they sent directly—Groll was a few months shy of his thirtieth birthday and perhaps leaner than the

Josef Groll, the first brewmaster of the Burghers' Brewery, had a reputation as a particularly skilled—and acerbic—craftsman from the rich Bavarian brewing tradition. COURTESY OF ARCHIVE OF PLZEŇSKÝ PRAZDROJ, A.S.

proportions he would take on later. But the dourness was likely there and probably a preference for work rather than socializing. Groll, even by age twenty-nine, had a reputation for being cantankerous and difficult to get along with, prone to outbursts and to melancholy—"the rudest man in Bavaria" was how his own father was said to have described Groll, perhaps jokingly.

That father ran a brewery in Vilshofen, a town in southeastern Bavaria on the Danube River. It was much smaller than Pilsen, but like any good Bavarian municipality then, Vilshofen needed a steady supply of lager. The Grolls' brewery was one of a handful that could provide. It was there that Groll learned the latest in brewing technology, gaining a bit of a reputation in the field, despite being "a simple man without any manners." Maybe such brusqueness and bumptiousness were simply signs of a latent genius, a man ahead of his time and therefore destined to be misunderstood. Or maybe his personality did not matter, or should not matter. Maybe Josef Groll was simply doing what Bavarian brewers were supposed to do—make good lager in the same ways over and over—and that ability led him to Pilsen about one hundred miles directly north.

Either way, Groll had a hand in helping Stelzer design the Burghers' Brewery in 1842. And, on October 5 of that year, at five o'clock in the morning, in the nearly fifteen-thousand-square-foot space, Groll and an assistant named Jan Eisner began brewing what would become the most popular beer style ever. It would be the palest lager yet, bright and golden, with heads of foamy fluffiness and a clarity that would have driven the Bavarians and the English to envy—and eventually did.

To this day, it is unclear whether Groll set about to change food and drink forever—whether he had some mad vision that saw around gustatory corners decades or centuries down the road—or whether he was simply going through the motions of his training in Vilshofen and got lucky because of the local conditions. There was obviously a trend in that part of Europe toward lagers of greater clarity and lighter color. Witness Anton Dreher's Vienna lager or Gabriel Sedlmayr's märzen in Groll's native Bavaria. Never mind the dunkels so long prevalent in that country and the pale ales from Albion. Those were unusually detritus-free in comparison to the millennia of ales that had come before, and Groll would have been familiar with all three by late 1842. Whatever the reasons, the beer Groll began brewing in the wee small hours of October 5, 1842 turned into the brilliantly golden, exceptionally effervescent lager tapped in at least three pubs and inns in Pilsen on the feast of Saint Martin of Tours on Friday, November 11, roughly five weeks later.

Pilsner's golden color was—and is—the style's most striking feature. This is a pour at the current Pilsner Urquell brewery in present-day Pilsen. Courtesy of Archive of Plzeňský Prazdroj, a.s.

That golden color came from the kilning techniques that Gabriel Sedlmayr had popularized in Bavaria—and surely from the kiln made in England by a manufacturer lost to history. Using that kiln, Groll had roasted local Bohemian barley, purchased at a weekly market, just so to impart a lighter hue to the finished beer. The fermentation and lagering lengths were likely similar in their weeks-long durations to those for others lagers, as were the temperatures Groll brewed at, for he was using techniques honed in lager-mad Bavaria. As for the golden result's sharply crisp taste, that came from the Bohemian-grown hops, purchased from a vendor based in the present-day Czech town of Mnichov (and interestingly, outside the Saaz hop-growing region that the original pilsner would come to be associated with so closely).

As for the golden lager's relatively light mouthfeel and effervescence, that was due to the soft water around Pilsen and to the yeast, which like the barley and hops was obtained in a very conventional way: purchased from a supplier in Bavaria, not smuggled over the frontier by an erstwhile monk. Really, in the end, Groll's finished product was a consequence of a marriage that the burghers had arranged and that might have come along eventually anyway given simple geography and lager's growing popularity. In other words, "Bavarian skill had met Czech ingredients," as one historian would put it centuries later, when the import of Groll's work in the fall of 1842 was clear.

His accomplishment was also a triumph of beer as a local foodstuff. Wine often overshadows beer in this regard, but what Groll accomplished was due not only to his skill, his supplies, the freshly made brewery he had at his disposal, and the innovations that he borrowed liberally from—they also came from the time and the place in which he toiled. Take away the water alone, and the outcome would have been different, maybe vastly so.

As it turned out, though, this was millennia-old beer going definitively in a new direction and about to take brewing with it. In its first twelve months, Pilsen's Bürgerbrauerei—or Burghers' Brewery (sometimes translated "Citizens' Brewery")—would produce just over three thousand barrels of its new lager in two different forms. One was a weaker version intended for everyday consumption and the other had more alcoholic punch. Both looked the same and tasted similar. More than three thousand barrels was a sizable amount for a brewery of that age and size. The volume would grow considerably, the increase reflecting the nearly immediate commercial hit that Pilsen's golden lager became. It was being served in Prague, the largest Czech city in the empire, two days' travel away, before the end of its birth year of 1842, and in the imperial capital of Vienna by 1856. In between, enough imitators of the new style—called "pilsner," meaning "from Pilsen"—had arisen that the Citizens' Brewery had to take out advertisements in Prague newspapers that implored consumers to look for the real deal:

> In the effort to put an end to practicing on non-resident consumers and perverting the sale of fake beer, we inform everybody who would like to buy genuine pilsner beer made by bottom-fermentation that the sale of this beer in transport barrels is exclusively provided by the administration of the Burghers' Brewery in Pilsen, who include the certificate of delivery with each supply. Therefore we beg you to turn to them only.

It didn't work. For the beer that Josef Groll created in the brewery that František Filaus built and that Groll designed with Martin Stelzer was born during a portentous time and in a particular place. Had the burghers of Pilsen grown desperate over the influx of Bavarian lager during any other decade, it is possible that Groll's creation would have stayed a local Bohemian curiosity for at least a few decades and maybe even longer, much as was the fate that befell märzen and dunkel, which remained staples of mostly southern

Germany alone into the late twentieth century. Or, if its popularity did have to spread, perhaps it would have been more gradual, maybe through corridors that other products forged, much like stout and porter seemed to find their ways anywhere a British naval or merchant ship sailed. As it was, the Austrian Empire did not engage in that kind of extensive trading or colonization, and no nation's navy could rival the British fleets of the mid-nineteenth century. Instead, because of its time and place, pilsner rocketed around the globe via other means—scientific, financial, and political.

The events between the burghers' manifesto in January 1839 and the tapping of the kegs in November 1842 would soon slip into brewing lore, enveloped in a cloud of legend that would not fully clear for well over one hundred years. Later generations would downplay or forget pilsner's evolutionary place among earlier lighter lagers, preferring instead to depict it as some sort of golden thunderbolt in a sky of inky-black ale. They would also flub all sorts of details about the birth of this most popular beer style—indeed, perhaps the most popular style of any alcoholic beverage ever—including details surrounding those who created it. Josef Groll would come to seem as legendary as that yeast-carting monk, though the former very much existed and the latter was a mere droplet in the ahistorical fog.

Groll himself lived just long enough to taste his creation's initial success, though he did not taste any real financial windfall from it. He had wanted to stay on as brewmaster after his contract ended on April 30, 1845, but he instead returned to Vilshofen in Bavaria. A trio of Bavarian brewmasters would succeed him, with the burghers not looking outside that German state for a head brewer until 1900. Perhaps Groll's personal brusqueness had caught up with him or maybe he could not deliver the savings that the burghers apparently demanded of their smashingly successful brewery. Whatever the reason for his return to Bavaria, Groll eventually inherited his father's brewery, and died in 1887, at age seventy-four, at the regulars' table of his favorite pub.

7

NEW WORLD, OLD BEER

1797–1842 | Mount Vernon, Virginia

In early July 1797 George Washington sat down at the desk in his first-floor office just off the grand entryway to his Mount Vernon estate in northern Virginia, near a set of keys to the liberated French prison the Bastille that the Marquis de Lafayette had given him, and wrote a reply to one of his nephews, Samuel Washington. Five days earlier, a letter from Samuel had arrived at Mount Vernon explaining to his uncle that he had lost "all my crop of small grain" during the past couple of harvests in present-day West Virginia. He was wondering if the older brother of his late father might loan Samuel "a sum of money such a one as you can conveniently spare."

His uncle would, without interest, but he wanted to make something perfectly clear. "I perceive by your letter of the 7th instant," the elder Washington wrote in his reply, "that you are under the same mistake that many others are, in supposing that I have money always at command. The case is so much the reverse of it."

The nation's first former president did not get the perks nor pensions of his successors in the late twentieth and twenty-first centuries. Nor had Washington taken a salary as commander of American forces during the Revolutionary War; he hadn't even been able to recoup many expenses he incurred in that role—including for a vast spy network that he himself paid for and understandably preferred to keep off the books. Washington, in short, needed money. Enter James Anderson, his Scottish-born plantation manager. Anderson—a father of seven who grew up on and around farms north of Edinburgh, and who rented a farm near Mount Vernon—took a look at Washington's cash crops and knew just what to do. Before the war, Washington had gradually started shifting away from the estate's longtime principal cash crop of tobacco, because it was particularly difficult to sell and because it was depleting the soil. He had instead begun planting grains, including rye, wheat, and oats. That proved a particularly smart decision, as other tobacco farmers in the vast Virginia commonwealth began to fall on hard times, not least because the war's outcome had cost them their prime tobacco trading partner, the British Empire. The grains were easier to sell whole or ground up—Washington had a new mill built in 1770—and the subpar leftovers could be fed to the estate's livestock. They could also, James Anderson thought, make a pretty fine whiskey.

Early in 1797, around the time Washington handed off the presidency to John Adams, Anderson persuaded his employer to start distilling some of Mount Vernon's grains to make a whiskey that Washington could sell. The idea was not so absurd. Whiskey distillation went back centuries in Anderson's native Scotland, and the spirit was a particular favorite of Americans. It was slowly displacing rum as the favored strong tipple of the new nation because access to the sugar cane from the British West Indies necessary for rum's production had dried up. (Neither Florida nor Louisiana, which would become major sources of sugar, were under American control then.) In the end, though, what likely swayed Washington was that postpresidency need for ready cash. By the spring of 1798 Anderson and six enslaved Mount Vernon workers—history records only their first names, Hanson, Peter, Nat, Daniel, James, and Timothy—were distilling whiskey, mostly from rye and wheat, in a converted cooperage on the estate. Soon, George Washington's distillery was either the biggest or one of the biggest distilleries in the United States, if not North America. It produced eleven thousand gallons in 1799, its first full year of production, and netted Washington the equivalent of $120,000 in today's dollars. The distillery would continue to reap dividends after his death in December 1799, after a nephew (not Samuel) took it over. But by the end of the first decade of the nineteenth century, the distillery, by then in a specially built stone house, had fallen into disrepair and disappeared.

That was a shame for the Washington family, for it was during that decade that whiskey really became the national drink. There were some thirty-six hundred distilleries in Virginia alone by 1810, likely about one-quarter of the total nationally, nearly all of them dedicated wholly or partially to producing whiskey. A new corn-based version of the stuff, eventually called bourbon, had come roaring out of the western hinterlands of Virginia—the part that became the Commonwealth of Kentucky in 1792—helping whiskey displace rum at America's spiritous zenith. Whiskey was relatively easy and cheap to make. No imported sugar cane or molasses necessary, just the grains one could grow and grist. It was also a cheaper and more efficient use of the grain itself, which might otherwise spoil on its way to market.

And what a market. "Distilling whiskey was good business because, to the astonishment of foreigners, nearly all Americans—men, women, children, and sometimes even babies—drank whiskey all day long," as the historian Gordon Wood put it. It is almost impossible to overstate how much Americans drank in the early days of the republic and how much of that was distilled spirits, whiskey in particular. Americans of all socioeconomic classes tippled to a degree that the nation has yet to supersede. A medical professor at Columbia in New York City complained around 1800 that nearly half the city's physicians were drunkards—who, like even their soberer counterparts, were likely prescribing the water of life for what ailed their patients, for whiskey was seen as a perfectly legitimate kind of medicine. Jugs of whiskey might be passed around during trials, including to the accused and the jury impaneled to judge him or her. "Whiskey accompanied every communal activity, including women's quilting bees," an observer noted. By 1820, the average American would put away nearly five gallons of spirits annually, most of it whiskey, up from two and a half thirty years before as a result of many drinkers starting in the morning and continuing through the day. As an English visitor then noted, "I am sure the American can fix nothing without a drink. If you meet you drink; if you part you drink; if you make an acquaintance you drink. If you close a bargain, you drink. They quarrel in their drink, and they make up with a drink."

This rise in whiskey in the early 1800s not only displaced rum, it all but finished off hard cider as a favored beverage among Americans, particularly those in apple-friendly areas such as New England and New York state. John Adams, a Massachusetts native, was said to down a tankard of cider nearly every morning, well into his eighties. Hard cider fueled some of the spread of Americans from the Eastern Seaboard westward, with another Massachusetts native, John Chapman, setting off in 1774 just one step ahead of other pioneers and planting hundreds of orchards as far west as Illinois. Chapman's orchards were of apples only good for pressing and fermenting—the sorts that people enjoyed eating would come decades later—but that did not stop him from gaining a nickname famous to schoolchildren to the present day: Johnny Appleseed. Away went cider as a major tipple, though, as whiskey shoved it into a historical black hole that it would not emerge from until the twenty-first century.

Whiskey also finished off what was left of a once relatively robust American brewing industry. The Pilgrims were said to have celebrated their first Christmas in the New World in 1620 aboard the Mayflower because their boat had a supply of beer from England and clean water in Massachusetts was proving difficult to find. Within fifteen years of that celebration, the colony had its first tavern, licensed to a Samuel Cole in Boston in 1634, and its first brewing law—a fine of one hundred English pounds for anyone caught brewing "beer, malt, or other beverages" without a license. And from Massachusetts on outward, brewing along the East Coast flourished, particularly in New York, New Jersey, and Pennsylvania. Before the Revolution, Pennsylvania's largest city was probably America's brewing capital, as Philadelphia's ales, porter especially, "had gained a remarkable reputation." But a shift in international trade of the grimmest kind caused a sort of first great extinction for American-made beer. The amount of beer exported from nation-leading Philadelphia, for instance, dropped to below one thousand barrels annually, from several times that just before the Revolution in the late 1770s.

What was the shift? New England merchants realized their cooler climate was particularly well suited to distilling rum from molasses and sugar cane imported from plantations in the British West Indies powered by slave labor. They began a triangular trade that involved importing raw materials from their fellow British colonies in the Caribbean, producing the rum for both sale on the mainland and as payment for enslaved laborers from West Africa, and then importing more slaves to produce the raw materials on plantations notorious down through history for their death rates. It was simply too good a killing for the New Englanders to pass up, and this sugar-rum-slave axis made some of the great family fortunes of that supposed regional hotbed of abolition. The American Revolution put an end to much of the triangular trade, at least in molasses and sugarcane from the British West Indies, but not before the rum craze of the late eighteenth century had dented American brewing.

The American beer industry would dust itself off in the early 1800s—thousands of Americans never lost their lust for beer—and the numbers of breweries started once again to climb until there were just under 130 breweries in ten states by 1810, 100 of them in Pennsylvania and New York. But that was nothing compared with the 3,600 distilleries in Virginia alone by the same year and the estimated 14,000 across the nation during the same period. Spirits consumption dwarfed beer drinking: Americans on average drank more than four times the volume of spirits in a given year than they did beer. The young country was pretty much a one-beverage nation in the beginning of the nineteenth century, like so many places with traditions of distillation and fermentation. In Mother England, beer—ale in particular, and porter to be specific—was the reigning alcohol. In France and much of southern Europe, it was wine both red and white. In the Continent's German-dominated central and north, it was beer—ale mostly there, too. In the Russian Empire and throughout Scandinavia, it was vodka, which was usually made from wheat or potatoes. In Japan, it was sake, a strong wine made from rice. To be sure, there were some notable runners-up in each place. The English had a famous taste for what they called claret—red wines from France's Bordeaux region—and for whiskey from Scotland and Ireland. Scandinavia had a rich brewing tradition, particularly the dense Finnish style known as *sahti*. But most countries and regions were one-drink towns when it came to alcohol. Like with bourbon on what was then the American frontier—and with many beer styles born in Europe—these drinks were distinct to certain times and places by the early nineteenth century.

And none were lager. That was a Bavarian thing, and a thing in places that Bavaria bordered. And none were golden-colored lager, because that did not exist until 1842, and it did not start traveling far until years after that. When it did—first via the old imperial trading routes that had long bolstered the prospects of its birthplace of Pilsen and then through mass emigration as Europeans fled a dismal continent—it did not stop until it conquered the world. In no place was pilsner's arrival more deeply felt than in a United States awash in whiskey. There, pilsner would change the culture, the economy, and the politics of a country on the wings of the world stage.

8

OF REVOLUTIONS AND COUNTERREVOLUTIONS

1845–1849 | Palermo, Sicily; Paris; Munich; Berlin

The manifesto circulating from the "revolutionary committee" set a date for the uprising: January 12, 1848, the birthday of King Ferdinand II of Naples.

"Sicilians!" the manifesto read. "The time for useless supplications is past. Protest, requests, and peaceful demonstrations are useless. Ferdinand has scorned them all." Instead, the committee, consisting of radical members of the educated and landed of Palermo, called for residents of Sicily's largest city to take up arms against the government based in Naples across the Strait of Messina. "The force of the people is omnipotent," they claimed. "The unity of the people will bring the fall of the king."

It did—for a time, at least. The despotic regime of Ferdinand II of the Spanish-based House of Bourbon was overthrown in Sicily, and for several months that island governed itself as best it could. Ferdinand would retake control in 1849, with the aid of foreign armies, but the uprising in an impoverished corner of a middling Continental power lit a fuse that sparked an explosion so incandescent the world took notice. For what happened in Palermo did not stay in Palermo. It became the common source of a series of revolutions and counterrevolutions that convulsed Europe for nearly two years, upending the old ways of governing, some of them centuries old, and, most important for the story of pilsner, sent millions of Europeans fleeing far, far from home, taking their ideas and habits with them.

The Napoleonic Wars at the start of the nineteenth century had killed several million soldiers, sailors, and civilians, devastated whole towns and cities, and disrupted trade for years. Those wars came on the heels of wars tied to the French Revolution at the end of the eighteenth century. So when an alliance that included Austria, the United Kingdom, several German states, and Russia finally defeated the French emperor at Waterloo in 1815, it fell to the victors to restore some semblance of order to a continent racked by a quarter century of violent conflict. They did so by trying to turn back the clock. Old regimes overthrown in the revolutionary tumult were restored to power. New states were created to ballast those old regimes, and a reactionary way of governing settled upon Europe, one that saw a kind of top-down law and order as the ultimate goal. The only nominal democracy was the United Kingdom's, and even that was restricted to landed gentry and other aristocracy. Europe's powers tried to put a lid on things in 1815, and it did not work. Piazzas and plazas were peppered with men disabled from the wars. Hunger and disease were rampant, child labor and exploitation common. Censorship and police surveillance were the norm, freedom of the press and of assembly unheard of in most European countries.

Things came to a head in the early 1840s when poor harvests and an economic downturn struck around the same time. Beginning in 1845, bacteria blighted potato harvests across northern Europe—most catastrophically in Ireland, where as many as one million people starved to death—and, in 1846, the wheat and rye harvests in central and northern Europe failed to yield nearly as much as expected. Food prices spiked and famine spread. These economic and physical calamities collided with a growing feeling that things had to change, a feeling that rapid changes in communication and transportation facilitated. Emperors, kings, archdukes, princes, and other leaders with dictatorial powers and little to no accountability were just not going to cut it anymore, not when people were starving to death en masse. Because of this, the revolutions were not unexpected, even if their eventual scope and effects surprised. Politicians, journalists, diplomats, and others had been warning since at least the late 1830s that something was going to give in Europe.

And so it came, first to Sicily, and then in a matter of weeks to nearly every other nation on the continent, more than fifty uprisings in all. The most significant was probably in France, where King Louis Philippe—himself brought to power by a revolution in 1830—fled out the back of the Tuileries Palace and into a common taxi with fifteen francs in his pocket. He chose as his moment the dead of night on February 24, 1848, as angry Parisians crashed in through the palace's front. News of Louis Philippe's hasty exit reached Vienna five days later, and revolution shook the Austrian Empire. Out went Emperor Ferdinand in favor of his nephew, Franz Joseph. The new emperor allowed his realm's growing middle class more say in governance, and even the peasantry—which accounted for most of Austria's population—received relief through a key change, one that likely resonated particularly loudly with the Czechs of Bohemia: the end of having to pay tribute in crops and work to nobles who were often ethnically German. In neighboring Prussia and Bavaria, the two biggest German states after Austria, the monarchs in Berlin and Munich, respectively, also cowered in the wake of unrest, and new rights emerged. These included a relatively free press in both and at least some forms of representative government, whereas before a cabal of courtiers and the kings themselves ran most everything.

But, like in Sicily, where it all started, these changes were short lived. A counterreaction swept most of the European capitals that the revolutions of 1848 had disrupted. Military might restored regimes, coups and crackdowns toppled hastily created republics, and the Continent returned to a familiar repressiveness and to sorting out international disagreements through war. From the early 1850s through the end of World War I in 1918, Europe would be in a near-constant state of armed conflict—Prussia alone would fight wars with Denmark in 1864, Austria in 1866, and France in 1870—with all the death, maiming, and destruction that came with it.

By then, though, a lot of Europeans, especially in those German states, had left. There was little to keep them there but the same grind and grisliness that the unrest of the 1840s had lain bare. Most who left crossed the Atlantic Ocean to settle in a fast-expanding United States. One million Germans would emigrate to America in the 1850s alone. A smaller number of Czechs as well as smatterings of Italians, Poles, and Slavs would also make a break for it in the mid-nineteenth century. It was the Germans, though, through their sheer numbers and their industriousness, who would come to dominate the wave of immigration. They would become the first large ethnic group to assimilate into established American culture. That assimilation would be a two-way street during the end of the 1800s and the dawn of the twentieth century. These hundreds of thousands of newly minted German Americans would, in other words, absorb much from their adopted land and would impart much as well, including their beer.

9

SPREAD

1845–1864 | Milwaukee, Wisconsin; Milan, Lombardy-Venetia

In February 1845, at a time when famine was starting to beset entire swaths of Europe, a new company in Milwaukee, Wisconsin, called Best & Company, Beer Brewery, Whiskey Distillery & Vinegar Refinery advertised in a local German-language newspaper that "herewith we give notice to our friends that henceforth we will have bottom fermentation beer for sale." The company's first offering was a light-looking and light-tasting lager that would not have been unfamiliar to the German speakers reading the ad. The beer would transform this modest operation on the then-outskirts of the United States into the largest brewery in the country by the close of the century.

That rise was partly a result of its birthplace. Milwaukee was one of the fastest-growing cities in America, located in a Wisconsin that was still nearly three years from statehood when Best & Co. launched. Milwaukee's location just up Lake Michigan from the even faster-growing Chicago and where the Menomonee and Milwaukee Rivers converged preordained it to facilitate trade between the more established parts of the United States and the expanding nation's frontier. Its location, too, made it ideal for brewing lager, given the long, cold winters—a fact that had helped draw German immigrants fleeing the tumult back home. Milwaukee's population followed a trend familiar to other cities on America's western fringes then: an influx of Germans more than doubled the city's population in the 1850s to more than forty-five thousand. "The public houses and streets are filled with newcomers and our old citizens are almost strangers in their own town," wrote one Milwaukee newspaper editor in the early 1840s. The Germans arrived sometimes by the dozens per day, steamers from Lake Michigan depositing them in a city and metropolitan area seeing rapid development of housing, roadways, railways, and all manner of commercial buildings, including breweries such as Best & Co.

Unlike so many of their fellow Germans, the Best family behind the new brewery had not been poor upon emigrating, but the hierarchal setup back home—in the Bests' case, the Grand Duchy of Hesse (in present-day southern Germany)—stifled their ambitions. Even successful Germans then lived "as if under lions and dragons, fearing every moment to be devoured by them," as one emigrant put it. Not so in America, where the Constitution enshrined basic rights, at least for white males, and even common workmen ate meat daily and owned a change of clothes. So, gradually, the Bests set out for the fringes of the unfolding American republic, with father Jacob Best Sr. decamping in 1844. Jacob Sr. had four sons, and at least some of the family appears to have emigrated via steamer up the Hudson River, by way of New York Harbor, to the 350-mile Erie Canal, a revolutionary bit of engineering that had opened in 1825 and that had cut by weeks the time it took to move goods and people from the Eastern Seaboard to the Great Lakes and beyond—including Milwaukee. This is where the Bests headed because the city was known as hospitable to Germans. As much as one-third of Milwaukee's population was said to be of German extraction by the mid-1840s, though one might also have heard Norwegian and Italian, even Welsh and Gaelic, on the unfurling city sidewalks.

Jacob Sr., an austere-looking man with a thin face and high cheekbones above a wiry beard, may have brewed in the old country, and was almost certainly familiar with the techniques and approaches gathering steam in southern German statelets such as Bavaria by the 1840s. The Bests had most certainly made wine, too, and had sold the fermenting juice that did not quite make the cut as vinegar, a common practice then. Since there was little demand for wine in their new home—either in the German-speaking parts of greater Milwaukee or in the wider United States, where the fruit of the vine had yet to captivate the masses—the Bests' first business in Milwaukee was a vinegary. The second was the brewery. They built it on Chestnut Street between a dense forest that led toward the then-territorial boondocks and the city's growing downtown, and started brewing in September 1844.

Like all breweries in America at the time, the Bests' L-shaped, one-story, brick operation was crude and man powered. Jacob Sr. and his sons personally did the laborious work of germinating and kilning the grains, which meant first soaking them, then drying them, then roasting them just so, before boiling the grains with hops—the hops likely came from upstate New York via the Great Lakes and the grains either from there or from nearby farmers. Then it was time to pitch the yeast—the Bests likely brought the initial strains from Germany or acquired them from other Milwaukee brewers—and await fermentation. Aging in barrels in a cellar beneath the brewery then followed ahead of the February 1845 release, which was promoted by their German-language newspaper ad. In the meantime, the family continued to make vinegar and also used leftover grains to distill unaged whiskey, a much quicker process than brewing.

Charles Best, one of Jacob Sr.'s four sons, was not heavily involved in the initial launch of this particular brewery. He instead continued to focus on his family's original vinegary. He sold that, though, in 1849, and got into the brewery business on his own with an operation in the Menomonee Valley west of Milwaukee. It was on what was called the Plank Road, and Best expected to sell beer to farmers coming in and out of the city. Breweries in the United States were local like that. For instance, the sharpest growth for the Bests' brewery on Chestnut Street was decades off, and early on, as one observer noted, "the product and sales of the brewery were necessarily small, being limited to two or three hundred barrels per year, and intended only to meet local demand." Charles Best's Plank Road Brewery ended up smaller than that and quickly fell into debt, and then bankruptcy, in part because of a dodgy business partner and because the farmer traffic did not prove remunerative enough.

Best's loss was the gain of one Friedrich Müller, who had emigrated from the Kingdom of Württemberg just to the west of Bavaria and who leased the Plank Road Brewery in 1855. The move turned out to be the gain, too, of the American brewing industry in general and that of the pilsner style in particular.

For it was pilsner that the tall, pear-shaped, mustachioed Müller—who anglicized his name to Frederick Miller even before the 1855 takeover of the Plank Road Brewery—would end up opting for. It would also become the style of choice for Jacob Best and family with the Chestnut Street operation. Their breweries in the 1840s and 1850s turned out lager, the umbrella style that Germans in the old country had come to prefer to the heavier ales of yester-year and that their breweries in the New World were expected to brew if they wanted to profit.

More important, these breweries turned out *lighter* lagers in terms of taste and appearance. It was barely a few short years since the births of Vienna lager, märzen, and pilsner, but brewers an ocean away in America were already bending that way by the late 1840s and throughout the 1850s. A Milwaukee newspaper article would in January 1861, in fact, describe Best's beer as "light" in terms of color—"light," not merely "lighter." By that time, right before the Civil War, there was a well-documented race among German-founded US breweries to streamline their lagers to make them that much clearer, consistent, and lighter, a race that after the war would lead to pilsner's stylistic triumph. Along the way, this contest would spur paradigm-shifting recipe changes and industry-changing competition. The very fact that Miller and

Frederick Miller founded one of the more enduring brewing dynasties in the United States. Courtesy of MillerCoors Archives

the Bests were able to produce lighter-colored lager early on without the aid of kilning techniques such as the ones that British and Bavarian brewers enjoyed suggests both an extraordinary perseverance on their part—for it was already hot, wet labor to begin with—and a recognition that that was what was necessary: go lighter or go home.

Then there was the simple decline in America during that time of ales and of darker beer in general. "The really important and successful breweries of the pre–Civil War period were ale manufacturers—though this was, unknown to them, their swan song," one historian wrote, about ninety years after the war. Even in that rollicking, lager-loving, German-infused boomtown of Milwaukee, Wisconsin, in the 1840s and 1850s, ale hung on as a serious presence. But by 1867 there was one ale producer left in the entire city. The disruption would repeat itself nationwide and all over the world as pilsner-chasing start-ups gobbled global and national market shares and other lighter lager styles found themselves shunted to only regional success.

One of the unlikeliest examples came from Italy around the same time that Best & Co. was well into its second year of operation. Sometime in 1846—the exact date is no longer known—Francesco Peroni set about brewing beer in the Milan area, in the Kingdom of Lombardy-Venetia, which fell directly under the Austrian Empire's control. Peroni was the youngest child in a family that owned a pasta-making outfit, and apparently he saw the potential for turning some of that production capacity toward brewing. Though it had long been associated with winemaking—and would be associated long after Peroni—the Italian peninsula did have a history with beer.

It went back to ancient Rome, whose empire exported brewing to the far corners of Europe after having discovered it upon contact with the Continent's Germanic peoples. A man named Giovanni Baldassarre Ketter launched the first modern brewery on the peninsula in 1789, in the northwest corner known as Piedmont, and the number of breweries would grow to around 140 within a hundred years. Many of these would come and go, subject to supply chains that ran thin and then broke, particularly when it came to the key ingredients of grains and hops, strained by the vicissitudes of Italian politics. A series of conflicts beginning in that all-important year of 1848 and lasting through the early 1860s would shake the peninsula from several statelets into one single Italian state under the king of Piedmont-Sardinia. The Austrian Empire had dominated many of the northern statelets, holding control over some areas even after Italian unification. During this time, the empire exported not only aristocrats to rule and soldiers to intimidate but also plenty of beer to drink. For instance, the family of Anton Dreher, which controlled the empire's biggest brewing operation, would open a brewery in Trieste, a city on the Adriatic coast that was predominantly Italian ethnically but that Austria used as its main port. The beers these Austrians made and exported were mostly ales or lagers that were light but not too light, and certainly not golden—the Vienna lagers that Dreher himself had pioneered and the dunkels so popular with Bavarians.

Francesco Peroni's operation became the largest example of a stylistic break in Italian beer and an unlikely early example of how pilsner, once introduced in a country—even one as steeped in wine as Italy—never lost its mass appeal. Peroni's initial offering in the late 1840s was the color of straw, and it was effervescent, not unlike the bubbliness that would become a staple of prosecco, the Italian sparkling wine, in the late nineteenth century. Peroni's beer was a lager—the brewery took advantage of its proximity to ice sources in the Alps for cooler fermentation and lagering—and, more to the point, it was a pilsner. It did not call itself pilsner, and it was not likely made with the same ingredients that Josef Groll had used earlier that decade in Bohemia—which, like Peroni's Lombardy-Venetia, was under Austria's thumb. But the original Peroni beer looked and tasted very similar.

It also proved very popular. Peroni's company would add a second brewery in Rome in 1864, and eventually move its headquarters there right around the time the Eternal City became the capital of a united Italy. From that fortuitous perch, Peroni beer spread over the next fifty years to every corner of the young nation. By the start of the twentieth century, bar posters for Peroni showed a golden beer, its honeycomb-light foam overflowing the rims of crystal-clear fluted glasses. It had become the first homegrown, mass-produced beer in Italy, and the first example of the pilsner style becoming synonymous with a nation's beer.

PART II

10

ANTI-IMMIGRANT FERMENT

1855–1865 | Chicago

On March 13, 1855, Levi Boone, a doctor with round spectacles, eleven children, and a thick white beard, was sworn in as mayor of Chicago, a fast-growing city of about thirty-five thousand on Lake Michigan in what was then the frontier state of Illinois. Boone had come to power as a Know-Nothing, a member of a virulently anti-immigrant party that was also invariably anti-Catholic because so many immigrants to America in the preceding decade were Catholics fleeing the revolutionary turmoil in Europe. "I cannot be blind to the existence in our midst of a powerful politico-religious organization, all its members owing, and its chief officers bound under an oath of allegiance to the temporal, as well as the spiritual supremacy of a foreign despot," Boone said in his inaugural remarks.

The "foreign despot" he referenced would have been clear to anyone following the politics of the day. It was the pope, whom the Know-Nothings assumed had a claim to the political and civic allegiance of all these Catholics overrunning the United States with their weird religious rituals and festivals, their heavy accents and choppy English, and this one habit that good, decent Protestants such as His Honor could not abide. "Who does not know that the most depraved, worthless, and irredeemable drunkards and sots which curse the community are Irish Catholics?" explained the Boone-backing *Chicago Tribune* in an editorial around the time of the inauguration.

As many as two million Irish fled famine, disease, and English harassment in the 1840s and 1850s, most for the United States, with over two hundred thousand arriving in the country in 1849 alone. Another one million Germans, most Catholics from southern statelets such as Bavaria, landed in the United States in the 1850s, hoping to escape the violent political turmoil that had disrupted so many statelets in northern and central Europe. This immigration was at a time when the overall US population was around twenty-three million, meaning that the arrival of these millions of foreigners was acutely felt.

They swelled the populations of cities, particularly in the Northeast and what became the Midwest, where their labor for the most menial and backbreaking jobs was in greater demand than in the South, where four million enslaved black people did the drudgery. An influx of Germans and Czechs drove the population of Chicago from around 30,000 at the start of the 1850s to nearly 130,000 at the end of the decade. At the time of Levi Boone's inauguration, foreign-born Chicagoans accounted for nearly half the city's residents.

They brought with them their own customs, their own ways of worshiping, of dressing, of working. All of it rankled Know-Nothings like Levi Boone and the editors of the *Chicago Tribune*, who in part saw their disgust as virtuous. After all, did they not have an obligation to America's Founding Fathers to educate and indoctrinate these newcomers on how to be real Americans? In other words, if the Know-Nothings could not stop the Germans and the Irish from coming—and they could not because of the demand for labor and because the rival Democrats welcomed the potential voters with open arms in ports such as New York and Boston—then at least they could school them in that good old-fashioned Protestant work ethic.

That meant in large part changing the drinking habits of these immigrants. It was for their own good, for the nativists blamed drink—especially strong drink—for everything from illiteracy to showing up late for work. Although America had been awash in whiskey during the first couple of decades of the nineteenth century—and although founders such as George Washington, John Adams, Thomas Jefferson, and Ben Franklin had themselves been omnibibulous, with Washington running one of the nation's largest distilleries—a temperance movement driven largely by fear of immigrants and a need to purify both them and the drunken nation had taken hold in the 1830s and 1840s. That explained why per capita consumption of alcohol—most of it skull-cracking spirits such as whiskey—dropped from an astounding seven gallons annually in 1830 to two gallons in the mid-1840s. That also explained the Know-Nothings' appeal and the rise of politicians such as Levi Boone.

So it came as little surprise when Boone decided to enforce a little-remembered provision that required taverns and bars to close on Sunday for the Christian Sabbath. This was in the era of the six-day workweek that might stretch to seventy hours or so as workers trudged to mines, factories, and elsewhere just after dawn and ceased toils only at nightfall. Sunday was their day off, and the Germans and the Irish, in particular, enjoyed a beer or something stronger to unwind. Boone and his allies knew that and knew that the enforcement of the Sabbath law would preclude much of the immigrant laborers' drinking—as most drinking was done outside the home, with tipples such as beer, wine, and spirits coming in barrels or kegs, not bottles and cans. For good measure, Boone upped the annual liquor license fee to $300 from $50 in an effort to drive out of business the city's 625 immigrant-owned taverns—roughly 90 percent of the total then in Chicago. The police generally left alone those taverns that native-born residents owned, even if they operated on Sundays.

Perhaps just as Boone and the Know-Nothings wanted, the Chicago police soon found themselves busting dozens of tavern owners for serving on the Sabbath. Authorities decided to make an example of one such owner by bringing him to trial on Saturday, April 21, barely five weeks after Levi Boone was sworn in. The start of the trial prompted a slow, steady march of Germans to city hall. "They filled the sidewalks and pushed the Americans . . . in the streets," the *Tribune* reported, the use of "Americans" a deliberate dig at the foreign origin of these particular Chicagoans. These were the relatively peaceful ones, however. The newspaper reported that a whole other host of additional Germans were holed up in taverns and "were engaged in loading their guns and preparing apparently for a fight."

It is not clear if this was merely hyperbole on the part of a newspaper allied with Boone and the nativists. But it was clear by what happened next that Germans had had it with the moralizing and were going to make an example, too. The Germans marched down Clark Street toward a bridge over the Chicago River that would lead to city hall. But a bridge tender drew up the span and delayed the Germans' march. In the meantime, Boone had sworn in more officers and had set up two cannons in front of city hall. When the demonstrators finally did make it across the river, they quickly clashed with police. In many cases, the fighting was hand to hand—or club to head. "One German was taken off the field of battle with his head pounded to a jelly," the *Tribune* reported. Another "had his nose almost entirely knocked off by a blow from the baton of one of the officers." Dozens more were injured, and one demonstrator lost his life.

What came to be called the Lager Beer Riot of 1855 typified the violence of the era between recently minted Americans and those who had been in the republic much longer, between those who saw a danger in the benches and taps of the pub and those who took them as reminders of better times back home, before the hunger and the wars. Similar violence would grip other US cities with growing German and Irish populations, including Cincinnati, Louisville, and Milwaukee—even as far afield as Portland, Maine, where local militia opened fire on a crowd trying to get into the state liquor authority, killing one and injuring seven. It was always the same as far as the dynamics: mostly immigrant—and Catholic—crowds versus civil and criminal authorities composed almost solely of native-born Protestant Americans. And the clashes hinged on alcohol, or the lack of it.

A temperance movement had been building in the United States since the start of the century, notching its first big win in Maine, which banned the sale and manufacture of alcohol in 1851. During the same period, a flush of religious revivalism, the likes of which America had not experienced as an independent nation, swept out of the Northeast and through the rest of the country, leading to jumps in membership for the Baptist and Methodist churches, and to the formation of Mormonism, each of which espoused either abstinence from alcohol or at least moderation. Millions of Americans turned, sober and forthright, toward that old-time religion to see them through the new century. This Second Great Awakening and the temperance movement joined consciously and unconsciously to power an even larger crusade, wherein the crusaders beheld some of the major changes afoot in the world—from the railroads and the steamships to the spread of democratic and republican ideas of government to the blossoming in communication from the telegraph and faster mail—and declared America would be at the forefront of it all. They had a duty to their fellow man, to God, especially given that by the middle of the 1800s, with the settling of the West Coast and the annexation of Texas and soon half of Mexico, it was clear the nation was destined to unfurl across an entire continent and become one of the largest and most powerful empires ever.

The wobbly ship of state then had to be steadied, its course firmly set toward self-improvement, before it blew its chance to lead the earth. "Campaigners railed against every conceivable national ill, from dueling and spitting to bad architecture and masturbation," as the historian Maureen Ogle noted. Some advocated free primary education and women's suffrage as solutions. Most, though, took dead aim at what they saw as public enemy number one: drinking. The so-called drys spoke of it as the common root of much of the nation's evil, and the history be damned. Few remembered, much less acknowledged, George Washington's distillery or John Adams' near-daily tankard of hard cider. All they knew was that excessive drinking was a problem—they had seen it in their own lives. It had to go. Other nations had temperance movements, but none combined religious revivalism with national improvement quite like America, where the movement also spread over an unusually large topography. "Intemperance in our land is not accidental," inveighed Lyman Beecher, a founder of the American Temperance Society and one of the nation's most prominent religious leaders, in a sermon from his Connecticut pulpit in 1825. "It is rolling in upon us by the violation of some great laws of human nature. In our views, and in our practice as a nation, there is something fundamentally wrong; and the remedy, like the evil, must be found in the correct application of general principles. It must be a universal and national remedy."

So it began: a ninety-five year march from Beecher's reprinted and widely circulated sermon to Prohibition. The march, though, turned out to be far from steady, and it was obviously very slow. What happened? In between the early 1820s and the end of the century, a much bigger ill, this one far less perceived and much more concrete, convulsed the nation. African slavery had been a presence on the American continent since the 1500s and had evolved into a particularly vicious chattel version of the practice. By the time of the Lager Beer Riot in Chicago in early 1855, slavery had become a distinctly north-south phenomenon, with most of America's four million enslaved found south of the Ohio River and the institution largely extinct beyond that. But the US victory in 1849 in the Mexican-American War opened up what would become California, Nevada, Utah, and much of Arizona, New Mexico, and Colorado to the possibility of slavery. Slavery proponents, in Washington and in state capitals, began agitating for further laws to protect its expansion. "I claim, sir, that slavery being property in the United States, and so recognized by the Constitution, a slaveholder has the right to go with that property into any part of the United States," Mississippi senator Jefferson Davis said in February 1850 from the Senate floor. "I deny, sir," he added, "that this government has the sovereign power to prohibit it from the territories." Men like Davis even called for annexing Cuba from Spain to add to American slavery's ranks—and for reopening the African slave trade that had enriched so many New Englanders in the eighteenth century.

Suddenly, with the very real prospect of slavery extending from sea to shining sea and beyond, keeping people from their next mug of beer or bourbon seemed far less important. The temperance movement ebbed as slavery consumed the body politic. A new party emerged in 1854 out of the Know-Nothings, one dedicated to curbing the spread of slavery and to infrastructural improvements that included a transcontinental railroad and land-grant colleges to boost agricultural science and production. The leaders of the new Republican Party knew these were tall orders in such charged times. They also knew they would need lots of votes to make their presence felt in the shadow of the dominant Democrats and the embers of the dying Know-Nothings. The Democrats had been signing up recently arrived

Irish immigrants in droves in eastern ports. The Republicans turned their attentions to the Germans chasing work westward to Chicago, Milwaukee, St. Louis, and elsewhere. An enterprising and ambitious young lawyer and former congressman from southern Illinois, in fact, quietly purchased part of a German-language newspaper in 1859 to drum up support for Republican policies and candidates.

Abraham Lincoln never lost his rapport with Germans and German Americans, least of all after he became president the following year. He called on not only German votes to win the White House and to secure a congressional majority for his fellow Republicans; he called on German lives to save the United States. Tens of thousands of German immigrants and sons of immigrants fought for the Union. Some were drafted, but the majority appear to have volunteered. The struggle—particularly how Lincoln often framed it, in terms of liberty for the slave and endurance for representative democracy—struck a chord with ordinary German soldiers old enough to either remember the repression back home or have heard about it from others who experienced it firsthand. "It isn't a war where two powers fight to win a piece of land," one German enlistee wrote in a wartime letter that was not atypical. "Instead it's about freedom or slavery, and you can well imagine, dear mother, I support the cause of freedom with all my might."

Their devotion to the Union cause and their sheer numbers following the war melted away much of the bigotry German immigrants and their families had encountered before. They had in the crucible of that conflict begun what would turn out to be a rapid and unusually thorough assimilation into American life. They were a ready gusher of votes for the reigning Republican Party—one the rival Democrats would soon try to tap—and after the war they were a source of cheap and efficient labor in a rapidly industrializing United States that had just freed millions of enslaved people. Political, business, and even religious leaders realized it was probably best not to hassle German Americans too much over their love of beer and their drinking habits, certainly not to the point of advocating prohibition, lest they throw their support and their muscle elsewhere. The embrace of Germans in America set the table for what turned out to be the biggest boom in brewing the world had ever seen, one that reverberates today, and one that pivoted on a veritable arms race among German Americans to mimic the great Bavarian-Czech style born earlier in the century.

The boom would also win unlikely converts. Levi Boone lost his reelection bid for Chicago mayor even before the war, the Lager Beer Riot of 1855 defining his brief tenure down through history. A postwar attempt by one of Boone's successors—Joseph Medill, who had been editor of the virulently anti-German *Chicago Tribune*—to reinstate the Sunday ban on operating taverns met with resounding opposition and eventual defeat. This was in 1874. By then, even Boone, "now mellow in old age," according to one chronicler, liked to listen to orchestral music while he "enjoys a glass of beer."

11

SCIENCE MEETS BREWING

1864 | Amsterdam

In 1864, the same year that a growing Peroni decamped for Rome and that millions of German Americans broke for Abraham Lincoln in the US presidential election, a twenty-one-year-old heir and entrepreneur finished purchasing Amsterdam's De Hooiberg brewery, which had been in operation since 1592 and which was the only one in the city to make full use of steam power. Gerard Heineken's family had been in the food business for several decades by the evening of June 30, 1863, when he sat down and wrote a letter to his mother asking for the funds to purchase De Hooiberg—which in English means "the Haystack" and referred to the brewery's most popular product, a weak, cloudy ale available year round in barrels and popular with both Amsterdam's growing throng of manufacturing workers and the Dutch kingdom's farm laborers. The mustachioed, mutton-chopped Gerard Heineken's grandfather had started a cheese and butter company in Amsterdam during the latter half of the previous century and had come to own several warehouses around the city as well. His son Cornelis—Gerard's father—grew up in the business, and Cornelis's son surely imbibed some of his acumen.

When De Hooiberg came up for sale in 1863, the year Cornelis died, the younger Heineken moved to take full control of the brewery—not just purchasing a majority stake—because he saw the potential in growing it beyond Amsterdam and its environs. "All! Or nothing! Otherwise it would be a waste of time," Gerard wrote his mother. Part of this exuberance sprang from the fact that excise taxes on brewing materials and production were falling in the Netherlands, and Heineken surely thought that that would translate into lower operation costs for his new acquisition. Another part was because, unlike with Francesco Peroni's Italy in southern Europe, the Netherlands in northern Europe had a rich brewing history by which beer played a major role not just in the daily diet but in culture as well. And yet another part

Gerard Heineken originally dreamed of exporting English-style ales to England itself. He pivoted to pilsner lager instead. COURTESY OF HEINEKEN USA

of the rationale for full control was the worldly young Heineken's dream of exporting English-style ales to England itself. De Hooiberg also made a porter, after all.

By the end of February 1864 Heineken had a deal with De Hooiberg's shareholders, and he quickly renamed the brewery after his family. He almost just as quickly disabused himself of exporting to the United Kingdom. The costs of that immediately proved too high, so Heineken refocused on the Dutch market—but with a twist. In 1867 he traveled to Bavaria to explore the brewing scene there. He met a brewmaster named Wilhelm Feltmann Jr., who had a reputation for being ornery—shades of Josef Groll perhaps—but very, very good. Interestingly, Feltmann was, like Heineken, also in his early twenties and that meant that the brewmaster could not remember a Bavarian brewing industry not influenced by the innovations of English brewers via the Germanic likes of Anton Dreher and Gabriel Sedlmayr beginning in the 1830s. Heineken hired Feltmann for the refocusing on the Dutch market and Feltmann in turn brought Bavarian brewing methods northward to the Netherlands.

Inevitably, then, Heineken the brewery started producing lighter-colored lagers in the Vienna and märzen traditions pioneered by Dreher and Sedlmayr, respectively. Heineken the man was particularly a fan of Dreher's, probably because that fellow heir and entrepreneur was well on his way in the 1860s to building his brewing company into the largest in the Austrian Empire. The young Heineken saw a similar track for himself. Into the 1880s his brewery rode Feltmann's expertise in producing Vienna lager and märzen to become the biggest brewing operation in the Netherlands. A second brewery—in Rotterdam, then as now Europe's largest port—allowed the company to start the larger-scale exports that had been so dear to Gerard Heineken's heart.

But it was a switch to pilsner production during that busy decade of the 1880s that really set Heineken on a course for major growth. If Francesco Peroni's operation represented the first time that an iteration of pilsner became synonymous with a nation's beer, then Gerard Heineken's operation represented the first time a brewery deliberately tried to take its own iteration to the masses beyond its borders. By the time he died in early 1893, Gerard Heineken had been witness to—and a catalyst of—the transformation of the Dutch brewing industry. Heineken and its handful of domestic competitors—all producing mostly pilsner by then, with Heineken featuring the very word prominently on bottle labels—had edged out not only Germanic imports from places such as Bavaria but also pretty much any Dutch beer that was not a conscious attempt to mimic the Czech-born style. When young Gerard acquired De Hooiberg in 1863 and 1864, its cloudy, weak ale was probably the Netherlands' most popular style, followed perhaps by a spin-off of the dark Bavarian lager called dunkel—which, in the Netherlands and other northern European countries was called some derivation of Bayer, after Bayern, German for "Bavaria."

As the nineteenth century barreled toward its finish, though, it was pilsner that cropped up in one form or another everywhere in the kingdom. Part of that was consumer taste. Part of it was that innovations during the second half of the century lent themselves to further popularizing pilsner at the expense of other styles. "It was not only the conversion to making pilsner which made Heineken and his fellow Dutch brewers successful," according to an analysis of Dutch brewing history. "They took advantage of existing technical knowledge and converted as quickly as possible to the latest methods and equipment."

Those latest methods and equipment ended up furthering the growth of pilsner throughout the United States and Europe, and then well beyond that. The methods and equipment, too, involved just about every step of the brewing process, including how beer drinkers encountered the style itself. Heineken did feature "pilsener" prominently on its glass bottles—the proliferation of such vessels an innovation in itself, one of the new methods from one of the new types of equipment in the late nineteenth century—but others did not. This was particularly true in the United States, where the arms race between German immigrant brewers ended up producing the most popular pilsner styles ever, though one would have been hard pressed to find the actual word on the labels.

On April 23, 1859—ironically enough, the same month and day that the Reinheitsgebot was first decreed 343 years before—the Burghers' Brewery in Pilsen registered the trademark "pilsner bier" with regional authorities to describe the style born there seventeen years earlier. But it was too late. By the time of the trademark, brewers such as Francesco Peroni and Gerard Heineken, and the likes of Frederick Miller and his fellow German Americans, were rattling in their entrepreneurial pens or well off on the commercial race. Just as innovations such as the steamship, the railroad, and the telegraph—and political earthquakes throughout Europe—aided pilsner's initial spread twenty years before, this entrepreneurship and these new methods aided its international takeover and its evolution in all sorts of directions. "This convergence of science with the hotbed of nineteenth-century brewing led to many imitators in a very short period of time, many of them calling themselves pilsner, but often with scant resemblance to the original," the critic K. Florian Klemp would note.

Interestingly, it was during that very consequential 1864, the year Peroni moved to Rome and Heineken debuted, that the most influential method of all came famously to light.

Heineken was one of few breweries to slap some version of the word *pilsner* prominently on its labels early on. Courtesy of Heineken USA

12

"BEER OF REVENGE"

1858–1876 | Lille, France

At noon on December 10, 1858, and the next day at 4:00 PM, Louis Pasteur meticulously noted what he observed in a little vial filled with brewer's yeast—namely, "the continual rising of extremely fine bubbles." He would make similarly precise notations throughout that December and into January 1859 as he studied what the yeast was doing in his laboratory at a university in Lille in northern France. The observation, and his own studies and immense knowledge of microbiology and chemistry to that point, would lead Pasteur to a revolutionary conclusion for the mid-nineteenth century: that the reproduction of living yeast cells spurs fermentation, the process that makes beer and other alcoholic beverages intoxicating. Or, as Pasteur put it before he even undertook his observations in late 1858, "For there can be no hesitation, yeast brings about fermentation, and not the other way around."

That was vintage Pasteur. He was born in 1822 in France's Jura region, a mountainous and then largely impoverished area near the Swiss frontier. His father had earned the prestigious Legion of Honor fighting as a non-commissioned officer in Napoleon's invasion of Spain, and he might have gone further in life once back home had he had an education. As it was, Pasteur's father worked as a tanner, though he did not let his relatively meager trade stand in the way of his son's prospects. He saw that young Louis got an education—or at least the opportunity for an education, for the younger Pasteur proved an average student early on. But, by his late twenties, the dogged, somewhat egotistical student had mastered a subbranch of chemistry called stereochemistry that dealt with how molecules compose things. "Thanks to Pasteur, scientists thus began to see that in living beings molecules constitute the functional units of every organism," a biographer would later explain. "Forming the cells and the tissues, they mediate all biological events."

This was heady stuff for a kid from the provinces to have pioneered, and Pasteur's fame grew as he contributed to other foundational aspects of modern biology, physiology, and medicine. Pasteur, a workaholic with a close-cropped beard beneath short hair and thin oval spectacles, closely guarded his reputation and fiercely defended the conclusions of his many hypotheses. Indeed, Pasteur was not above challenging his challengers to public reviews of their findings that invariably attracted press attention that in turn buoyed Pasteur's reputation further when he was proved right. Had he lived and worked a century and a half later, he might have been called a self-promoter. But there was real fire behind the smoke. Pasteur's discoveries truly were groundbreaking.

By the time he set about his study of brewer's yeast at the end of the 1850s, he was one of France's—if not the world's—top scientists. Had Pasteur's only achievement been unlocking yeast's role in fermentation, brewers and beer fans would still remember him to this day. At the time, there was little understanding of the microbiology and chemistry behind brewing. Even the most experienced brewers barely understood the role of yeast in the process. Take the friend of Pasteur's who ran a family brewery near the center of France. The brewer was celebrated for his skill at creating popular beers—all ales—for patrons of local cafés. He told Pasteur that he discarded his yeast when it was no longer good. How could he determine that? Pasteur asked his friend. When people from the cafés start complaining about the quality of the beer, the brewer replied. Beyond that, even this skilled practitioner of the ancient practice knew little of the mercurial microorganism's role. "At most, people knew that if beer was to be healthful and tasty," a Pasteur biographer would note, "it must be clear, but there were wide differences in alcohol content, depending on the country and on local customs."

The French beer of Pasteur's time was mostly ale of iffy quality. France was not a beer country on the scale of the United Kingdom or German states such as Bavaria. It was known for wine, though beer was making inroads into the wider French marketplace in the mid-nineteenth century, fanning out from frontier regions such as Alsace next to the Germanic lands and Artois and Flanders next to Belgium. Beer consumption among the French grew tenfold over sixty years during the 1800s. The diversity of styles offered, if not the quality, markedly improved, especially for the café set in the cities. But beer would never overtake wine in the French marketplace.

For as long as anyone alive could remember, wine had held a vaunted place in French culture and commercialism. The suitability of the country's soil for any number of wine grapes made it the world's leader in both production and diversity. As with whiskey once in America, wine was pretty much omnipresent in France when Pasteur was coming of age. "Every good bourgeois owed it to himself to have, if not his own vineyard, then at least his own wine cellar," went one description. "In the countryside, a meal without a pitcher of wine on the table would have been unthinkable." Like with beer, though, the quality of French wine could vary greatly, and not just once it was in the barrel, for most wine in France was served straight from the barrel into glasses, mugs, or jugs well into the twentieth century. Wine might turn to vinegar during fermentation, whole batches of expensively harvested grapes ending up much too sour for sale. Until Pasteur came along, this changeover was thought to be largely a luck of the draw tied solely to raw materials such as grapes and water. Despite France's reputation in the field, "it was still widely thought that winemaking had nothing to do with science," according to one historian of the industry. Winemaking was instead seen as an art form, one where winemakers treated ingredients like paint or pencil—things had to be just so to achieve a good barrel. Balance was key. Vinegary results and other signs of spoilage were a by-product of a lack of equilibrium and once set in motion simply could not be reversed.

Pasteur saw things differently. Steeped in chemistry, he saw the unpredictability of French wine—and French beer, for that matter—as a result of either exposure to oxygen at the wrong times or infection with germs. Better techniques, including a better understanding of the role of yeast in fermentation, could help winemakers avoid spoilage and produce wines of more consistent quality. One technique that Pasteur eventually recommended, and that would have immense effects on beer and wine down through the ages, was heating wine to a certain degree for certain lengths of time and at certain points in the winemaking process. What came to be called pasteurization grew out of a request from Emperor Napoleon III—the nephew of the sovereign who had awarded Pasteur's father the Legion of Honor—for Pasteur to please look at what was spoiling so much wine across his empire. An aide to Napoleon III wrote to Pasteur in the summer of 1863. The aide cited the scientist's work on the effects of infection on wine and asked Pasteur to try to find ways to stop it. His Majesty and his advisers were also likely aware of Pasteur's research into the role of yeast in fermentation. In short, if anyone could end centuries of happenstance in French winemaking, it was Louis Pasteur. "The Emperor is firmly convinced that it would be of the highest importance that you turn your attention in this direction at the time of the grape harvest," the aide wrote.

Flattered by the attention—not a difficult thing to achieve with Pasteur—the scientist threw himself into the task. Since the grape harvest was right around the corner from the summer, he quickly enlisted three assistants and decamped from Lille, where he ran the science faculty at the University of Douai (later the University of Lille), for his childhood home in Jura. Local leaders offered to set up their famous native son with a laboratory, but Pasteur instead set up his research in the back of a local café in the town of Arbois. There, in a sparse laboratory over long working days and with the help of a vineyard he purchased with Napoleon III's largesse, Pasteur set about studying how to prevent the spoilage of that almighty French wine. He and his assistants read earlier research on the subject, collected and studied samples in the back of that Arbois café, and consulted area winemakers and drinkers from the surrounding Jura region and beyond. By early 1864 Pasteur was ready to present his findings, which he did during an April gathering at the University of Paris. In the late fall of 1865 Pasteur discussed his findings on pasteurization and the prevention of the spoilage of wine with Napoleon III himself during a days-long visit with other notables to the grand royal retreat in Compiègne a few hours northeast of Paris by train. His Majesty was impressed with Pasteur's doggedness in defense of the realm's most famous product. "Are you continuing your studies?" Napoleon III asked Pasteur during a meet and greet before he presented his findings. "They are so important."

"I endeavor, Sire, to keep to the same road," Pasteur replied modestly. "It is only by pursuing the same studies for a long time that one can hope to see a little better than one's predecessors."

"You are so right," the emperor said before moving on to the next Compiègne guest.

In the short term, the wine industry took enthusiastically to pasteurization—and not just in France. "Pasteur is as popular with the vintners of California as the president of the United States," a trade group representative wrote at the time. "If he were here, they would appoint him to a big job." Vintners in northern Italy and in Hungary, then under Austrian rule, also adopted pasteurization early on. French wine showcased at the International Exposition in 1867, which drew to Paris entrants from forty-two nations and visitors from across the world, benefited from the technique to Napoleon III's delight. (He may have already been planning the exposition—an answer to a similarly grandiose effort in London in 1862—when he had his people approach Pasteur about studying wine spoilage.) Ultimately, however, Pasteur's work on the hygienics of wine had little long-term effect on the industry, especially in France. That country's production processes continued to be uneven, with predictably uneven results, and it soon faced a much more vengeful foe than bacteria: a vine-munching parasite called phylloxera. It would not be until the twentieth century that the French wine industry recovered.

By then, the emphasis in winemaking had moved beyond trying to prevent spoilage through pasteurization to instead preventing it through greater care of the grapes before they were harvested and greater cleanliness throughout the winemaking process. "The practice of heating fell into disuse among the vintners, who experienced far greater distress," as one historian notes.

Pasteurization instead proved much more popular and durable among brewers. "Within a few short years," an observer wrote, "pasteurization became a neologism which rapidly attained status in technical language among brewers and nonbrewers alike." Beer, in fact, came to occupy a lot more of Louis Pasteur's time than wine in the late 1860s and the 1870s. That was because it had become personal. The mighty Prussian military—fresh from victories against Austria and Denmark during the previous half-dozen years—muscled into France in August 1870 and soon laid siege to Paris, where a revolutionary government had deposed Napoleon III (whom the Prussians had taken hostage anyway). The capital sank into anarchy for several months, first because of the siege and then because of a power struggle. Some famished residents grew so desperate they resorted to eating zoo animals before the siege eased. Hundreds of thousands of Parisians would flee the city permanently, relocating to a diminished set of French provinces, for the Prussians had taken Alsace and Lorraine in the east as trophies. Among other attributes, the pair of provinces had served as the primary source of hops for French brewing. Now the Germans had them—and had a Continent-dominating empire, which they proclaimed in the palace of Versailles near Paris in 1871. The former French hop fields became just another weapon in the Germans' already formidable brewing arsenal. It rankled a dedicated patriot such as Pasteur. "I was inspired to do this research by our misfortunes," he explained. "I began working on it immediately after the war of 1870 and have ceaselessly pursued it since that time, determined to carry it far enough to bring durable advances to an industry in which Germany is superior to us." In short, he wished for what Pasteur called "beer of revenge."

While France would never equal Germany in its brewing lore or success, Pasteur's further research into the subject ended up revolutionizing it that much further in a nineteenth century full of mini-earthquakes for beer. Before Pasteur, research was whatever brewers and prospective brewers could cage and crib through experience, visits to competitors, or word of mouth. After Pasteur, it was, in short, more scientific. Or at least the approach to solving problems was more scientific. Yeast was a prime example. He did not isolate usable strains—that would happen soon enough based on his work—but Pasteur showed the usefulness of doing so and the role such strains could play in brewing if brewers took care of the mercurial microorganisms. Pasteurization was another example. They did not have to do it, but it gave brewers a way to preserve beers for the marketplace, especially if a particular part of that marketplace was far from the brewery itself.

Such research had more impact on producers of lighter-colored, lighter-bodied lagers, pilsner in particular, because the diseases it combated were so much easier to spot and to taste than in thicker, heavier ales. Whether Pasteur intended his research to end up aiding lager producers—so many of whom were German or German-influenced—is not known, but those brewers especially took the scientist's work on healthy yeasts and well-preserved beer to heart and into their own laboratories. The same went for pasteurization, which tended to work better and make more sense for lagers because they had to be aged longer than ales and because their growing popularity meant they were often shipped farther and wider than their richer ale cousins. In the end, Pasteur's *Études sur la bière*, published in French in 1876 and translated into several languages, became a kind of bible in the brewing industry, and the scientist's other research to that point added to the canon. By then, Pasteur's most fervent disciples could be found well outside France—including probably the most influential disciple of all, who happened to live in a city named for a French king.

13

THE ETERNAL OPTIMIST

1865–1876 | St. Louis

In August 1861 a twenty-two-year-old immigrant from the Germanic duchy of Hesse was mustered out of the United States Army, where during a little more than three months of service in northern Missouri he had risen to corporal in an infantry unit that fought in minor skirmishes in the early part of the American Civil War. Trim and serious looking, with big, sad eyes and dark black hair that peaked at different points like mountains on his head, the corporal was one of more than 216,000 German immigrants who fought for the Union. Many served out of patriotism for their adopted land, others because officials impelled them to fight. It is likely the corporal served because of the former, and his 1861 exit from the army meant that he missed the worst of a war that evolved from a relatively restrained fight to restore the United States as it was to a grim slog to destroy slavery and remold the nation. It also meant that he could set about more quickly building one of America's great fortunes, a fortune based almost entirely upon pilsner.

Adolphus Busch had emigrated to the United States in 1857. He was the second to last of twenty-two children of a successful wholesaler in Hesse who also owned thousands of acres of lucrative vineyards and forests. Busch, too, had been formally educated, including at the Collegiate Institute of Brussels in Belgium, where he picked up French, and had worked as an apprentice at two trades, including in a mercantile house in Cologne and under an uncle in his brewery. So, unlike many Germans fleeing revolution and counterrevolution and the misery it brought, Busch came to America with some prospects, some marketable skills, and a little financial backing. It was not much—there were twenty-two children, after all, most of whom lived into adulthood—but by all accounts, the eighteen-year-old Busch and three of his brothers settled in St. Louis with relative ease, Adolphus reaching the city via steamboat up the Mississippi from New Orleans.

The Missouri city was booming then, its population expanding from 20,000 clustered in a handful of neighborhoods in 1840 to more than 160,000 the year the Busch brothers arrived. It was America's eighth-biggest city, larger even than Chicago and the capital of Washington. German arrivals such as the Busches drove much of this growth. "We found it almost necessary to learn the German language before we could ride in an omnibus, or buy a pair of breeches, and absolutely necessary to drink beer at a Sunday concert," a local newspaper editorialist wrote in June 1857, shortly before Adolphus Busch arrived.

It was that last part, the part about beer, that came to be associated most closely with the German arrivals and their immediate descendants. As was the case in other then-western US cities such as Milwaukee and Chicago, German Americans could not get enough of lager, and soon Americans with deeper family roots in the nation could not either. Beer from St. Louis's thirty to forty pre–Civil War breweries—many of them owned and operated by German immigrants and most producing lighter-colored, lighter-tasting lager based on the pilsner style—had been "well nigh universally adopted by the English-speaking population of St. Louis," one observer noted, "and the spacious bier Halles and extensive gardens nightly show that the Americans are as fond of the Gambrinian liquid as are those who have introduced it." Less salutary reactions had greeted the rise in lager's popularity in 1850s America, of course, with Chicago's Lager Beer Riot of 1855 probably the best example of nativist backlash. But German Americans' service in the war in the early 1860s and the sheer size of their brewing operations in many cities quenched most of the thirst for any such pushback by the time the Civil War ended in April 1865.

St. Louis followed what became a trend in Americans' fandom for beer. The city entered the nineteenth century like much of the United States: whiskey territory. This was not least because the city was a major port along the Mississippi River and therefore a loading and unloading point for that new-fangled bourbon whiskey that had begun pouring out of Kentucky via the Ohio River during the previous century. Beer grew in popularity, though an unreliable supply of barley in particular made its quality spotty and demand for it uneven. That all started to change in 1842—the same year Josef Groll more than half a world away unveiled Pilsen's take on Bavarian lager.

That was the year when a German immigrant to St. Louis named Johann Adam Lemp, along with his son William, started turning out consistently good lager from a new brewery on Second Street. Lemp aged the beer in this pre-refrigeration era in a natural cave south of St. Louis. "This light, clear, pleasant-tasting, bottom-fermented brew quickly captured the public fancy," a historian of the city writes. The "lighter" referred to its color relative to the darker lagers and much darker ales available, and the "clear" to its clarity in a beer world where detritus might still be common. By the following decade, lager "had captured the lion's share of the local market." Two dozen St. Louis breweries brewed 60,000 barrels of the stuff in 1854, and between thirty and forty breweries produced nearly 190,000 barrels six years later. A newspaper partial to the recently formed Republican Party noted that eighteen million glasses of lager were drunk in St. Louis during the warmer months of 1854—March 1 to September 17, "when the lager beer gave out." That time span would have made sense to William Lemp, who would have been familiar not only with government regulations from back home that lager be brewed only during a certain part of the calendar but also with the practice of taking advantage of the cooler months to both brew and age a type of beer that did not take kindly to heat.

One of the St. Louis breweries churning out this brew for sale during the spring and summer belonged to Adolphus Busch's future father-in-law, Eberhard Anheuser. Busch met Anheuser through a brewing supply business that Busch and partners had started in 1859, and Busch married Anheuser's daughter Lilly in April 1861—shortly before both men ended up in the same Missouri infantry regiment. Before the business and the marriage, the recently arrived Busch scraped by in St. Louis as a riverboat clerk. The death of his father back in Europe in 1859, however, provided him the capital to cofound the supply company. As for Anheuser, he owned a struggling concern on St. Louis's far south side called, simply, the Bavarian Brewery. Anheuser had made a tidy local fortune in soap- and candle-making—and he came from a family that back in Europe owned successful vineyards. He also earned interest loaning money to various fellow German Americans, including the owners of the Bavarian Brewery. To pay off their debts, the owners turned the keys over to him. The brewery was already struggling financially to produce about four thousand barrels of lager a year—St. Louis's largest operations turned out a few times that annually—and Anheuser himself fell into debt to Busch's supply company sometime around the outbreak of the conflict between North and South.

Oddly enough, the Civil War proved a godsend financially, and not just to Anheuser's teetering brewery. St. Louis was the largest city in a slave state that could have gone for the Union or the Confederacy. Missouri's governor and other top leaders, in fact, broke for the latter early on, and it was only the imposition of martial law and the Union's seizure of federal arsenals that kept the state essentially neutral for the duration—technically still part of the United States, but with plenty of well-armed Confederate sympathizers. That was enough to ensure that a sort of brutal anarchy reigned over much of Missouri for much of the war. "The war in Missouri was more violent, more chaotic than anywhere else," one historian wrote. The Lincoln administration did what it could to protect this strategic spot halfway along the Mississippi River, meaning that from early on in the four-year conflict Missouri teemed with Union soldiers and sailors. And those servicemen drank. "Everybody—almost—drinks," a visiting physician observed of Missouri during the war. "Beer shops and gardens are numerous." Lager was the particular favorite of these soldiers and sailors, and of the United States military in general, which classified it as nonintoxicating and far more preferable to much stronger whiskey. Hundreds of breweries in Missouri and elsewhere contracted with the military to provide lager, which lasted longer and traveled better than ale. And the United States Sanitary Commission, a civilian organization that worked to ensure better care for military personnel, even recommended lager as healthy, with one commission physician noting that it was "a valuable substitute for vegetables" in preventing constipation.

The war also proved a roundabout boon to industry cooperation. At its start in 1861, American breweries—invariably family-owned and family-run, on the small side, and distributing not far from the brewery walls—operated mostly in isolation. At times there was some informal cooperation when necessary, like the sharing of new techniques and sources of material such as ice and grains. But breweries in the United States did not cooperate on any grand scale. Those in the Hudson Valley knew little of the challenges of those in the Ohio Valley. The war changed that, and it would have far-reaching effects not only for brewing but for American business in general.

On August 1, 1862, the Lincoln administration enacted a recently passed tax of one dollar per thirty-one-gallon barrel of "beer, lager beer, ale, porter and other similar fermented liquors, by whatever name such liquors may be called." It was the first national excise tax on beer, and it was meant to raise money quickly for the prosecution of the war. This was a time when it was unclear who would win, when international powers such as France and Britain dithered on whether to recognize the Confederacy, and before Lincoln and his generals started fighting what they called a "hard war" to force submission—and the end of slavery—versus one merely to bind up the nation as it had been. Beer was not alone as a target for taxation. Leaders in Washington aimed the levy at other so-called luxury items, everything from billiard tables and playing cards to yachts and carriages. The regulations on beer also required brewers to purchase a federal manufacturer's license for one hundred dollars if they produced at least five hundred barrels annually, and fifty dollars if they made half that—both the equivalent of several thousand dollars in 2019 money. In the end, it worked, raising cash quickly for munitions, soldiers' pay, etcetera. The newly created Office of the Commissioner of Internal Revenue cleared $369 million in taxes in the last three years of the Civil War, some $8 million of that from the ballooning beer industry.

Brewers, loyal to the United States though many were, saw the tax as a threat to their booming business. They quickly organized in a way that was unusual for American business at the time. European economies had their guilds, wherein merchants and artisans in the same field banded together to set standards and prices, and to generally protect the status quo if it was worth protecting. Such a system had yet to catch on in a younger, much more geographically diffuse America. The meeting of a few dozen—one report pegged it at thirty-seven—New York City–area brewers at Pythagoras Hall on the Lower East Side on August 21, 1862, three weeks after Lincoln signed the tax into law, therefore marked a watershed for American business, certainly for American food manufacturing.

No one could know it at the time, but what became the United States Brewers' Association was charting new territory in lobbying for business. Lager brewers and Americans of German descent constituted nearly the entire trade group, so much so that early meetings were recorded in German rather than English. The association enjoyed a coup almost immediately, too. Its lobbying helped persuade Congress to cut the per-barrel tax 40 percent, though before the war's 1865 end it crept back to one dollar. Nevertheless, "the brewers learned a valuable lesson: better to cooperate than to resist; to educate the nation's lawmakers than to ignore them," one historian wrote. It was a lesson brewers and businesspeople in other industries would take to heart.

That included the eventual savior of Eberhard Anheuser's St. Louis brewery. Whatever boon the Civil War provided in terms of fresh demand, Anheuser's debts followed him right through the conflict. So he provided his son-in-law a management role at the brewery around the time of the war's end in 1865. It proved a shrewd move on Anheuser's part and a monumental one for national and international business. Within a decade, Busch helped turn around the Bavarian Brewery (then called the E. Anheuser & Co.)—being able to ease its debts to the supply company he co-owned surely helped—and in the first years of the 1870s the brewery was one of the most profitable and largest in St. Louis, then, as now, a brewing hub for all America. The brewery was producing twenty-seven thousand barrels annually by 1873, nearly all of it lighter-colored and lighter-tasting lager, and nearly all of it for consumption in the St. Louis area. Production would grow exponentially under Busch's firm guidance, as would geographic reach. In 1879 Anheuser made Busch a minority partner in what the older man rechristened the Anheuser-Busch Brewing Association. And when he died in May 1880, at age seventy-three, Anheuser left his son-in-law and daughter with a majority of the company's shares.

Until that point, the brewery that Anheuser and Busch owned had been in turnaround mode largely because of St. Louis's postwar population boom, particularly its echoing boom in residents of German descent (Adolphus and Lilly Busch themselves would have three children during their rise to prominence in the city and thirteen total). The beer these German Americans and others put away in St. Louis and other growing American cities was invariably lighter-colored, lighter-tasting lager and not necessarily of any particular lager style. After 1880, though, the beer that German Americans favored, and that the nation as a whole would come to favor, became inextricably linked with

A polymath with a keen business sense, Adolphus Busch always wanted his beer to appeal to a wide audience. COURTESY OF AND USED WITH PERMISSION OF ANHEUSER-BUSCH. ALL RIGHTS RESERVED

the style born in Pilsen in the Austrian Empire's Bohemia region in 1842. And that would be because Adolphus Busch threw his brewery keenly behind a recipe from that region. He tweaked it to American tastes and adjusted it to American agriculture. Fluent in French—among other languages—he read Louis Pasteur's groundbreaking 1876 work on yeast and the diseases of beer, and he seized every imaginable emerging technology and trend to blast his version of pilsner to the nation and then the world.

For more than three decades, pilsner had run alongside lager in general, the golden child of predecessors that were light but not as light, effervescent but not as effervescent, crisp but still with a malty mouthfeel not unlike that of ales. Breweries such as Heineken featured the word *pilsner* prominently on its packaging, but the word in any of its spellings had not really broken through within the industry and certainly not with the public. Before the 1870s few outside central and northern Europe spoke of pilsner as a distinct style of lager. Even then, the references might be more to the geography of the beer than to its makeup. Pilsner was that golden lager from Bohemia, much as Anton Dreher's Vienna lager was the reddish lager of the Austrian capital or Gabriel Sedlmayr's orangish märzen was the lightest Bavarian offering.

After the 1870s, however, owing to the exertions of Adolphus Busch and a handful of others, never mind the ready audience of millions of German transplants, pilsner's distinctness and influence became impossible to ignore. It was well on its way then to conquering alcohol sales worldwide and to altering the business of food and drink forever. If its dominance seemed improbable, or at least unlikely given that pilsner had spent over three decades emerging, it was. "I am an eternal optimist," Adolphus Busch would explain toward the end of his life in the next century, when pilsner had made him the largest brewer in history and one of the richest men on earth. "[I] never lean in the least to the other side, and I am always coming out right."

14

INTERNATIONAL SPLASH

1873–1874 | Vienna; St. Louis

There were fifty-three thousand exhibitors from thirty-five countries within 575 acres inside Vienna's Prater, a vast park near the Danube River. The site of the fifth World Exhibition from May 1 to October 31 in 1873 was physically larger than the previous four in London and Paris combined. More than 7.2 million visitors—about a dozen times the population of the Austrian capital itself—would pour through the four grand halls of the exhibition, each dedicated to a particular facet of human endeavor or ingenuity: industry, machines, agriculture, and art.

For that was what these world expos were supposed to do: highlight the march of human progress. At the first one, in London in 1851, Mathew Brady demonstrated his innovations in photography and Samuel Colt showed off his new six-shooter, which fitted perfectly in a holster on a man's belt. At the fourth one in Paris in 1867, attendees got to see a hydraulics-powered elevator and reinforced concrete. They also got to see—and to taste—the latest in beer. Gabriel Sedlmayr's Spaten brewery in Munich took home a medal from that world expo, complete with a relief of Emperor Napoleon III in profile, for its märzen, a medal the brewery displays to this day in a cavernous malting hall turned museum. The 1867 expo's organizers also awarded medals to other breweries from other countries, a sign that beer, like wine, was seen as a beverage truly international in its variety and appeal and one worthy of analysis.

That approach continued in 1873 on a grander scale. Austria, after all, was much more of a beer country than wine-centric France. "Of course all the great breweries in diverse parts of the complex Austrian empire, with the celebrated Dreher at their head, took part in the competition," wrote one British visitor after the expo. There were also beers from throughout Europe, including Poland, Russia, Italy, Romania, and Spain, never mind Germany. Brazil and China sent samples, and some beer came from as far away as

New Zealand. In a wing of the expo's agriculture hall, visitors were able to examine and, in many cases, to taste these offerings amid flamboyant decorations. One of the Austrian breweries decorated its exhibit with "a pyramid of beer casks, interspersed with bottles of Märzen beer, its four-corner pedestals being decorated with typical topers colored to resemble life, and representing a student, a soldier, a peasant, and a priest." Another Austrian exhibit "was constructed in the form of a cave, above which the mythical beer-imbibing king Gambrinus, resplendent in red, green, and yellow, and holding a foaming beaker of ale in lieu of a scepter in his hand, was seen seated on a throne, while within the cave itself half a dozen inebriated gnomes in the guise of medieval cellarmen, were battling over a barrel of beer with their overturned flagons littering the ground." Beer also proved popular beyond the expo in a Vienna that was then at its late-nineteenth-century peak. "The restaurants and beer halls were crowded," wrote an attendee, "and thousands were walking about enjoying the sight of the many novel objects and constructions on all sides."

As for how the beer at the 1873 Vienna expo actually tasted, that was a mixed bag. The offerings from places such as Romania and Switzerland were treated as curiosities. The Brits sniffed that it was unfair to judge their ales, which had traveled nearly one thousand miles, against the fresher lagers from the Continent. The Austrian and German offerings fared the best among international judges, brewers themselves, and the general public. "The Austrian beers, like all the light beers of Germany, are brewed in accordance with the Bavarian system, and are generally a very superior class of beverage," went one assessment. The expo's breakout beer, though, was only technically Austrian in that it fell within the imperial realm, and only tangentially related to Germany in that its origins lay with a brewmaster from Bavaria and the techniques he picked up there. In a formal report presented to the British parliament in 1874, an official observer sang hosannas to what to London ears then was still a largely unsung style. Writer and publisher Henry Richard Vizetelly entered into the public record through that parliamentary presentation perhaps the most complete description of pilsner from the late nineteenth century:

> Most of the Austrian beers have a mild and soft flavour, and it is rarely that any of them are so bitter as the English pale ales. An exception, however, must be made with regard to the so-called Pilsner beer brewed in Pilsen, in Bohemia, on a very extensive scale, and much in favour with the Viennese, who do not object to paying a slightly high price for it. This beer is exceedingly pale in colour as

well as remarkably light, being even weaker than the Vienna beer [Vienna lager] and contains a considerable amount of carbonic acid [carbonation]. Its distinguishing quality, however, is its strong, indeed almost medicinal bitter flavour, due to the Saaz hops, held in the highest esteem in the locality.

Vizetelly's report then went on to note the "medal for progress" that the expo's organizers awarded to the "Citizens' brewery at Pilsen" that had invented the style. The brewery that launched in 1842 was by the time of the 1873 expo "the most extensive brewing establishment in Bohemia"—no small feat as the amount of beer produced in the region had increased 76 percent since 1860, according to Vizetelly. The Burghers' Brewery produced "by far the largest quantity" of pilsner, and it now had imitators up and down the Continent, and fans as far afield as America. But while it stepped into a kind of imperial spotlight at this fifth World Exposition in a peaking Vienna, pilsner still remained enough of a novelty that a well-versed Englishman like Vizetelly felt the need to describe it in such detail for one of the world's biggest beer-drinking nations, the United Kingdom.

Maybe that was a function of the British beer market, in which darkly sweet porters and stouts, along with bitter brown and pale ales, still dominated. A bitterer iteration of pale ale called India pale ale was very much in vogue, too, in the 1860s and 1870s. IPA was "the drink of fashionable London, a 'wine of malt' that was prescribed by doctors for stomach complaints and general well-being," as one critic would later note. Lighter-colored, lighter-tasting, less-bitter pilsner would have a hard time cracking that market. Maybe pilsner's relative novelty in the 1870s had to do with the fact that its imitators rarely called their imitations "pilsner." Heineken did during the period, displaying the word prominently on packaging and on what later generations might call marketing material such as advertisements. Peroni and others did not. "Lager" sufficed for explaining this growing trend in lighter-colored, lighter-tasting, higher-carbonated beer. Vizetelly's description from 1874 remains so memorable precisely because it was so rare in identifying for a wider audience the style (pilsner) with the place (Pilsen) that had given it its name.

That was about to change in a big way. For the Vienna expo attracted visitors from Missouri. They took the railroad to New York, and steamers over to Europe, and then more railroads to the Austrian capital. One of them was Otto Lademan, who attended as Missouri's official representative to the international confab. Lademan had emigrated from Prussia in 1856, served four years in the Union Army, and then married the daughter of a St. Louis brewer named Joseph Uhrig in 1865. It is likely that Lademan at least heard about, if not tasted, pilsner and its imitations while in Vienna. He might have been familiar with the style—though not the name—even before his train pulled out of St. Louis. His father-in-law's brewery was one of the growing number in the city specializing in lighter lagers. Lademan then very likely discussed his Viennese adventures with St. Louis's German American brewing community upon his return, perhaps at one of St. Louis's popular beer gardens. Among that St. Louis brewing community, of course, was the entrepreneurial Adolphus Busch. It is unclear if Busch himself went to Vienna. He might have. But it is clear that he and Lademan thereafter familiarized themselves thoroughly with pilsners, including one Lademan learned about at the expo that came from a small Bohemian city called České Budějovice—or Budweis in German.

15

BEYOND ICE

1871–1876 | Munich; Trieste; Milwaukee

In the summer of 1871, Carl Linde, a mechanical engineering professor at the Technical University in Munich, reached agreements with the Dreher Brewery in Trieste, the Austrian Empire's major port, and the Spaten brewery in Munich itself to install an artificial refrigeration machine to keep lagers cool during fermentation and aging. Linde—an earnest-looking Bavarian native one year shy of his thirtieth birthday, with a thick black beard and tiny oval spectacles—had first come upon the idea of artificial refrigeration while competing in a university contest to cool paraffin wax. Artificial refrigeration was not a new idea. Tinkerers had known for centuries that the surest way to cool something was to extract heat from it, usually through decompression or evaporation—but it had yet to be done in a consistent, safe, and reliable way. "The thought immediately struck me: here was an area of mechanical thermodynamics that had not yet been fully explored," Linde would write in his memoir decades later. He set about researching the challenge in between lecturing at the university.

Linde published his initial research in 1870 and 1871 in a well-known Bavarian trade journal—which he also edited—and the research quickly caught the attention of those pillars of the southern German economy: brewers. In particular, Gabriel Sedlmayr, the revolutionary owner of Munich's largest brewery, reached out to Linde, with whom he was already on friendly terms. Would Linde like to try out what the professor called his "improved ice and refrigeration machine" at the Spaten brewery? That brewery that had done so much to advance beer and brewing, particularly of the lighter-colored, lighter-tasting variety, was one of the world's most modern. Yet, despite innovations such as a switch to steam power and a vast expansion at a new location in the early 1850s, Spaten still relied on ice and cellars for keeping its famous lager cool. For all the march of technology and time, Spaten's brewers were still brewing with a technique that the legendary monks who founded

Munich in the Dark Ages would have been familiar with. The same went for the Dreher Brewery in Trieste, which Anton Dreher's son had launched in 1869 and which had become the largest in the Austrian Empire. If Linde's research—which hinged on using a liquid refrigerant to absorb and remove heat from an enclosed space—could be put into practice in a lager brewery, the increasingly popular beer could be reliably made year round and the practice adopted by pretty much any industry that needed it.

Spaten was the first test case. Linde's earliest machine was installed there in January 1874. It was dangerously flawed, though, and Linde's chosen refrigerant, methyl ether, leaked from a faulty seal. "This design was not a suitable solution for the requirements of practical use," Linde noted with his typical dry scientific exactitude. "So it seemed imperative to build a second machine." Build it he and his partners did—this time with a sturdier glycerin seal and more consistent ammonia as the refrigerant. Linde tested it throughout late 1875, and in March 1876 received a Bavarian patent. The same year, the Dreher Brewery bought the first commercial machine. The brewery started using it to cool fermentation and aging rooms in the spring of 1877, and it ran more than thirty years. In 1879 Linde quit the Technical University in Munich and went full-time into the artificial refrigeration business, becoming an ever-innovating giant in the field and a part of German nobility in 1897, when the kaiser knighted him and he could add "von" to "Linde."

The great leap ahead in commercial refrigeration in the 1870s came almost entirely from Linde's relationship with German brewers of lighter-colored, lighter-tasting lager. Had there been no relationship, it is clear that the advance of artificial, or mechanical, refrigeration would have taken much longer. Instead, in these brewers, Linde seemed to find kindred entrepreneurial spirits willing to try new things and unafraid of setbacks. "It was Linde's close relationship to the use-oriented brewers which permitted the development of a complete refrigeration system, first for breweries and then for numerous manufacturers of foodstuffs," according to a history of Linde's company, which lasted into the twenty-first century. "Without this kind of contact, Linde probably would not have found the simple yet strong solutions that made his equipment stand out."

Further innovations in artificial refrigeration followed in the 1870s and 1880s. John De La Vergne, a grocer turned brewer, developed a much-imitated ammonia-driven refrigeration system that became a standard in the brewing industry, starting at New York City's old Herman Brewery on Manhattan's West Eighteenth Street, which De La Vergne co-owned and which hosted his company's first machine in 1880. Brewers' adoption of artificial refrigeration on both sides of the Atlantic—Heineken in the Netherlands would install a system in 1881—furthered that nascent industry and helped other foodstuff producers see its value. Brewers themselves had been skeptical, and some remained so into the waning days of the nineteenth century. Though acquiring and shipping tons of ice to keep lager cool while it fermented and aged could be an expensive headache—especially during warmer months—the positively medieval method was seen as more reliable than some of the early stabs at refrigeration. Still, experience triumphed and earlier adopters such as Heineken were rewarded with expanding production capacity and distribution potential. "My cellars and fermenting rooms are kept cool as I desire, while the air in them is dry and fresh," raved one early adopter of De La Vergne's machines, "a marked contrast with the condition when ice is used and which only a brewer can appreciate."

One brewer who really appreciated the potential of refrigeration—probably more than any other soul in any industry during refrigeration's nineteenth-century salad days—was Adolphus Busch. Well into his thirties by the 1870s and gradually amassing a baronial presence in St. Louis, complete with mansions there and as far afield as California and Germany, Busch was pushing the boundaries of how far his lighter lager could be shipped and how long it could be packaged before consumption. Just as Busch had seized upon Pasteur's research into spoilage and become the first American brewer to pasteurize his beer (with the inaugural pasteurized Anheuser-Busch beer reaching dusty, hot Texas as early as 1872), he seized on the refrigeration trend. Through the 1870s and 1880s, Busch would build a fleet of 250 railroad cars outfitted with refrigeration. The fleet replaced a vast system of roadside icehouses that Busch had already built up and that the railcars gradually rendered obsolete. The growing Anheuser-Busch brewery in St. Louis also adopted refrigeration in the 1870s. Soon, Busch's beers could be shipped farther than any American-made beer had ever been shipped in large quantities, and Anheuser-Busch was well on its way to becoming one of the world's largest breweries by the close of the century, with more than one million barrels of beer produced annually. It was a far cry from the struggling operation Busch joined in the 1860s at his father-in-law's behest.

Adolphus Busch's biggest rival during this period came in the form of Frederick Pabst, a fellow German immigrant. Born in March 1836, Pabst emigrated with his parents from Prussia's Saxony region during the continental upheavals of 1848. Cholera took his mother a year later, and father and son scratched out a living in Chicago as a cook and a waiter, respectively, at the old Mansion House hotel. The younger Pabst moved on, probably before his twentieth birthday, to working on the newfangled steamships that regularly plied the coast of western Lake Michigan, many depositing German immigrants such as himself in growing port cities. By 1857, Pabst was co-owner of a ship he called the *Huron*. People called him "Captain," a nickname he never lost, and they routinely described him as affable and generous. A photograph shortly after this period showed a stout young man with curly brown hair and curly brown goatee, his eyes almost twinkling, his face as if trying to suppress a wide smile. Pabst very likely would have remained a minor and contented tycoon on the Great Lakes were it not for a terrible storm on December 16, 1863. Waves and wind lashed a new ship of his called the *Sea Bird*, with Lake Michigan threatening to macerate and swallow the vessel, taking down not only Pabst but also his passengers and crew. Pabst beached the ship in Whitefish Bay just north of Milwaukee. He saved everyone's life, but it would take $20,000—a small fortune in those days—to fix the *Sea Bird* and resume his business.

Lucky for Pabst, he had a plan B. During one of the *Huron*'s voyages—perhaps while docked in Chicago—Pabst had met fellow Teutonic transplant Phillip Best. Best was down from Milwaukee, where he had taken over the family business Best & Co. and renamed it Phillip Best Brewing Co. That operation had grown into one of Milwaukee's more notable breweries, but it had yet to really break out beyond the city and its surrounding region. Plus, like other breweries that had sprung up behind lighter lager and the German immigration wave in the 1840s and 1850s, the Best brewery had quickly run up quite a bit of debt to suppliers and other vendors. Still, for all he knew, when he met Phillip Best, Frederick Pabst was meeting another German American who had done good in his adopted land. What's more, Phillip Best had a daughter in her late teens named Maria, whom Pabst fell for—the pair married in March 1862, when the groom was twenty-six and the bride nineteen.

After the storm the following year mauled the *Sea Bird*, Pabst went to work for his in-laws' brewery in Milwaukee, quickly becoming a partner in the venture and then co-owner with another Phillip Best son-in-law, Emil Schandein, before the 1860s were out. Pabst would take the lead, however, turning the Best brewery around financially and seizing on some of the same scientific and technological advances as his eventual rival Adolphus Busch seized on to make his own father-in-law's operation successful.

By the mid-1870s, the two men would dominate not only American brewing but, increasingly, world brewing as well. They adopted pilsner as their main style and went from respective operations of perhaps a dozen employees each to conglomerates involving phalanxes of workers in brewhouses, offices, and along distribution channels. It was their respective embraces of the style, moves born of customer demand and technological change, that were the decisive factor in pilsner vanquishing other lighter lager styles. As imperious as their favored style was becoming, both Pabst and Busch were each the sort of man who "commanded any room he entered," as the historian Maureen Ogle noted. They were imposing, courtly, charming, and ruthless—and, much like the beer style they rode to wealth and renown, they came along at just the right time. For artificial refrigeration was far from the only leap forward that pilsner prompted.

16

FARTHER AND WIDER

1872–1880 | St. Louis

Toward the end of 1877, the *Western Brewer* journal, then the leading trade publication about the US brewing industry, reported that an entire barge loaded with glass beer bottles had departed Pittsburgh for a long journey down the Ohio River and then up the Mississippi toward St. Louis. The cargo was bound for the Anheuser-Busch brewery.

Unsatisfied with being simply one of the largest breweries in the St. Louis area, Adolphus Busch's operation had been faster than any to embrace bottling its own beer for shipment over great distances. Some rivals had tried it—most famously Anheuser-Busch's archrival out of Milwaukee, Best Brewing led by Frederick Pabst—but no sizable American brewery had stuck with it. The Best brewery, for one, transferred its bottling to an outside bottling company after only one year doing it in house. And George Ehret's Hell Gate Brewery in Manhattan, by the late 1870s the largest operation in the US, also turned to an outside bottler. Not Anheuser-Busch. Its leader saw the potential that bottling brought in an era of both expanding beer consumption and technological innovation. The groundbreaking research of Louis Pasteur, especially the development of pasteurization, made it immensely easier for brewers to keep their lagers fresher and effervescent for longer. The unspooling of vast rail networks and the rise of artificial refrigeration made it that much easier to ship that pasteurized lager farther and wider. Then there were the bottles themselves, born of research and innovation—and helped along in their rise by a pilsner style that looked particularly good in bottles.

Bottled beer was not new in the late nineteenth century. Brewers in Europe, especially in the United Kingdom, had been doing it for centuries, with a notable pickup in the 1700s, though the beers bottled were often heavier ales meant for more immediate consumption and not for shipment far from the brewery. What's more, the consistency and the quality of these bottled beers tended to vary greatly. The bottling was laborious—done by hand and susceptible then to every mistake in the book, from bacterial contamination to uneven fills across a single batch. Plus, bottles were expensive for most brewers to obtain and reliable sources could be scarce. Unsurprisingly, most beer in the United States and elsewhere was still drunk from the tap when Adolphus Busch set about his audacious plan in the 1870s to sell his beer widely not only in bottles but in bottles he produced.

Originally, like other breweries, Anheuser-Busch filled any bottles it sold by hand. Workers used a rubber hose to fill the bottles and capped them with a cork stopper—invariably just as foam started to seep out. The workers then wired the bottles shut, and their contents underwent pasteurization to guard against spoilage. Out the door they went in wooden crates, usually six dozen quart bottles or ten pint bottles per crate. It was not exactly a packaging recipe for world domination.

This was in the early 1870s. By the end of the 1870s, Anheuser-Busch boasted the largest bottling plant in the United States—for any industry, brewing or otherwise. The two-story bottling plant that went up in south St. Louis could turn out one hundred thousand bottles a day. Workers still sealed these quart and pint bottles by hand, but by then they were using a screw topper made of a very hard rubber called ebonite that an Englishman named Henry Barrett had developed. The stopper allowed for more rapid turnout of bottles, leading Anheuser-Busch to gradually pivot toward such packaging and away from selling its beers by the barrel or cask. Not that the company did not have access to plenty of those. Anheuser-Busch's explosive growth in the 1870s and 1880s included two new cooperages at the corner of Eighth and Pestalozzi in St. Louis, which were in turn part of a massive complex that was quickly on its way to becoming the world's largest brewery. In the late 1870s Adolphus Busch's juggernaut "embarked upon a building program that never seemed to be entirely completed," as one chronicler put it. Seven new buildings or additions would go up at the St. Louis headquarters between October 1, 1877, and September 31, 1878, at a then-astounding cost of nearly $59,000. These included a brick brewhouse and a refrigerated beer vault in addition to the bottling plant.

Steam powered much of the Anheuser-Busch complex, an approach that European brewers had adopted years ago but that might have still seemed novel to many US brewers. Steam even helped set the right temperatures in the brewing kettles, providing a uniformity in the process never possible before. Steam would pump the fermented beer from the kettles to the aging tanks, and then send the beer to the bottles, which would clank along on machinery that must have seemed otherworldly to many. It was all so state of the art for the era, so much so that breweries such as Anheuser-Busch were an inspiration for Henry Ford's automobile assembly lines thirty years later. Even the office portion of the expanding Anheuser-Busch complex was groundbreaking—"a model to other businessmen," a historian of the era writes. It facilitated quick communications in house and with the outside world—the office included a special Western Union telegraph wire—at a time when American business was trending toward speed, efficiency, and repetition.

What was happening within Anheuser-Busch's seven-acre south St. Louis footprint was illustrative, if not among the vanguard, of what was happening across America as the now-continental nation industrialized. Millions of its citizens were relocating from the farm to the factory, which meant relocating to the city—and the influx of immigrants continued unabated, this time mostly from China and southern Europe rather than central and northern Europe like a generation before. From 1870 to 1900 the share of the nation's population living in cities grew from about one-fourth to well over one-third. The shift occurred partly because mechanized reapers and plows had rendered a lot of farm labor obsolete. A larger factor, though, was that automated production of goods was clearly the future and already the present. American factories were belching out goods as varied as porcelain toilets and bottled condiments, typewriters and canned food, bath tubs and crackers.

And they were doing so at unprecedented rates. The McCormick Harvesting Machine Company turned out fifty thousand reapers annually by the 1880s. Campbell produced millions of cans of soup a year on its way to more than fifteen million yearly by the turn of the century. And on it went, with an increasing share of these mass-produced goods leaving the country: American exports would triple between 1860 and 1900. The economic drivers of the United States circa 1878 would have been unrecognizable to someone from fifty years before stepping from a time machine, and the social changes—not least the shift from farm to factory, and the grinding, often dangerous drudgery that millions of industrial workers toiling usually six to seven days a week endured—would have astounded. The brewing industry was no different. In its permanent rearview mirror now were smaller operations of a dozen workers, max, making small batches that did not come out uniformly similar—never mind identical—and that did not stay drinkable that long after they exited the brewery.

Now the industry was more automated than ever and more focused than ever on producing beers that tasted the same batch after batch. They also had to look the same—transparently clean, for just as glass bottles were becoming popular with brewers, glassware was becoming popular with consumers.

Finally, they had to pour the same, which invariably meant bubbly and with a thick, lasting head at the top. That was a problem for many American breweries—and there were nearly twenty-seven hundred in 1876, the most there would ever be until the twenty-first century and almost all thanks to the rise in popularity of lighter-tasting, lighter-colored lager. That was because "much of the local beer sold in the nineteenth century was of poor quality, inconsistent, sour, or flavorless," a student of the era noted.

That was not just some quirk of the gods. It was a result of many American brewers simply not keeping up with the latest leaps forward, particularly in the science of brewing that Louis Pasteur pioneered. A brewer wrote to the editor of *Western Brewer* in 1881 to ask how the beer from Best Brewing—Frederick Pabst's fast-growing Milwaukee outfit—sustained its foamy head for so long. "We use bicarbonate," the brewer wrote, "but the beer won't carry like the Milwaukee [beer]." The editor replied that Best's enviable head "depends not so much on addition of foreign substances as on the quality of the malt, the mode of mashing," and other factors, including a particularly meticulous fermentation process and top-notch facilities. Breweries willing to expend time and capital to brew a consistently solid lager did so, borrowing where necessary from banks eager to involve themselves in a growing industry or, more often than not, sinking profits into research and development. "I wish it understood that I must have nothing but the very best and finest picks," Adolphus Busch once wrote to a hops dealer. He meant it.

Then there were the ale brewers that the craze for lager—pilsner in particular—was leaving in the commercial dust. There simply were not many brewers of ale left in the United States. The shift to lager had been swift and pronounced after the Civil War ended in 1865 as the Germanic influence spread. Ale was disappearing beneath an ocean of lager; brewers were producing some nine million barrels of lager annually by 1877, the *New York Times* reported, "by far the greater part of which flows down American gullets," rather than those of Germans, whom the *Times* apparently considered distinct from other Americans. Not only was lager sweeping all before it in a changing American brewing industry; it was a particular sort of lighter-tasting lager that was doing so. This one was not aged as long and tasted "sweeter" as well as "softer," according to the *Times*. An older lager might taste "hard," "sour," and "bitter," the newspaper reported, and since "one American beer-drinker consumes more, on an average, than three Germans," brewers had no choice but to respond to the demand. "Of course the Americans are to blame for this," the newspaper lamented. "They have never yet got to generally like the real lager flavor."

No matter. The wide trade in what the world would come to know as pilsner was the future of beer. The statistics did not lie. In 1880 three-fourths of American brewers produced fewer than four thousand barrels annually; half produced fewer than one thousand. Most of that beer, the majority of it lighter lager, made it maybe a couple of miles from the brewery itself, usually to local taverns and hotels. Operations such as Frederick Pabst's Best Brewing and Adolphus Busch's Anheuser-Busch turned out so much more—200,000 barrels in the case of the former, 141,000 in the case of the latter. Nothing reflected this growing dominance more than the introduction of the year-round, widespread shipping of pasteurized lager in glass bottles during this period. The very emergence of bottled beer on a grand scale changed where beer could be consumed and by whom, altering forever the trajectory of a beverage thousands of years old. The distribution, too, allowed breweries such as Best and Anheuser-Busch in America, and Heineken especially in Europe, to expand their footprints and to scale their financial growth like no other breweries had before. Even mighty Guinness with its dark stout ale out of the United Kingdom never enjoyed the consistent reach of these producers. By the end of the 1870s—and following the introduction of one brand of pilsner in particular—bottles of Busch's beer could be found as far afield as Japan, India, Mexico, and Brazil. Once extended, too, the reach would never shrink.

17

HOW IT SPARKLES

1876–1895 | St. Louis

C arl Conrad was not a beer man necessarily. He liked wine; the stout Hessian immigrant with a wide face, closely cropped hair, and a wiry goatee imported wine and champagne into the United States in the 1860s and 1870s via C. Conrad & Co. out of offices in St. Louis and Germany. He was also said to have worked on the business side of the restaurant trade. Good German that he was, whatever his affinity for wine, Conrad did know about beer, and he almost assuredly partook in the beverage. It was hard not to in St. Louis in those days. Plus Conrad, thirty years old in 1873, ran in the same social circles as the city's brewers. One simply had to hoist a stein from time to time.

That was how Conrad came to know Adolphus Busch, whose brewery was probably the largest in the St. Louis region at the time, with plans to grow even larger behind steam power, artificial refrigeration, the railroad, and pasteurization. Busch's brewery was best known by the early 1870s for its Bavarian lager, a darker, albeit still light-tasting brew, though Busch had started to tinker with lighter-colored pilsners. The first that the Anheuser-Busch Brewing Association released was called St. Louis Lager, a conscious imitation of what was coming to be called both pilsner and Bohemian pilsner—and that would also come to be known as continental lager, among other names. Developed by Busch's longtime brewmaster and minor company shareholder Erwin Spraul, St. Louis Lager used rice as well as the more traditional barley to undergird its body and give it its color. That was because the six-row barley so common in North America—and therefore so readily used by American brewers—had a lot more protein than could be processed out during the brewing process. Simply put, the yeast could only convert so much of the broken-down six-row barley's sugars. That was fine for darker lagers. The colors could mask any detritus that might make it through. For golden and paler lagers, that would not do. "A glass of sparkling, translucent Bohemian lager . . . functioned as a klieg light that illuminated every blob of unprecipitated protein, every tendril of undissolved yeast," historian Maureen Ogle wrote. Lagers chasing the Pilsen ideal had to be clear and clean, like they were in Europe, where brewers were blessed with copious volumes of the less protein-rich two-row barley (six-row rarely appeared in any great quantities in Europe).

While later history and popular culture would bang on about Busch and other larger brewers leading American brewing's embrace of six-row barley alternatives, called adjuncts, the truth was that brewers big and small in the United States had been working on end-runs around the mercurial six-row for a while. For much of the nineteenth century, brewers used white and yellow corn as well as white rice as adjuncts. Both corn and rice were rich in starch that could be converted to sugar. Unlike six-row barley, though, neither had a lot of protein. These adjuncts then were reliable additions for a fast fermentation and a relatively clean-looking finished product.

Rice had the added advantage of being less oily than corn, so rice it was that Adolphus Busch and his swelling domain settled on for its pilsner knockoffs. The first had been that St. Louis Lager, which was definitely a nod to the original pilsner born in the Austrian Empire's Bohemia. Not only had Adolphus Busch first heard about it either when Otto Lademan returned from the Vienna expo or during his own European travels, but Spraul was also steeped in Bavarian lagering. The second pilsner homage, however, would turn out to be thoroughly American, even though it too traced its roots to Europe—to Bohemia, in fact.

Adolphus Busch got the idea for the new beer from Carl Conrad. It appears lost to history as to where Conrad himself got the idea. The legend has it that Conrad, a frequent voyager to Europe via steamship, dined at a monastery in Bohemia that made its own version of pilsner. That is not unlikely, given the style's spread during the middle and latter parts of the nineteenth century and its very birth in Bohemia itself. Conrad is said to have pronounced that beer "the best he ever tasted." He brought the memory back with him to St. Louis and ordered from his friend Adolphus Busch a similar-tasting and similar-looking beer. While that monastic pilsner may have indeed so bowled over Conrad—pilsner tended to turn heads early on—it seems more likely that the immigrant entrepreneur who already traded in both still and sparkling wine wanted in on St. Louis's burgeoning beer scene, which showed no signs of abating. The epic violence of the Civil War in Missouri was years past, and the completion of the transcontinental railroad in 1869 made St. Louis—already a key transportation hub because of its location on the Mississippi River—that much more integral to the growing nation's fortunes. And that nation was growing. The 1870 census pegged the population at more than 38.5 million. That figure would nearly double to 76 million just thirty years later. Adolphus Busch and a handful of others were riding technology's wave to deliver beer to these masses. It seems Conrad wanted his piece.

The recipe he hired the Anheuser brewery to brew relied on Saaz hops from Bohemia and on a special strain of Bohemian yeast. The brewery used lightly malted barley, of course, to give the beer its golden color, and rice too—about eight pounds of rice per batch to every five bushels of barley. The brewery also aged the beer in vats with beechwood strips on the bottoms for filtration to trap any last bits of detritus such as errant yeast. When the aging was complete, Busch's men transferred the beer to kegs coated with a pitch made from pine, to impart what Busch himself described as a kind of aromatic "special characteristic." As for the rest of what went into Conrad's beer—and the proportions and the times involved in the mash, fermentation, and aging—he, Busch, and brewmaster Spraul kept that to themselves. "Taking [the grain] out of the water mash & boiling it & putting it back in the water mash again makes a much better mash, & gives the Beer a better flavor," was how Busch blandly explained his reasoning about the process when later questioned.

The finished product became the bestselling pilsner beer of all time, and it still stands among the world's top handful of beers in terms of sales. They named it after that small Bohemian city in the Austrian Empire called České Budějovice—Budweis in German—that neither Conrad nor Busch had ever visited but that they knew from its reputation for making a slightly more golden-hued pilsner than that from the original source of Pilsen. Again, that knowledge might have come via the travels of Otto Lademan or of Conrad himself. Much as travel had revolutionized brewing fifty years before—when men such as Anton Dreher and Gabriel Sedlmayr squirreled away the latest information in English brewing for use on the Continent—it had done so again with the creation of Budweiser. The golden, crisp, effervescent lager that C. Conrad & Co. introduced beginning in March 1876 was a marriage of European tradition and American disruption.

And it proved ravishingly popular from the get-go. Conrad cagily decided to sell his new beer in bottles rather than in casks and kegs, with wired-shut champagne corks so as to emphasize the fizziness and the clarity. He also touted how it "sparkles," and how it was "not so heavy" compared with other lagers (and certainly with ales). "It has a very pretty flavor," he wrote, and he pushed his product hard, though it eventually seemed to sell itself, first in the St. Louis area and then all over the United States. Conrad's company would sell a quarter of a million bottles of Budweiser during its first twelve months, an astonishing figure for the time. Anheuser's brewery would produce six thousand barrels of the pilsner during its first two years, another astonishing figure considering that the vast majority of American breweries produced fewer than one thousand barrels total each year.

Though it did not yet own the brand—it was Conrad's product and the bottles were stamped with the name of Conrad's company—Budweiser helped the Anheuser-Busch Brewing Association on its way to becoming one of the globe's largest brewers. Even its largest competitors had trouble playing catch-up. "Can't you give us a paler, purer beer?" a distributor in Chicago wrote to Frederick Pabst's Best Brewing of Milwaukee. A client of the distributor had "sent us word he could not use our beer any longer, its being so dark." Pabst urgently wrote his brewmaster, who had trained in the Bavarian school of darker lagers made from recipes that did not necessarily include adjuncts such as rice, "There is no doubt in my mind if that kind of [dark] beer keeps on, we will lose a great deal of trade which had cost us a great deal of trouble and money to get." Pabst then noted that he, like Adolphus Busch, furnished his brewers with the best in technology and matériel, "and I can only look at this as either carelessness or not the necessary knowledge of the business." Pabst then added, "I want to be understood that we *cannot afford* to have anything of this kind repeated."

"The business" in the United States was pivoting to pilsner, which was sweeping all before it. Frederick Pabst's operation swung, too, hiring brewers knowledgeable in the latest Bohemian techniques and implementing the newest innovations in mashing, yeast pitching, and cooling. Soon, the Phillip Best Brewing Co.—which the company directors would rename after Pabst in March 1889—was on its way to becoming for a time the world's largest brewer with its own pilsner interpretations, including one called "Select" and another called "Bohemian Beer." These and others on their own would never capture the market quite like Budweiser by itself, but together they were enough to drive the renamed Pabst Brewing Company to unheard-of heights in brewing in the Western Hemisphere. "We have done & are doing a good deal of Building, but we are in Shape now to sell 1,200,000 bbls by only putting two more kettles in the Brew House, which will be done this fall," Pabst wrote in early 1891 to his cousin Charles Best Jr., who worked as the brewery's secretary. "Our sales this year will *very likely* reach 800,000 bbls." That was, of course, a phenomenal figure for American brewing—for any country's brewing industry—though it alas proved a little too ambitious on Pabst's part.

The company missed its master's sales goal for 1891, but Pabst was still able to sniffily write to Best, "We will lead Busch over 100,000 bbls." Indeed, a list from 1895 of the largest American breweries by barrels produced would have the Pabst Brewing Company squarely at the top, just ahead of the Anheuser-Busch Brewing Association and the Jos. Schlitz Brewing Company—like Pabst, a German immigrant–run Milwaukee outfit that specialized in pilsner.

The 1870s and the 1880s, the latter half of that first decade especially, were when pilsner really gathered its forces. As beer consumption increased during the latter half of the nineteenth century, larger operations such as Anheuser-Busch and Best/Pabst set out aggressively to gobble as much market share as they could. In the United States annual per capita beer consumption would more than double from 1870 to 1890, to more than thirteen gallons. The brewers' ambitions marched hand in glove with innovations such as artificial refrigeration, pasteurization, vastly improved cleanliness at breweries, and all that went into producing a securely bottled beer. Without these, and earlier innovations in kilning and filtration as well as mass immigration in the 1840s and 1850s, it is unlikely that pilsner would have turned around once it reached the United States and set itself upon the world. One further innovation in far-off Denmark, at a brewery run by an even bigger fan of Louis Pasteur than Adolphus Busch, would seal pilsner's fate and that of the international brewing industry.

18

"ALL THE OLD STYLES WERE ALL BUT GONE"
1883 | Valby, Denmark

Emil Christian Hansen was born in May 1842 in a house built partially from logs in the town of Ribe on Denmark's then sparsely populated western edge. A rapacious reader at a time of widespread illiteracy, Hansen originally proved a promising student and dreamed of becoming a stage actor or a portrait artist. But the family circumstances—his father was poor, had many children, and was an alcoholic—ruled out such endeavors and forced the son to turn to full-time work in his teenage years, including at a grocer and then as a journeyman housepainter much like his father. An attempt to achieve university-level training in the arts failed around that time, seeming to seal the young man's fate. (Some accounts of his life have his father not only as a housepainter but also as a designer of theatrical sets, which is perhaps where the younger Hansen picked up his artistic ambitions.) Hansen kept up his reading, however, and around his twentieth birthday he got a job tutoring the children of the caretaker of a vast estate on the island of Zealand, not far from Denmark's capital of Copenhagen.

This job not only brought Hansen—by now a tall, slender man with large blue eyes and the beginnings of a full beard he would keep for life—in closer proximity to the kingdom's ruling elite but also allowed him to fill in the gaps in his own education, as one biographical account put it. He learned Latin and became particularly fascinated by the subject of botany. Hansen at twenty-two decided to pursue a degree in natural history from the University of Copenhagen. Patronage from wealthy Danes who saw the young man's potential paid part of his way. The other part came from articles that Hansen wrote for almanacs and magazines under the name EC Hansen. He was also said to have penned novels, though none seem to have survived in print. Whatever the funding, by 1870 Hansen had a degree in hand and had started a meteoric ascent in the scientific world, where he would become best known for his isolation of lager yeast.

A mixture of professional frustration and the ambition of a young man very aware that he came from the provinces drove Hansen's ascent. Early on, he had done groundbreaking research into beech trees, a major feature of the Danish landscape, but Hansen felt he never got the proper credit for it. He quit his research job because of the slight—real or perceived, no one knows—and earned a living again through writing. This time it was coauthoring a Danish translation of Charles Darwin's memoirs of sailing and studying aboard the HMS *Beagle*, the work that laid the foundation for Darwin's theories on evolution and natural selection. Now past thirty, Hansen appeared to be on his way to becoming a kind of itinerant scientist in much the same way he had bounced from painting job to painting job. His research continued into microorganisms and fungi, and in 1877 the cliquey world of Danish scientists handed him a plum assignment: Hansen was invited to work in the University of Copenhagen laboratory of Peter Ludvig Panum, one of the kingdom's most famous scientists. Panum was best known then for his research into a measles outbreak on the Danish-controlled Faroe Islands in the North Atlantic. It was while working at Panum's lab that Hansen's career took another fortuitous turn. The scientist who he had felt slighted his research into beech trees recommended Hansen for a new position at an in-house laboratory at a brewery just outside Copenhagen. The scientist's motives were unclear—perhaps Hansen had been right and his former mentor was making up for the earlier slight—but in July 1878, Hansen got a job at the Carlsberg brewery that he would hold the rest of his life.

It was there that he honed in on the microorganisms that make beer: yeast. For years, thanks to Louis Pasteur, brewers had had a better understanding of what caused beer to spoil after fermentation or to emerge from the process a little sour and otherwise foul tasting. They had also had a sense of how to prevent such spoilage, and therefore how to preserve that much more beer. But even as late as the late 1870s, when brewing juggernauts such as Best (Pabst), Anheuser-Busch, and Heineken were cranking up shipments of pilsner in thousands and then hundreds of thousands of bottles, brewers still struggled with consistency. It was a supreme triumph of the larger breweries—and one of the reasons they *were* the larger breweries—that so much of their beer was fermented and aged so consistently. They had bent millennia of experimentation to their will and turned beer into just another industrial good that factory-sized breweries turned out. But there was still room for error—too much room sometimes. In early 1882 the distributor of Frederick Pabst's Best Brewing in Kansas City, Missouri, one of the nation's largest markets, refused to send out a batch of pilsner because it had turned hazy in transit, possibly because of suspended yeast that had not settled out fully during either fermentation or pasteurization. Along with figuring out how to better preserve packaged beer, much of the research at breweries around this time was on yeast and making the little organisms that much more effective and easier to harness.

Perhaps no brewery in the world was more committed to this than the originally humble Carlsberg. Danish aristocrat Jacob Christian Jacobsen had been running a brewery he inherited from his father that made ales. The younger Jacobsen had become enamored of the bottom-fermenting Bavarian lagers, however, and sought to popularize them in his own country. To do that, he needed the perfect space and the right materials. He built a new brewery in the mid-1840s on a small mountain (*berg* in Danish) in an area called Valby that was then on the outskirts of Copenhagen. The area provided fantastic springwater, and Jacobsen could age his beer in cellars dug into the hill. As for material, he tapped the same barley markets as he had been using for the smaller alehouse his father had started. For the yeast, Jacobsen journeyed into Europe's Germanic center and, in an echo of Anton Dreher and Gabriel Sedlmayr's thievery from English breweries, came back with a hatbox full of lager yeast, supposedly from Sedlmayr's Spaten brewery in Munich. Hansen did his best to keep it cold with regular douses of water, and once home tested making the new lager in his mother's bathtub. It was her death that provided the funds for Jacobsen to finally open the mountaintop brewery in 1847, which he named after his five-year-old son Carl and the brewery's topographical home. Carlsberg introduced its first lager, a darker Bavarian-style dunkel, in November 1847. It was apparently "an instant success," and the tall, pear-shaped, thirty-six-year-old Jacob Christian (J.C.) Jacobsen was on his way to becoming one of the most successful businessmen in a Denmark, which, like much of Europe and America, was rapidly industrializing.

Until Carlsberg's lagers, ale had reigned in Denmark just as it had reigned pretty much wherever beer had been drunk anywhere in the world. Danish brewers were known in particular for using honey and pollen in the brewing of their beer—at least until medieval monarchs and monks shifted to hops as the primary seasoning. The honey and pollen—and bog myrtle and fruits such as cranberries and cowberries—still showed up in Danish ales from time to time, but the lagers of Carlsberg and other subsequent producers "swept quickly through Denmark and soon all the old styles were all but gone," left to await rediscovery more than a century on in our own time. Like with the launch of Heineken in the neighboring Netherlands, Carlsberg turned its home nation into a lager-drinking one. By 1868, too, Carlsberg was exporting its lager as far afield as South America and East Asia, never mind forging distribution inroads in the ale-heavy United Kingdom.

A big part of this was through Jacobsen's commitment to the science of brewing. Son of a self-trained brewer himself and a fan of Louis Pasteur's groundbreaking work, Jacobsen sought to codify the scientific study of beer through the establishment of a laboratory in 1875. It was the first of its kind in the world: a brewery-owned and brewery-run research facility. Other breweries had their own research operations, of course, but Carlsberg's would be a standalone lab for trial and error. "J.C. believed that the art of brewing could be vastly improved by applying a scientific approach, and he was very open to new developments in brewing," a later admirer wrote. Jacobsen was right in his belief and generous in his approach. Anything of substance that his laboratory produced Carlsberg would share with the rest of the brewing world—or so went the lab's mission statement. A good thing, too, for his newly minted top scientist, Emil Christian Hansen, made a monumental discovery within a few years of his coming aboard in 1877.

Hansen had a hunch that only some of the cells in various strains of brewer's yeast really contributed to fermentation. The rest were unreliable or uselessly dormant. Isolate and reproduce the productive cells, Hansen hypothesized, and a brewer could ensure consistent and clean fermentations time after time using the same strain of yeast. So that was what Hansen did over several years at the Carlsberg laboratory. Using spent yeast from the brewery, he isolated single productive yeast cells and then produced colonies of them through mixture with a sterile form of the unfermented beer called wort. Hansen then had batches of beer brewed with different yeast colonies until he could decide which were the true stars—the strains that would produce that clean, consistent lager time after time. It was hot, wet, sometimes tedious work, but it paid off. "In 1883, the work was completed, and, at the Carlsberg Brewery, for the first time in history, commercial beer was brewed using a pure culture of the best lager yeast available," a later Danish brewer would note, echoing the awe in which Hansen's achievement was still held even more than a century later.

Crucially, Hansen's boss, Jacobsen, shared the discovery and its application. That included with Tuborg, a brewery that two fellow industrialists, Philip W. Heiman and C. F. Tietgen, started in 1875 just north of Copenhagen. Tuborg had introduced the first beer in Denmark marketed as a pilsner, and with Carlsberg's yeast strain Grøn Tuborg—or Tuborg Green, in its signature green bottles—became that much clearer and that much more consistent. It would become Denmark's bestselling beer.

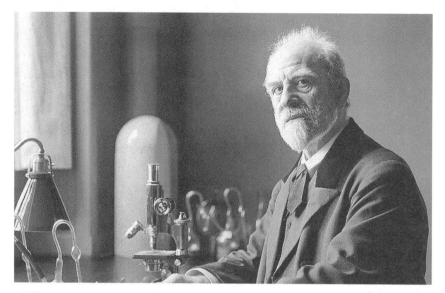

Emil Christian Hansen's research at Carlsberg made high-quality brewer's yeast consistently and widely available for the first time, a milestone central to the dominance of pilsner in the twentieth century. Courtesy of Carlsberg Foundation

Within five years of Carlsberg first using Hansen's "pure culture of the best lager yeast available" in November 1883, every brewery in Denmark and Norway was using it. The strain—which Hansen named *Saccharomyces carlsbergensis* and which is now known as *Saccharomyces uvarum* (Latin for "sugar-mold grapes")—eventually became a parent of yeast strains that breweries as far afield as France, Italy, and North America developed and propagated. More than anything, Hansen's work ushered in the era of high-quality commercially available brewer's yeast, one that even the lowliest homebrewer today can partake in with gusto. Gone forever were the days of scraping off the previous batch's foamy fermentation leftovers and trying to make a go with it for subsequent ones. Brewing—lager brewing and pilsner brewing in particular, given how the style benefited from cleaner, consistent fermentation—became that much more scientific. By the early 1890s, less than a decade after Hansen the would-be artist turned scientist performed his painstaking chemical magic, operations such as Anheuser and Pabst were producing hundreds of thousands of liters of pure yeast strains on their own, using Hansen's original. His isolation work in Carlsberg's lab was the last major piece of the pilsner puzzle as the golden style rushed into its golden age.

PART III

19

THE RIGHT KIND OF LAGER

1877–1895 | Newark, New Jersey; Munich

Peter Ballantine was born in November 1791 in Dundee, then a particularly hardscrabble town along the Firth of Tay in eastern Scotland. Little is known about Ballantine's early life, but when he was twenty-eight he emigrated to the United States—as thousands of Scots were doing in the early 1800s—and settled in upstate New York. He appears in Albany in 1820, and by the early years of the following decade Ballantine owned a local brewery in New York state's capital. Albany, like pretty much all beer-drinking America in the early 1830s, was ale country. Brewers in the city and the surrounding Hudson Valley had originally been known for beers made from wheat—likely a vestige of the Dutch who originally colonized that area before ceding it to the English in the late 1600s. When Ballantine came along, Albany brewers used mostly barley to underpin their hearty, English-style ale, and it was that kind of brewing the Scottish immigrant imbibed, first as an apprentice brewer and later as a brewery owner.

Ballantine brewed in Albany until 1840, and then left to set up first a malthouse and then a brewery in Newark, which with about seventeen thousand residents was New Jersey's largest city and a major port. It is not entirely clear why Ballantine made the leap down the Hudson River, but his decision to either build a new brewery or acquire and then upgrade an existing one—that too is unclear—proved fortuitous. By the mid-1870s, P. Ballantine & Sons was the nation's fourth-largest brewer, turning out more than 107,000 barrels a year. The nation's largest—George Ehret's Hell Gate Brewery, just across the Hudson in Manhattan—was turning out more than 138,000. But Ehret and, for that matter, the number-two US brewery, Frederick Pabst's Best in Milwaukee, were producing lagers, and lighter-looking and lighter-tasting ones at that. Ballantine was producing ales, probably exclusively, making it the largest such brewery left in the nation. More important than its status as America's largest ale producer was the type of ale for which Ballantine was known: India pale ale.

The style grew out of English pale ale in the late 1700s and early 1800s. It probably got its name from exports of pale ale to the Indian subcontinent, which by the latter half of the nineteenth century—with tacit and active support from the British government—mercenaries and executives from the East India Company had essentially colonized. A range of myths have shrouded IPA since. One has it that a particular English brewer near East India's headquarters, George Hodgson, invented the style specifically for the British market in India. This theory has a corollary: that Hodgson used copious amounts of hops to preserve his pale ale on its months-long journey to India, and that was what gave it both its name and its distinctive bitterness. As it stands, IPA appears to have arisen much more organically. It was simply a bitterer offshoot of pale ale, one that developed gradually and that responded to market demand. It had little to do with long journeys to India—beer that was more lightly hopped routinely made the trek just fine. Instead, it seemed that drinkers in the United Kingdom and in the areas its people colonized, including the eventual United States, simply liked their pale ale with a little bite now and then.

That was certainly the case for Ballantine's customers. The breweries that Peter Ballantine and his sons built up in Albany and Newark they built up around thicker, richer ales, and not lagers. "The Messers. Ballantine manufacture strong Burton and India pale ales, which rival those of Bass and Alsop to such a degree that experts can seldom tell them apart," one New York City newspaper writer noted in May 1878. It must have gratified the Scotland-born Ballantine to be mentioned in such august British company, despite the rise of the sea of lager all around his industry. But such acclaim was not enough to carry the nation's leading ale producer for long. Its place among America's largest brewers began slipping even before Peter Ballantine's death in January 1883 at age ninety-one. Curiously, when a leading trade journal tallied the nation's largest brewers in 1895, a brewery called Ballantine & Co. of Newark, New Jersey, was number five with five to six hundred thousand barrels annually. (Pabst Brewing Co. was number one with between nine hundred thousand and one million.) But Ballantine & Co. was not the ale producer that Peter Ballantine had built up. Rather, it was a subsidiary created when P. Ballantine & Sons purchased a lager-brewing Newark rival in 1879. And that subsidiary ranked squarely among the nation's largest breweries by 1895. As for P. Ballantine & Sons, which had made the list only sixteen years before behind hearty ales in the grand English (and non-Germanic) tradition, it was nowhere to be found.

Perhaps Peter Ballantine and his three sons saw the writing on the wall and shifted resources and focus to their lager-brewing subsidiary in the 1880s.

There would appear to be no records of their decision-making at the time, but they certainly would have been familiar with the major leaps forward by then, including pasteurization, pure yeast strains, and mechanical refrigeration, never mind bottling for wider distribution, which they did for their ales. Moreover, Ballantine and progeny lived and worked in the New York City area, the nation's largest commercial market for beer—for most products—one whose consumption figures dwarfed those of the likes of Milwaukee and St. Louis. The Ballantines would have been able to sample every trend in brewing that passed their way, and they surely knew of pilsner's rise behind the influx of Germans into America. In the end, that was probably it—pilsner was coming like a great wave from the Midwest, ready to swamp the East Coast evermore, and the Ballantines wanted in. So up went their lager operation and down went their ale one. The vaunted Ballantine IPA would gradually peter out sales- and production-wise in the twentieth century under different owners. Not until smaller commercial brewers and homebrewers resurrected the India pale ale style beginning in the late 1970s would Ballantine ale be any kind of a force in the beer world.

Such was the fate of ale beginning in the late nineteenth century in a United States that was fast becoming the world's largest market for beer. Barrel counts by city showed lager overtaking ale in place after place. In the fast-growing cities of the Midwest such as St. Louis and Milwaukee it was a rout, with ale production pretty much disappearing. In the East, ale held on, for the brewing tradition stretched back much further and British (not German) transplants such as Peter Ballantine had originally animated it. M. Vassar & Company in Poughkeepsie, New York, about a three-hour train ride due north from Manhattan, had since the first decade of the 1800s been one of the largest breweries in the Northeast. Its steady production of rich English-style ales had enabled its England-born namesake and founder, Matthew Vassar, to endow a women's college on the banks of the Hudson River. Throughout the latter half of the century, though, the Vassar brewery's sales declined as its distribution shrank. Unlike Ballantine, Vassar had never embraced lager. By 1899 the brewery was all but gone, left to stagger on for a decade until its equipment was sold for parts.

It was not just stubborn ale producers like M. Vassar & Company whom lager picked off. Other lager producers felt the commercial sting of not producing the right *kind* of lager—that is, pilsner. F. & M. Schaefer Brewing Company, which two brothers from Prussia started in the 1840s and which occupied not only a large chunk of Manhattan's Park Avenue for its brewery complex but several lagering caves dug into the banks of the East River, answered the march of pilsners such as Budweiser with a "genuine old lager" free of adjuncts and reliant instead on traditional malts and hops, a kind of dunkel in the Bavarian mold. Alas, it was too much of a throwback. Void of "the rich, creamy broth" of the more popular pilsners and especially hoppy and bitter, Schaefer's lager flopped—greeted by the drinking public with "a general growl," as one observer put it. The brewery spent the end of the century pivoting to lighter lager fare in order to compete.

It was the same story in Europe, but there brewers and their guilds put up more of a fight. In the Prussian city of Cologne, brewers reinvigorated the local style known simply as *kölsch*, after the German word for the Cologne (or Köln) dialect. Born as it was in the Middle Ages, long before lager's ascent, kölsch was an ale. But when Cologne brewers reintroduced it in the late nineteenth century as a rebuttal to pilsner, they made it brighter and lighter, in part through aging it in colder conditions. It was a kind of lager-ale hybrid in that regard and aimed squarely at countering the rise of lighter-tasting pilsner. While through its introduction "pilsner was thus stopped at the gates," kölsch's commercial reach until the very late twentieth century would not extend much beyond Cologne's environs.

Not so an altogether new style that anxious brewers in all-important Munich developed around the same time. The city and its surrounding region had birthed progressively lighter-colored versions of dunkel, including a conscious pilsner imitation called Münchener Gold from Hackerbräu in 1893. None of these really overtook sales of traditional dunkel, which remained the everyday tipple of the average Bavarian, even amid the slow creep of pilsner from across the border. Then, in March 1894, the Spaten brewery, now run by Gabriel Sedlmayr's three sons and operating out of the same massive complex along Munich's Marsstraße that it would be using in the twenty-first century, introduced a style it called *helles*, after the German word for bright. The beer was a straw-colored lager with a lighter taste than dunkel. It, too, was a conscious imitation of pilsner, and it was a commercial success from the time Spaten first introduced it in the northern German port of Hamburg under the trademarked name Helles Lagerbier. Munich fans would get their first tastes in June 1895. A Munich competitor called Thomasbräu released its own helles the same year and advertised what it called quite bluntly "Thomasbräu-Pilsner" with the tag "recognized as the most complete substitute for Bohemian Pilsner."

It was all so very unmistakable and one of the surest signs of pilsner's success so far. For nearly half a century Bavaria had commanded the vanguard of brewing. Ever since Gabriel Sedlmayr had returned from his fact-finding mission in the United Kingdom, it had been a region that outside brewing concerns looked to for their brewmasters and for the latest methods. After all that, they were now pivoting toward lighter-tasting, lighter-looking lagers that imitated in appearance, technique, and even name a style born because brewery owners in Bohemia's Pilsen had in the late 1830s been concerned about the market domination of Bavarian beer. In many ways, the teacher had become the student. Bavarian brewers would, like those in the rest of the world, continue to chase pilsner's success until helles and pilsner each held about one-quarter of the region's market share.

The pursuit was not without controversy, of course. In November 1895, after Spaten's and Thomasbräu's helles releases proved that lighter beers could sell briskly in the kingdom of dunkel, the owners of some of the largest breweries there "declared that they had no intention of making any pale lagers in the near future" during a contentious meeting of the Association of Munich Breweries, a leading trade group. Helles might have become an evolutionary dead end in beer style then and there. Bavaria provided most of the beer for what since 1871 was the German Empire, the Continent's reigning power militarily and economically—and still the world's largest beer market, despite the rise of the United States, with more than thirty-six million barrels produced in 1885 and a per capita consumption of nearly twenty-four gallons a year, more than twice that of the United States. If those larger Bavarian brewery owners had succeeded in their plan to block the spread of the local answer to pilsner, it might have stopped the growth of helles permanently, and perhaps made Germany in general a backwater for innovation in brewing. As it was, the brewers agreed to disagree, and those who wanted to pursue that helles answer to pilsner did so. Those who did not stuck with dunkel and other older styles, including the smoky-tasting *rauchbier* popularized in Bamberg and the crisp, heavy *alt* from Dusseldorf—or, for that matter, Bavaria's indigenous wheat beers. None of these, though—not kölsch, helles, dunkel, nor the others—would prove as durable and adaptable in Europe or among European breweries as pilsner. It would condemn all these styles and others to be mere regional favorites—or, worse, curiosities—until the late twentieth century's craft beer boom led to their rediscoveries.

And what of wine, the Continent's other great tipple? Winemakers could not very well adjust to counter pilsner's rise directly in their realm. They worked with the grape, after all, not the grain. But, just as technological innovations and scientific advances converged to help pilsner along, so too did the bizarrely tenacious yellow bug that loved wine as much as the French—or at least loved the vines of wine grapes. Phylloxera was not the first plague to curse vineyardists and winemakers in Europe in the nineteenth century. There had been a fungal spore called oidium in the 1840s, downy mildew about thirty years later, and finally black rot in the late 1880s, which was exactly what it sounded like: a fungal disease that rotted grapevines. All three of these caused major hiccups in European wine production, rendering thousands upon thousands of acres of vineyards largely useless. But phylloxera, a bug barely visible to even the discerning eye, did far more damage.

It all started sometime just before the late 1860s, probably thanks to the speed of steamships, which by that era could ply the Atlantic so fast that insects and assorted parasites on imported plants could easily survive the voyage, ready to thrive in habitats for which they were never intended. Phylloxera was one. It seemed only to thrive at the roots of European grapevines—though it probably arrived on American ones—feeding off the sap found there and eventually stunting whole stalks. Grapes could not blossom and grow. Phylloxera spread quickly through cracks in the soil and through farm machinery as well as simply by wind. And this particular aphid was also absurdly fertile. A single female phylloxera could birth more than twenty-five billion descendants in eight months.

Starting in France's famed Languedoc wine region, phylloxera spread over two decades to vineyards as far afield as North Africa and the present-day Republic of Georgia. By 1884 it had destroyed two and a half million acres of French vineyards alone, nearly crippling the world's leading wine-producing nation. A cartoon in the British satirical magazine *Punch* from 1890 showed a plump phylloxera in a tuxedo sampling from several bottles of vino. The caption read: "The phylloxera, a true gourmet, finds out the best vineyards and attaches itself to the best wines." Just as it seemed like phylloxera would finish off oenophilic France completely—and much of Spain and Italy's wine industry as well—winemakers, government officials, and researchers settled upon a solution: grafting seemingly resistant American grapevine roots onto European vines. Enter again the speed of the steamships. American rootstocks were carefully yet quickly imported, and the munching march of the merciless lice was stopped.

But that was not before it had seriously dented wine and brandy production in Europe. Though hard figures remain difficult to come by, all anecdotal evidence from and about European wine production in the 1870s and 1880s, including of the famed French brandy known as cognac, tells of slumping sales amid low supply and skyrocketing prices. Unscrupulous practices, too, ran amok, with producers trying to run around the crisis with watered-down offerings and clearly misleading labels. The fallout from the phylloxera infestation, in fact, led to France's groundbreaking regulation of its wine labeling. To this day, French wines bear designations to strictly certify that they are what they say they are and come from where they say they come from, a practice that several other nations have adopted. The slender supply, the higher prices, the dodgy marketing—it left a bad taste with consumers.

So they turned elsewhere for their tipples. Whiskey from the United Kingdom—especially Scotland and an Ireland that was then a de facto colony—did particularly well in the wake of phylloxera. It was not that more people drank more whiskey—though anecdotally that appeared to be the case—it was that more people turned to the fortified Spanish wine sherry and that whiskey distilleries in turn used those emptied sherry casks to age their wares, creating some of the roundest, most palatable Scottish and Irish whiskies ever. As for beer, and pilsner in particular, it would never be clear if the great wine blight was a boon. Many of the nations and regions where pilsner was gaining fastest in popularity were not really wine markets, and nations such as Belgium and Denmark had no real wine industries to speak of. It certainly did not hurt pilsner to have wine regions such as Bordeaux and Bourgogne sidelined for several years and their industries in disarray, however. It likely emboldened distribution of pilsner that much further. Breweries such as Carlsberg and Heineken were moving aggressively into markets beyond their national frontiers during this time, and, in the United States, pilsner was fast becoming the fastest-selling alcoholic beverage. "By the 1870s," a historian concluded, "the American drinking public had made a clear choice for lager beer over ale, porter, and the other English beers. What was more, the Americans preferred a lager closer to the Pilsen than the Munich type: i.e., a pale, light-bodied, clear and effervescent beer, relatively low in alcoholic content." Indeed, behind pilsner, America was becoming the largest market for beer in the world as every other ethanol competitor, wine included, stumbled to the margins. By 1910 the United States would surpass the United Kingdom as the globe's second-biggest beer market, and it would only be a matter of time before it bested Germany.

It was a remarkable march in retrospect. When entrepreneurs such as Peter Ballantine and Matthew Vassar started up in the early part of the nineteenth century, beer ran perhaps a distant third to whiskey and cider among American tipples. Even as late as 1850, if anything in the domestic alcohol universe seemed new and exciting, it was the continued rise of bourbon out of Kentucky and Tennessee. Then lager disrupted things, and pilsner disrupted things some more, until America tipped toward century's end to becoming a beer country—and not only a beer country, *the* beer country. For the next century, American tastes and techniques would drive the world beer market and much of the alcoholic-beverages market in general. And the driver in America would be pilsner and how to get that much more of it into that many more mouths. The giants of the age now ending—entrepreneurs such as Adolphus Busch and Frederick Pabst—were about to shuffle off the global stage they had helped set, but not before one last big bravura performance.

20

TOWARD A BETTER PILSNER

1893 | Chicago

The opening day of the World's Columbian Exposition in Chicago on May 1, 1893, broke cold and misty. Rain threatened. That would not stop the festivities, which had been more than three years in the making, ever since Congress awarded the Midwest's largest city the chance to host the exposi- tional homage to Christopher Columbus four hundred years after his first trips to the New World. Chicago had beaten out several comers, including archrival New York, and saw the world's latest exposition as a chance to seize its brightest international spotlight yet, only twenty years after a fire had devastated much of the city. "Millions of people would come to appreciate that here, indeed, was a great metropolis, a rival not only of New York, but also of Paris and London," a historian of the exposition noted.

The World's Columbian Exposition of 1893 would carry on the grand traditions of other such conclaves stretching back to the first one in London in 1851. In doing so, it would consciously assert the industrial muscle and prowess of an America keenly aware that it, too, was about to step into its brightest spotlight ever. With the divisions of the Civil War largely repaired— or at least papered over—the nation was one of unfathomable productive capacity, factories and farms belching and churning with cheap labor and ready capital from sea to shining sea. So the 1893 exposition would serve, as one observer put it, as "a coming out not only for Chicago, but for all the nation. The industrial and technical exhibits, the confidence of the architec- ture, and the grand scale of the enterprise together signaled a new, vigorous world power, bristling with innovation and self-assurance."

How grand it was. The last world expo, in Paris in 1889, had stretched to 160 acres. Chicago's would cover more than 630, enough to wear out even "the most stalwart legs"—which spurred some industrious college students to charge forty cents an hour to push festivalgoers around in rolling chairs. And the buildings within this Chicago acreage in Jackson Park on Lake Michigan were designed to drive home the exposition's grandiosity. "Never before have I realized the effect which could be produced by architecture," a British journalist wrote. "The Court of Honour, with its palaces surrounding the great fountain, the slender columns of the peristyle . . . and the golden dome of the Administration Building, formed a picture the like of which the world has not seen before."

Some 130,000 people would stream through the so-called White City in Jackson Park that opening day in May, starting with a group led by President Grover Cleveland and his vice president, Adlai Stevenson the eldest, and including two direct descendants of Columbus himself. As Cleveland's retinue made its way down Michigan Avenue, "aflame with flags and bunting and alive with cheering thousands," the sun started to emerge as if on cue, according to a Chicago reporter. Representatives of numerous nations and communities greeted the president's approach with cheering "like that of distant thunder." Following a brief speech in which he trumpeted the "stupendous results of American enterprise," Cleveland pressed a golden button—it was really a gilded telegraph key—and set the World's Columbian Exposition officially in motion. Electric lights came on, steam machines started up, and fountains spouted.

And what exactly—beyond the colossal architecture and the teeming grounds—was all this accentuating and illuminating? The official guide classifying the expo ran to 104 pages, and it listed 968 classifications, everything from "cheese and its manufacture" to "electroliers and electric lamps" to "bridge engineering" to "religious organizations and systems." As a later chronicler of the Chicago gathering would describe it, "This was an exposition in the true sense of the term—not an amusement park, but an encyclopedic display of contemporary life and enterprise." Among this display, under the "fermented beverages" classification, were twenty-four brewers and their beers—and atop this libationary collection, the pair that all others looked to and that journalists and attendees in the know followed most keenly, were Adolphus Busch's Anheuser-Busch Brewing Association and Frederick Pabst's Pabst Brewing Company. "Adolphus Busch as well as other brewers regarded this international fair as most important and rivalry became very keen," a historian of Anheuser-Busch wrote seventy years later.

It can be difficult for contemporary audiences to appreciate the import poured into these world expos of the late nineteenth and early twentieth century. "In an era before mass commercialization, it wasn't easy to present new products to the public; the public had to travel to them," wrote podcast producer Nick Andersen in the *Boston Globe* in 2018. The expos were in effect giant commercials for the cities that hosted them and for the exhibitors' products and innovations. They were not unlike the modern Olympic Games in terms of the international attention they commanded.

The twenty-four participating breweries seized on this opportunity, none more so than Busch and Pabst. They were older men now, if not old men for their time—Busch was fifty-three and Pabst fifty-seven—and preparing to hand the reins of their multifaceted pilsner-producing empires to their heirs. With vast estates, private train cars, yachts, and armies of servants, they enjoyed stunning wealth on par with other business barons of the Gilded Age such as steel magnate Andrew Carnegie and oil giant John D. Rockefeller. Busch's favorite of his many estates was a thirty-acre expanse in Pasadena, California, that included fourteen miles of garden trails—the future Busch Gardens amusement park. Pabst and his family maintained a 225-acre horse farm west of Milwaukee—near enough for easy getaways from the clan's city mansion, which they spent the equivalent of $5 million constructing and outfitting. Along with such wealth came chummy relationships with the great leaders of the day, including a string of US presidents, governors, and senators, and Kaiser Wilhelm II of Germany and his family. It must have been particularly gratifying for Busch and other successful German American brewers to receive plaudits from a fatherland they left as largely anonymous, if not penniless, and returned to decades later as among the world's most successful businessmen.

The beer they produced, most of it modeled after pilsner, was reaching farther than ever before. In a major way, then, the Chicago expo would be pilsner's star turn just before the century's curtains. Barely fifty years old, it was the ascendant beer style and one of the bestselling alcoholic beverages ever. It had dropped in on the Vienna expo twenty years before as a kind of curiosity, one that had to be explained at length and one that was still closely associated with its Bohemian birthplace. In 1893 it was just . . . beer. The straw- to golden-colored, bubbly, crisp, lower-in-alcohol style had pushed others such as India pale ale and porter to the commercial margins and really only had to look over its shoulder at whiskey sales. At the top of the triumph was Adolphus Busch's Budweiser—the rights to which he had obtained from a financially struggling Carl Conrad in 1891, a year in which Busch sold some fourteen million bottles of beer total. Frederick Pabst's pilsner was up there, too, moving a similar amount in 1891.

So while Busch and Pabst—and their children and grandchildren—did not need to work, these immigrants turned tycoons could not resist the stage that Chicago had set. The twenty-two other breweries' expositions

ended up "puny" compared with those of the nation's two leading breweries, which were, according to contemporary accounts, among the more
ornate exhibitions of any at the expo. The Anheuser-Busch one featured a
twenty-five-foot-high iron and steel pavilion flecked in gold and housing
a twenty-five-square-foot replica of the St. Louis brewery that was "correct
to the minutest detail," according to one journalist, with replicas of every
brick, window, stack, and turret as well as the Busch family mansion and
its stable. The Pabst exhibit was even more grandiose, with a terra-cotta
pavilion that included granite steps and gold-leaf adornments. Inside was a
model of the Milwaukee brewery plated in twenty-four-karat gold at a cost
to Pabst of the contemporary equivalent of $2 million and accessories such
as streetcar and railroad tracks running over streets literally paved in gold.
Like Busch's, the details were precise, thanks largely to the three dozen Italian
artisans whom Pabst had hired to craft everything over four months. "Nothing
has been omitted," the same journalist who assessed Busch's pavilion noted,
"from the figure of Gambrinus that crowns the arch over the Chestnut street
[sic] entrance to the ornamental work about the top of the towering boiler
house chimney."

As ornate as the Busch and Pabst pavilions were, a contest over who
had the best beer would overshadow everything. The expo's organizers had
empaneled five judges from the United States and Europe to use a one-
hundred-point scale to judge submitted beers' purity, color, and flavor. The
actual numerical totals were supposed to remain secret, but it was understood
that any brewery that scored at least eighty points would receive a bronze
medal and a parchment attesting to their success at the World's Columbian
Exposition—a kind of low bar for a participation trophy. The judges balked.
They would rank the entries on a scale of their own creation, including points
for such benchmarks as "chemical purity," "brilliancy," and "commercial
importance." The entry or entries that finished with the highest number of
points would win. What exactly they would win remained uncertain. All that
was clear was that early on in the months-long expo, the judges had gone
rogue. What's more, all five judges were connected in some way or another
with Pabst or Busch. It was all a recipe for controversy, and that was exactly
what ensued.

The "commercial importance" bit caused the most rancor, with smaller
breweries accusing the judges of using it to favor the bigger players (which
was probably true). In the end, Anheuser-Busch entered the final round of
judging in October with a two-point edge over Pabst. This final round arrived
after expo organizers had begun affixing black-and-gold cards to exhibitions,

the placeholders for the bronze medals just about everyone would take home. It also came *before* organizers—using chemists from the United States Department of Agriculture—had finished a chemical assessment of the entered beers. No matter. Adolphus Busch on October 27, as the expo was wrapping up, took out advertisements in newspapers in Chicago and beyond proclaiming his Budweiser the recipient of a nonexistent grand prize and himself the "King of Brewers." Whether this was a conscious attempt at inverting the old Bohemian description of pilsner as the "Beer of Kings," we do not know, but the ads left no mistake about what an aging Busch thought of his prized possession. ANHEUSER BUSCH WINS, went the big, bold font at the top of the ad. "No award has ever been made so gratifying to [the] St. Louis people and so justly merited as the one given today by the Columbian jury of the World's Fair, consisting of connoisseurs and chemists of the highest rank, to the Anheuser-Busch Brewing Association." The judges were not necessarily connoisseurs—they were businessmen more than anything—and they certainly were not chemists; the chemical analysis was not done. And there was no actual top award for beer, or for any fermented beverages at the expo, or for anything really. The congressional directive that awarded Chicago the expo had wanted the gathering to be a showcase of the best and the brightest, not a descent into some kind of grubby lunge for prizes.

But that is what happened, at least when it came to who supposedly had the world's best beer. "The stuff published by Busch of St. Louis is rot of the worst kind," a Pabst-allied judge told a journalist following the Busch ad, the frankness typical of the coverage of the controversy. "It was simply presumption on his part." That indeed seemed to be the case after the chemical analysis turned up supposed additives in Budweiser and tipped the final points tally to Frederick Pabst. Now it was his turn to brag—PABST MILWAUKEE BEER WINS, went an ad in the *Milwaukee Sentinel*. Pabst draped his brewery in blue ribbon and gave his workers a rare non-Sunday day off. Never mind that there still was no grand prize to fight over, and that the judges had taken it upon themselves to gin up a points system that ensured one or another of their patrons would win. Busch petitioned the exposition's appeals court to reverse the reversal and once again declare his Budweiser the best. The court adjourned after a five-day hearing and reconvened just before Christmas 1893 to render its decision. That decision turned out to be a muddle of officialdom hand-washing. There was no top medal—no best beer in America award—the court reminded Busch, and therefore all this squabbling made little sense. They would not rejigger the judges' points tally again, so Pabst's pyrrhic victory stood.

That might have been the end as far as the exposition was concerned, but it was not the end for Adolphus Busch. Worried that the ruling would taint his bestselling beer's reputation and not wanting to be seen as an also-ran to his archrival—just another brewery with a participation trophy from the World's Columbian Fair—he steamed to Europe in the spring of 1894 to track down an H. Lichtenfeld, one of the judges. Busch went first to Berlin, then to Paris, then to Baden-Baden in southern Germany, where he found Lichtenfeld and treated him to a sumptuous meal, complete with wines from 1862. What did Busch want from the judge? He wanted a sworn deposition that his Budweiser was made with only the normal beer ingredients—adjuncts such as rice, fine, but no exotic additives. This was an era before truth-in-advertising regulations. Busch's rivals could say whatever they wanted about his company and his only recourse would be to respond in kind. There was no formalized appeal for negative or erroneous marketing.

Busch got the deposition affirming the purity of his beer—and so much more. "You have no idea what tricks were resorted to," he wrote to his son August of his dinner with Lichtenfeld. "Pabst wanted to win at all hazards and at any cost." And Pabst did, at least as the events surrounding beer at the 1893 expo faded into a fog of often inaccurate legend. Even armed with Lichtenfeld's sworn statement, the outcome of the Busch appeal stood, and into the twenty-first century Pabst Blue Ribbon pilsners would carry the tag "Selected as America's Best in 1893." For a time, Busch considered ditching the expos altogether. He would relent and exhibit at expos in Prague and Berlin in the coming two decades and at one in St. Louis in 1904, which he had a major hand in organizing.

Pilsner was big business now, after all, and the world fairs were its biggest stage. Ever since the accolades from Vienna in 1873, the style had gained notoriety and presumably fans from its appearances at these spectacles. The spectacles, too, had afforded pilsner purveyors such as Busch and Pabst a forum for showing off how they made such clean, crisp lager over and over on a scale unimaginable to brewers only thirty or forty years before. The thirst for pilsner had helped drive all sorts of trends and milestones by the early 1890s, including mechanical refrigeration; steam usage on an industrial scale; German assimilation into the United States; glass production and everything that came with it, including bottle tops; vertical integration, by which businesses such as Anheuser-Busch owned various stages of production and distribution, from grain mills to bottle factories to railroad cars; and a sizable chunk of what we would later call food science. Whether the forces behind them realized it at the time, these trends were all toward building a better pilsner. And it worked. The style was spreading globally during this era.

Another persistent creep during the same period would disrupt everything, though. It started, funnily enough, with another event in 1893, one that got far less ink initially than the back-and-forth in Chicago over a nonexistent grand prize.

21

THE INEVITABLE BEER

Anders Ohlsson was doing pretty well for himself by 1880. The stout mustachioed Swede with a receding hairline and creeping jowls had emigrated to southern Africa in 1864, at age twenty-three, from his native Norway, which was then part of a kingdom that included Sweden. In that, Ohlsson was like millions of other young men in a hurry. He had used his modest means to travel far from home to stake some sort of a claim to commercial success. In his case, that originally meant setting himself up as a merchant specializing in importing steel and timber from the lush Damaraland in present-day central Namibia. Ohlsson and a partner, also from Scandinavia, did a brisk trade in moving the goods between Damaraland, the British colony of Cape Town in present-day South Africa, and Europe. A tribal war in 1880, though, put a dead stop to this trade. The Swede looked around for something else to do.

Enter brewing. By the time Ohlsson's trading initiative collapsed, Germans were starting to colonize Damaraland and its surroundings in a typically brutal fashion, violently subduing and marginalizing the local populations and funneling much of any ensuing profits from exploiting their natural resources back to the fatherland. The German chancellor Otto von Bismarck had called a conference of European powers in Berlin in 1883 and 1884 that in effect divided up much of Africa between them. Among the spoils, the Germans got what became known as German South West Africa—present-day Namibia—and the British got to tighten their control over colonies that would one day become South Africa.

Anywhere Germans ended up in the world in the late nineteenth century, so too did pilsner. Much of the trade internal and external in German South West Africa was in alcohol in general. In 1884, the first year Germany really began to assert its control over the colony, a remarkable 64 percent of the total weight of exports from the major German port of Hamburg to Africa was alcohol, including pilsner. Large piles of empty beer bottles outside the colony's lucrative diamond mines would attest to this thirst, as would the sheer number of booze-producing concerns in German South West Africa by the turn of the century. Of the 167 companies and firms licensed there by 1903, fifty-three would exclusively or mainly deal in producing or trading alcohol. Such a tidal wave ensured that Europeans like Ohlsson knew of pilsner and knew of Germans' jones for the Bohemian-born lager. But when it came time for Ohlsson to move on to his next venture—a brewery—he picked the less volatile Cape Town colony that the British controlled. And there ale from the mother isles ruled. Ohlsson's commercial trajectory, though, would bend toward lager and toward pilsner in particular—and that trajectory serves as an excellent example of how pilsner bent beer markets the world over to its will, especially when those markets brushed up against Germans.

The European population of Cape Town and much of the surrounding British territory was mostly that: British. The other European group, the tens of thousands of Dutch-descended settlers known as Afrikaners or Boers, had either moved on to other southern African colonies, or had lived under a kind of forced Anglicization under the encroaching British. This included learning to love the heavier, richer, bitterer ales from the United Kingdom. In much the same way that Continental brewers had sought the expertise of their English counterparts in the 1830s and 1840s, South African colonialists did arduous reconnaissance in England as well, traveling back and forth for the latest research and matériel until they were able to produce ales akin to those back in London and other such locales. "In the 1830s, the British produced the best quality beer and their brewing methods were considered the best in the world," noted one historian of the period. So when it came time for Anders Ohlsson in 1880 to get in on the action in Cape Town, he hired a London firm well known for designing and rigging English breweries. "They used an English brewery design, built with English oak, and installed English brewing equipment," a chronicler put it. And Ohlsson dispatched one of his brewers to study the latest techniques back in England and later hired another one from there. These engineers and brewers were steeped in traditional methods of brewing that predated the research of Louis Pasteur and Emil Hansen. Theirs was still a world of brewing as part art. No matter—nothing succeeds like success. Throughout the 1880s, the pale ales, porters, and stouts from Ohlsson's Anneberg Brewery in Cape Town gained a reputation as particularly delicious. Ohlsson acquired other breweries—and icehouses and a mill—and he and his ales soon bestrode the South African market. He even exported to other nearby European colonies.

Then the ground under Ohlsson and other South African ale producers shifted. Gold rushes and migrations brought in Germans from German South West Africa and from Germany itself. With them traveled not only those voluminous amounts of lighter lager, including pilsner, but the techniques and the equipment behind them. So began a gradual shift in South Africa—as in so many other places, the United States most prominently—away from traditionally crafted English ales to more technologically turned-out lagers. Why, the treasurer-general of Cape Town inquired in 1885, was the head brewer at Cloete's Brewery, a rival of Ohlsson's, not a "scientific brewer"? Cloete's principal owner, John Spence, replied that it did not really matter. His "practical brewer" might not be better than one with a scientific background, but he was just as good. The treasurer-general pressed Spence further. He thought that the more scientific methods developed and tested on the Continent were superior to those from yesteryear used in England. Spence once again defended his brewer and his methods, but he did acknowledge that Cloete's adoption of some of those Continental methods had been good for business of late. That was due in large part to the growing demand for lighter lagers among the German arrivals.

That was certainly what spurred Englishmen Frederick Mead and George Henry Raw to switch from ales to lagers in the early 1890s. The pair had arrived for the gold and stayed to make beer, eventually acquiring the existing Castle Brewery in Johannesburg and raising capital back in London to found in 1892 what they called South African United Breweries—later known as South African Breweries (SAB). The new operation aimed squarely at lager, at pilsner in particular, importing the ingredients and the equipment necessary to essentially corner the market, a market that Mead and Raw knew Germans dominated. Early advertisements for South African United beers in the large Transvaal region of South Africa, for instance—including for Castle Lager, a light-tasting, effervescent concoction clearly modeled after pilsner—were in both English and German due to the "large and beer-loving Teutonic section of [that] populace." At the same time, pilsners produced in northern Europe poured into southern Africa at a pace never seen before.

Ohlsson, the African tip's beer king, saw the writing on the wall and pivoted as aggressively as possible to lagers after trying to stave off South African United and the imports through buying up retail outlets, including pubs, and making them serve his ales. By 1900 Ohlsson was laying the foundations of the first brewery built in Cape Town specifically for lager production. In barely twenty years, South Africa's brewing industry had shifted from English-style ales to Czech-born pilsner. According to a reporter who attended an official groundbreaking for the lager brewery in July 1900, Ohlsson himself acknowl-edged that "there was no comparison between the beer which he found [upon his arrival in 1864] and that of the present day." Ohlsson also praised the scientific and technological advancements that "had been called in to make the undertaking a success by securing a lager beer equal in all respects to the best brands now being imported into the colony."

It was all such a familiar arc, one that was repeating itself all over the world in the last decades of the nineteenth century. In August 1903 a group of British and German investors formed a joint stock company based in Hong Kong and called quite simply the Anglo-German Brewing Company. The venture used its capital to build a brewery within the German naval base at Qingdao, a port on the Yellow Sea. European countries and Japan had been divvying up bits of eastern China into spheres of influence—or into outright colonies as in the case of the United Kingdom's Hong Kong—and that had brought demand for beer, pilsner in particular. "They wanted the relief only a cool pilsner could bring them," one modern observer wrote of the founders of the new brewery at Qingdao. The light, bubbly pilsner would come to be called Tsingtao and would eventually become China's most popular exported beer. Unsurprisingly, it made use of German equipment, techniques, and expertise.

Ralph and William Foster followed a similar approach. The brothers, Americans of Irish descent, decamped from New York in the late 1880s for a several weeks' journey to Australia and launched an eponymous brewery in Melbourne with the aid of a German brewmaster. The company's first release in November 1888 was another conscious imitation of pilsner—and rightfully so. Australia was a largely inhospitable backwater of the British Empire, with notoriously toasty, dry, and long summers that rendered unpalatable the ales imported from the metropole or made off English recipes. Lager "supplied in the proper way, in bulk, cold and fully charged with carbonic acid," was the wave of Australia's future as one journalist at the time put it. The Fosters' pilsner became an almost overnight success. Within a year, lager importers had lowered their prices so much that the brothers were basically drummed out of the Aussie market. They sold their brewery to a business consortium for less than what it cost them to build it and were back in New York by the start of the 1890s.

Still, the experience of the Fosters and of the Anglo-German Brewing Company, and of Anders Ohlsson, were typical of brewery start-ups globally in the 1880s and 1890s. They might begin as ale producers or amid a frothy market for ales. But they invariably bent toward lagers, and lighter ones at that, modeled after the pilsner style. A few features clearly demarcated this style, one that imitations and iterations that might be created thousands and thousands of miles away from one another shared. Brewers by 1900 understood pilsner to be light in color and light in mouthfeel. From its first days under Josef Groll's watchful Bavarian eyes in the early 1840s, pilsner had always been light in color—golden almost—and lighter-tasting than most beers drinkers would encounter their entire lives. It was also bubbly. "Effervescent" comes up a lot in descriptions of the style during its first three quarters of a century. It was no accident that Carl Conrad, a master marketer, corked his early St. Louis–made Budweiser in champagne bottles. Pilsner was also invariably not as strong in alcohol as most of its compatriots, a feature that journalists covering those German beer gardens in American cities invariably pointed out. Drinkers of pilsner and other lighter lagers got drunk, but not *too* drunk too fast. All this was a result of the origins of the style—features, after all, defined any beer style—but also the embrace of new technology and new research that ensured a uniformity in production that most ale predecessors had yet to adopt. "When consumers ordered a pilsner, they could be sure they would receive the same clear beverage every time," wrote one historian of the style at the dawn of the twentieth century, "unlike when ordering a British beer that would be of higher alcohol, very hoppy, and likely full of sediment due to the lack of extended aging of the beer." This uniformity sped pilsner on its way to becoming "the first global beer style in terms of taste."

So did the technology behind it and the capital marshaled on its behalf in areas as disparate as the American Midwest, the Netherlands, southern Africa, and eastern China. Pilsner had the good fortune to be born at a time when Europe exploded economically, technologically, and politically. That good fortune extended to its arrival in an America that was just beginning to roll to the Pacific Coast, through some of the most verdant farmland in the world, ground that provided copious ingredients for industrious immigrant brewers. And pilsner's rise coincided with an industrialization that prized repetition and reach. Consumers wanted products that were the same time and again, and producers wanted to get those products to new markets. Fresh technologies and fresh trade routes—many forged through brutal imperialism, others simply through old-fashioned salesmanship—made both the consistency and the reach possible in the late nineteenth century.

Finally, pilsner rose to this wide-ranging popularity in a relatively short time despite its great cost. Before and even in the years after the spread of artificial refrigeration, "lager brewing required large quantities of ice in summer, large cellars for aging the beer in cold temperatures, and entailed a much slower turnover of capital." Ale was easier. Ale yeast was heartier.

Any temperature would do, short of boiling hot. Ale aged quicker and was ready for market faster. People knew ale like their great-grandparents had known ale. Lager was none of these things. It was unfamiliar initially outside southern Germany. But it surpassed ale in popularity nonetheless. What's more, its most mercurial manifestation yet—pilsner, a lager that through its clearness could show every mistake a brewer made—succeeded more than any other lager set up against it. It was the "Yesterday" of beers—the most widely covered style of its day. Riffs on its basic bubbly lightness popped up globally in the late nineteenth century. And nothing seemed able nor likely to stop its spread in the twentieth—except history. History had other plans for pilsner.

22

THE BIGGEST THREAT

1893–1914 | Oberlin, Ohio; Washington, DC

On May 24, 1893—twenty-three days after President Grover Cleveland flipped the switch on the World's Columbian Expo in Chicago—a new group formed in Oberlin, a small city about forty miles southwest of Cleveland and best known as the home of a prominent liberal arts college. The group was dedicated to an issue that had lain dormant nationally for decades but that had never truly died on the local and state levels: temperance. This new group in Oberlin was another state-level organization. The name said it all—the Ohio Anti-Saloon League—but its founder, a born public speaker and lawyer turned Congregational minister named Howard Hyde Russell, made clear that the league had national aspirations, ones that would change the world if realized.

Russell, a native Minnesotan who studied the law in Iowa before marrying a deeply religious woman in Ohio who spurred his move to the ministry in 1888, loved to tell audiences of how he came to the temperance movement after that. It started when a Sunday-school student of his arrived at the church classroom crying. The student told Russell that his mother had died of pneumonia after being "only sick three days," leaving behind her husband and two young children. Russell went with the boy to visit the home. There, in his own words, Russell discovered "the father intoxicated [along with] three or four neighbor women with liquor upon their breath." The minister quickly deduced what had really happened to the boy's mother. "Do you know what caused your mother's death? It was the drink. Are you going to drink my boy?" The boy looked up at Russell's warm eyes and round face bookmarked by two big ears and capped even in his thirties with snowy white hair. "I'll never touch it," the boy replied, clenching his fist. Moved, the minister vowed then and there "to go out to my brothers and sisters of the churches, regardless of their name and creed, and I will appeal to them to join their hearts and hands in a movement to destroy this murderous curse."

Russell's promise and the eventual nationwide platform of the Ohio league he started bespoke what the temperance advocates were aiming for from the 1880s onward. This was not your father's temperance movement, the one that in the beginning of the century had wrapped opposition to strong drink in an American flag. That temperance movement had smugly concluded that drunken hooliganism went hand in hand with the vast number of immigrants arriving in the United States at the time—most of whom, conveniently enough, just happened to be Germans and Irish who practiced the Catholic faith.

Temperance Movement 2.0 did see a connection between drunkenness and Catholic immigration—this time via the approximately four million Italians, many of them wine drinkers, who would arrive in America between 1880 and 1920. Rather than alienate potential allies among the ranks of immigrants and their immediate descendants and waste energy fighting a two-pronged front against immigrants and alcohol, the new movement saw success in a path paved with inclusivity and education. The new wave of temperance advocates sought to draw allies "regardless of their name and creed" with persuasive arguments against the ills of drink itself and not necessarily about the ills of the drinkers. And buoyed as they were by successful efforts to end slavery and to expand the American empire from the Atlantic to the Pacific—and beyond, with the acquisition of Alaska in 1867 and other territories—they had their sights set on a truly national stage. In December 1895 the Ohio Anti-Saloon League joined with a similar organization that had started in Washington, DC, to form the National Anti-Saloon League, which eventually became the Anti-Saloon League of America.

The names reflected the ambitions. "It has not come," one early leader explained, "simply to build a little local sentiment or to secure the passage of a few laws, or yet to vote the saloons from a few hundred towns. These are mere incidents in its progress. It has come to solve the liquor problem." It would do so through fomenting some much-needed coordination, one historian notes, using an almost corporate structure and some of that old-time religion to try to draw the broadest public support possible. To that end, the Anti-Saloon League would combine the power of various prohibition organizations with the more fervent wings of evangelical Protestantism—and it would brook no dissent once it got going. The group took as its motto "The saloon must go."

Brewers hardly noticed. They were in the midst of a remarkable run of growth, after all, of burgeoning sales and expanding reach, trends that the over-the-top exhibits and controversy at the Chicago expo had emphasized. This growth came not just from putting pilsner in front of more mouths. As with a lot of what drove this style's meteoric rise, there were new innovations. In particular, an Ireland-born Baltimore inventor named William Painter came up with what he called "crown corks," the precursor to the common bottle top. Painter would die in 1906 with more than eighty patents—including for an ejection seat from trains and a machine for folding paper—but none would have the enduring and personally enriching influence of this bottle top. "They were designed for one-time use, they were inexpensive, and they were completely leak-proof," a student of Painter's life put it. What's more, before the end of the century, he also patented an opener for his crown corks and a foot-powered contraption to affix them quickly to bottles. It was all a vast improvement on the stopper, which had itself been a vast improvement on cork, and pilsner producers would prove particularly enthusiastic fans of Painter's bottle top. It was yet another way to reach more consumers and to gain a financial advantage over competitors in an increasingly dog-eat-dog industry.

In the late nineteenth century, a wave of consolidation swept the brewing industry in America. The nation hosted more than forty-one hundred breweries in 1873, eight years after the Civil War's end, but at the start of the next century it would have fewer than half that number. Part of that was through mergers and acquisitions—Adolphus Busch owned or had sizable stakes in several breweries in Texas alone—and part of it came from a deep economic recession, which began in 1893 and lasted four years. Such growth and consolidation amid economic strife kept brewers busy, as did trying to thwart an excise tax increase to help pay for the Spanish-American War while dealing with a relatively new phenomenon in the country: organized labor.

Several unions of skilled tradesmen, including brewery workers, formed the American Federation of Labor in 1881. From then on, the group and its allies used all manner of strikes and slowdowns to agitate for better working conditions and better pay. For the most part, ownership and their government allies responded with violence. Several hundred workers and strikebreakers would die in strike-related violence between the early 1870s and the early 1920s—usually at the hands of local police, state militias, or hired mercenaries, but also sometimes the US Army. It was a fact of American civic life: agitation, a strike, publicity, a crackdown (often involving police firing directly into crowds), arrests, trials, and sentencing and fallout. Though the United States "has had the bloodiest labor history of any industrial nation," as one study noted, the confrontations between brewery owners and their employees were comparatively nonviolent, almost calm. That was because brewery workers tended to make more already than the average factory laborer and because brewery workers' unions—led by the National Union of the Brewers of the United States, formed in 1886—opted for boycotts of their owners' products versus outright confrontation outside the factories and in the streets. High-profile, sometimes yearlong boycotts of the likes of Anheuser-Busch and Pabst brought fewer working hours and higher pay—boycott-driven negotiations with the brewery union in Milwaukee, for instance, put an extra two dollars a month in workers' pockets. Capital and labor barreled toward the twentieth century in an uneasy alliance that still proved workable enough to make America the second-biggest beer producer behind Germany.

The final reason that brewers barely noticed the resurgent and reconfigured temperance movement was that it all seemed so ineffective and disjointed. The last temperance wave had crashed not only against the shoals of the Civil War and the assimilation of German immigrants that the conflict helped accelerate but also against the very setup of the nation. It enjoyed sporadic success with saloon fees as well as sales and manufacturing bans in this or that city, county, or state, but it never came close to a national prohibition against booze. Nor did it enjoy much cohesion in either organization or ideas. Some wanted high licensing fees for saloons—which ironically made bigger breweries major saloon owners as smaller proprietors could not absorb the higher costs—and some wanted a blanket ban. Some were content to let beer be, lower-alcohol lagers such as pilsner in particular, and instead focus on head-splitting rotgut such as whiskey and rum. And then there was a great swath of the nation that could never quite fathom the crusaders' zeal. "I drink beer and light wines myself," President Cleveland said in 1887, "and I think I feel all the better for them, but I do not recommend their use to others, because I believe every man should be a law unto himself in this matter." That was not what the so-called drys wanted. Though how to get what they did want remained elusive for decade upon decade.

It has become easy to see the temperance movement in the United States—and globally, for other nations would go dry too during the same era—as a straight line, as inevitable, something that was going to happen regardless of the opposition and the circumstances. After all, the temperance movement that the Anti-Saloon League embodied had, like pilsner, picked a great time to be born. Other reformist movements were chugging along on both sides of the Atlantic. Suffragists wanted to enfranchise women. Labor leaders wanted to not only ameliorate those working conditions and boost pay but also end forever odious practices such as child labor and six- or seven-day workweeks of indefinite hours. Marginalized groups around the world, from black people in America to the minority populations within the great

European colonial empires, wanted basic rights and a voice, if not full-on independence. The Jewish diaspora wanted a homeland—the modern Zionist movement arose in the 1890s. And crusading journalists, particularly in America, wanted good stories that would change the world. They found them, perhaps most prominently, in exposés of the nation's working conditions. Most prominently among that set was a thinly veiled work of fiction about the abysmal conditions among immigrant laborers in Chicago's meatpacking industry and the often-nauseating results of the squalor. Upton Sinclair's *The Jungle* dropped in 1906 and became an immediate sensation. "It pierces the thickest skull and most leathery heart," wrote a young English politician named Winston Churchill. President Theodore Roosevelt used *The Jungle* as a spur for driving through the creation of the Food and Drug Administration the same year Sinclair's novel came out.

It would have appeared, then, that the drys could not lose in this climate, heated as it was by great and often successful movements for change. If the federal government could extend its reach to the dinner table and into the kitchen icebox, then why could that same hand of Uncle Sam not grip every liquor bottle in the land and smash it to pieces? The drys even channeled a bit of Upton Sinclair. They were behind "a steady stream of newspaper and magazine articles" on "the liquor problem," surely pitching some of the angles themselves if not surreptitiously planting the stories outright. This prompted the United States Brewers' Association at its forty-eighth annual convention in Milwaukee in 1908 to publicly condemn what the drys saw as the root of the "problem"—namely, real or imagined illegality inside saloons, many of them owned and operated in conjunction with the biggest pilsner producers of the day. "Divorce the saloon from the brewers and liquor supply house," Adolphus Busch said in a curt statement issued from a steamship on the Atlantic as he traveled between his American and German estates.

Brewers, at least publicly, appeared perfectly willing to enforce regulations promoting general decency and the moderate consumption of alcohol, particularly their bestselling pilsner. They even put money behind efforts to educate the public not just on the joys of moderate consumption but the economic impact that the brewing industry had on America. Anheuser-Busch alone would put the modern equivalent of more than $16 million behind this learned push.

But that was all that the brewers would do. That was because it still seemed that the longtime disjointedness and infighting that Howard Hyde Russell's Anti-Saloon League had yet to fix would continue to hobble the temperance movement for the foreseeable future. By 1900 only Kansas, Maine, and North Dakota maintained prohibition. Worse for the drys, states and counties vacillated on the issue throughout the 1890s and early 1900s. A newly elected governor in Alabama—whom the liquor industry had backed—repealed prohibition there in 1911. A year before, voters in Florida rejected by a wide margin an amendment to the Sunshine State's constitution that would have banned "all intoxicating liquors and beverages, whether spirituous, vinous or malt." Such losses came despite growing support among business leaders. Industrial titans of the age such as Henry Ford, John D. Rockefeller Jr., and Andrew Carnegie embraced prohibition both for sincere reasons (they thought it would make America that much better) and for self-interested ones (a sober workforce might be a more malleable and productive one). The losses kept coming, though. The drys suffered defeats similar to the one in Florida in Missouri, Oregon, Arkansas, and Texas.

The political losses made it starkly clear that the only way the Anti-Saloon League and its allies might triumph was through that rarest of civil changes: an amendment to the US Constitution. But that had only been done seventeen times in well over a century, with the only two paths to success through either state-by-state legislative or convention votes, or the nation's first constitutional convention since 1787. The first would be tortuous and the second seemed improbable. Plus, the drys could not catch a real break at the national level. "You will hardly suspect me of being a prohibitionist crank," Theodore Roosevelt wrote to William Howard Taft as the latter prepared to succeed him in the White House in 1909, "but such hideous misery does come from drink that I cordially sympathize with any successful effort to do away with it or minimize its effects. . . . My experience with prohibitionists, however, is that the best way to deal with them is to ignore them."

Taft certainly tried. He vetoed legislation that would have prohibited the shipment of alcohol from "wet" to dry states (though Congress overrode his veto). His agriculture secretary spoke at an international conference of brewers in Chicago in 1911, which caused temperance advocates to go berserk. Taft couldn't have cared less. In a privately circulated memo responding to the Anti-Saloon League's protest of the cabinet secretary's appearance, Taft scrawled, "I can not & will not interfere—I think the societies might be about more useful business than clearing such phantoms."

Taft's successor, the Democrat Woodrow Wilson, offered little more in support. Wilson, an outwardly austere ex-academic and the son of a Presbyterian minister from the South, was nevertheless known to keep his own stash of wine and whiskey at the White House and in his private residences. "I notice in the papers that the States wanted to confiscate liquors and wines that have been stored in private residences," he once remarked to an associate. "I think that is interfering with personal privileges." Still, the year Wilson took office, the drys made their most dramatic stand yet in terms of pushing for prohibition. On December 10, 1913, four thousand men and women marched up Pennsylvania Avenue to the United States Capitol to personally submit a proposed constitutional amendment that the Anti-Saloon League had drawn up banning alcohol production and sales. It failed to gain the necessary two-thirds votes in Congress to go from there to individual states. The drys were vocal and earnest, but they lacked the congressional support, never mind the support of a national chief executive who would need to enforce any legislative or constitutional change regarding alcohol.

What's more, brewers were awakening to the threat—especially after the December 1913 rally and the gains in dry congressmen and senators during the 1912 elections. They fought dry propaganda with propaganda of their own. In particular, brewers leaned on images and elocution about the mild stimulating effects their pilsner-inspired beers had on drinkers. Theirs was a convivial, even healthful beverage. It was not hard liquor or jug wine. Plus, the nation's hundreds of breweries generated jobs and economic activity, and, because of vertical integration, it had its hands in myriad other industries, from agriculture to bottle production to the railroads to refrigeration to advertising to hospitality. Brewing over the past century—particularly since the first waves of German immigrants in the 1840s—had become one of the most important industries in an industrial America. And it was up to brewers to make the public and public officials aware of that, a point Boston mayor John F. Fitzgerald drove home in remarks to the United States Brewers' Association when it held its annual convention in that city in 1912. The maternal grandfather of President John F. Kennedy warned brewers "to take care that the lawmakers of state and nation are correctly informed as to your business, the character of the men engaged in it, the amount of capital involved, [and] the kind of men who are in organizations like this, having as its object to see that the business is properly conducted."

Brewers were determined to do so, but they seemed to understand that there would be no march of thousands of pilsner fanatics down Pennsylvania Avenue. Theirs was a position that was clearly about preserving business, whereas the drys could tug on all sorts of emotional heartstrings related to hearth and home—and house of worship. All that organizations such as the United States Brewers' Association could do was get their industry's views in front of eyeballs through advertising and sympathetic press coverage, and then hope for the best. "There is no doubt of the soundness of this method," the association's president said at a convention during this period, "but, unfortunately, everything related to the use of alcohol is the subject of such bitter controversy that the mass of the people find themselves involved in such a maze of contradictions that the truth is obscured." Lucky for brewers, though, even with all the marches and sermons, it just seemed like the drys would never get anywhere near the legislative numbers necessary, nor have a true ally in the White House for national prohibition. Or at least not any time soon.

Then a sickly nineteen-year-old shot a plumed nobleman few Americans had ever heard of, and everything changed.

23

WAR

1898–1919 | Sarajevo; Washington

When in late 1914 the German army took the small Belgian city of Hamont-Achel on the pastoral Dutch-Belgian border during World War I, it took with it a brewery there that monks of the severely ascetic Cistercian, or Trappist, order had been running since the 1850s. Because of its location, a portion of the brewery, known as Achel, was in Belgium and a portion was in the Netherlands. And, because imperial Germany respected the neutrality of the Netherlands but not of Belgium, the part of Achel that fell within the latter was basically destroyed with the monks looking on. The Germans smelted the brewery's copper kettles and other apparatus for war matériel, and the Achel brewery would not reopen until the late 1990s.

What happened at Achel was a small but telling example of what happened to brewing overall during what quickly became known as the Great War. Slavic nationalist Gavrilo Princip's June 1914 assassination of Archduke Franz Ferdinand, heir to the Austrian-Hungarian throne, in Sarajevo, Bosnia, touched off a conflagration the likes of which the world had never seen. An estimated twenty million people would die in the war that the killing triggered, and many more millions would die from its aftershocks, including a flu pandemic that swept the globe and the excessively violent revolution that destroyed czarist Russia. The fighting, done on an almost cinematic scale with weaponry and tactics previously never seen, would wound millions more, of course—estimates place that total at twenty-one million, not including the psychological scars that shadowed an entire generation and its children. Nations and regimes were decimated and entire industries disrupted.

Brewing was among those industries, and, while the fate of beer obviously pales in the face of such barbarous human carnage, the fact remains that World War I altered brewing in lasting ways. The most lasting was the change in trajectory for pilsner. The world's most popular beer style by the start of the war in August 1914 found itself on the commercial run within a few short years.

The war bookended that first golden age of pilsner that began with the mass emigration of Germans to the United States and that peaked amid scientific and industrial leaps forward in the 1870s and 1880s. That was an era when the race to brew clearer, crisper, lower-alcohol lagers based on and around pilsner fueled the rise of great fortunes and enduring brands. That era continued in all its bubbly glory until the war, despite the mortal exits of several monumental figures of the period. Gerard Heineken, who had built a marginal Dutch brewery into one of the Continent's biggest presences behind a green-bottled main brand that he proudly labeled pilsner, died at his desk, so to speak. One late morning in March 1893, as he was preparing to address Heineken's shareholders, the seemingly healthy fifty-one-year-old collapsed "without letting out the slightest sound," a journalist who witnessed it noted. Frederick Miller, the German immigrant who took the Best family's Plank Road Brewery near Milwaukee and put it on course to become one of the five biggest breweries in his adopted homeland and the largest in the world for a time, died five years before Heineken, in May 1888 at age sixty-three. Gabriel Sedlmayr died in October 1891 at age eighty. His long life witnessed and spurred some of the greatest changes in brewing via his family's Spaten brewery in Munich, which by the time of the Great War was under his grandsons' management.

Finally, the most portentous death—because of who it was and coming when it did—was that of Adolphus Busch. He had been ailing for years when he died in October 1913 in Hesse, Germany, at age seventy-four. It was as if the nineteenth-century era of brewing needed a proper coda before the effects of World War I commenced less than a year later. "The epitome of the dynastic brewer," as one chronicler put it, Busch commanded an empire that stretched to multiple breweries and nations before his death. A pioneer in everything from mechanical refrigeration to pasteurization to bottling to distribution to the use of adjuncts such as rice to vertical integration, the workaholic, imperious German immigrant had transformed his industry, and industry in general. By the time he died, Busch's Anheuser-Busch, the management of which his will entrusted to his eldest son August A. Busch, was turning out well over one million barrels a year and had stakes in multiple other breweries as well as distribution companies, and it had its own bottling sources. That production figure was a phenomenal sum. It likely made Anheuser-Busch the largest brewery in the United States—running neck and neck with Pabst—and perhaps the largest in the world. Most of the beer it turned out was still Budweiser, the brewery's take on the pilsner that Carl Conrad was said to have tasted in a monastery in Bohemia. Most of it, too, looked, tasted, and smelled the same no matter where it was shipped, an engineering marvel that would have stunned brewers a couple of generations back.

Busch's success, of course, made him immensely wealthy, a baronial presence that managed to stand out even in a gilded age that produced the likes of John D. Rockefeller and Andrew Carnegie, never mind Henry Ford, whose car factories of the early twentieth century may have consciously mimicked the early assembly lines of the main Busch brewery in St. Louis. When Busch and his wife, Lilly, celebrated their golden wedding anniversary in March 1911, the celebration in St. Louis "was said to have been unprecedented for its elaborateness in the world's history," according to the *New York Times*. Presidents William Howard Taft—who had nicknamed Busch "Prince Adolphus"—and Theodore Roosevelt sent gifts, as did old friend Kaiser Wilhelm II of Germany.

And, speaking of gifts, Busch gave his wife a gold crown studded with diamonds and pearls and said to be worth $200,000 in 1911 money. He also gave some five thousand St. Louis employees a holiday and made myriad charitable donations to mark the anniversary party. The *New York Times*' obituary for "St. Louis's millionaire brewer" estimated his wealth at some $60 million, the equivalent of $1.5 billion a hundred years later (and surely an underestimate on the *Times*' part given the value of Busch's real estate alone). Such wealth manifested itself in little ways as well as big ones. "Our gardens in California," wrote one of Busch's granddaughters, referring to the greenery around neighboring estates in Pasadena, "were really like a scene from 'Midsummer Night's Dream.' We employed forty to fifty gardeners." There was a private train car called "Adolphus"—that era's equivalent of owning a private wide-body jet—and the St. Louis Anheuser-Busch headquarters at 1 Busch Place. When a Busch child was born, cannons at the headquarters fired salutes. It was all a kind of hop-fueled fairy tale.

The war that started less than a year after Adolphus Busch died threatened to upend it forever. The most immediate and obvious effect was an interruption in the flow of beer. The march of armies, the battles larger than anyone alive had ever beheld, unrestrained submarine warfare on the part of the Germans, and the displacement of entire towns, cities, and regions as populaces fled the fighting—it all contributed to upending the normal manufacture and distribution of beer. So, too, did rationing. Every major European belligerent prioritized feeding its military, and that meant widespread grain scarcities for everything else, including for brewing. What's more, the Germans, who quickly swept through Belgium and Luxembourg and much of northeastern France, appropriated and repurposed perhaps hundreds of breweries in their conquered territories. A few were allowed to continue to operate—mostly to supply the German military with beer—but most found themselves used as stables, bathing facilities, laundries, dewatering stations, even slaughterhouses. The owners were almost never compensated, and many went off to the front anyway along with their workers. That was another side effect of the war—the loss of manpower in the literal sense.

Sometimes the effects were dramatic. The original Burghers' Brewery in Pilsen, where pilsner was born nearly seventy-five years before, had become perhaps the largest brewery in continental Europe by the start of the war, with its production hitting more than 825,000 barrels in 1913. It had ridden the popularity of its signature creation, including via railroad tracks that unspooled through western Bohemia in the early 1860s. It had also grown through exports. The majority of the brewery's output was being exported as early as 1865—including to the United States, starting in the early 1870s in Racine, Wisconsin, where a sizable Czech expat community lived—and that would continue to be the case right up to the war. In part to protect its reach amid a growing thirst for pilsner, the shareholders who still controlled the Burghers' Brewery successfully obtained that 1859 "pilsner bier" trademark for the original brew from Pilsen. But an attempt around that time to stem the use of "pilsner" or words like it to describe the style failed. A further trademark on February 8, 1898—this time "Pilsner Urquell," which means roughly "genuine pilsner" and which would become synonymous with the brewery—would do little to check either the rise in breweries calling their beers pilsner or their brewing of that style. It had spread too far too relatively fast. Only a conflagration like the Great War—which involved Pilsen's home nation of Austria-Hungary allying with Germany—could really trip it up, and it did. Pilsner Urquell's production would drop after the start of the war, and it would not scratch its early-century barrelage high again until the late 1990s.

All this was bad for European brewers. On the other side of the Atlantic, it was another story. "The sudden outbreak of the Great War cut Europe's beer exports to America, creating a market opportunity for quality domestic brewers," Alfred W. McCoy, a descendant of the German American founders of Piels Brewery in Brooklyn, New York, would write. America was officially neutral for the first thirty months of the war, even if public sentiment gradually swung behind the Allied cause that the United Kingdom and France led. Its brewers could go on brewing as they had before Franz Ferdinand's fateful assassination. They could even expand their reach as imports from Europe dried up. Anheuser-Busch helpfully offered to fill the void for German-made beers in France and the United Kingdom, both of which had no intention of allowing imports of perhaps their enemy's most famous product. August A. Busch even wrote a personal letter to American diplomatic consuls at various foreign ports, offering his company's pilsner, and other styles, in place of German beers that might never make it out of the Reich because of the war. The Piels Brewery ran a quarter-page advertisement in a New York newspaper just after hostilities broke out in August 1914, promising stateside lovers of good European styles such as pilsner that Piels' beers would "prove indistinguishable from the finest imported."

The results were immediate, at least domestically (the war prevented dreams of immediate European growth from coming true). Burgeoning world war or not, Americans wanted their beer. "The pilsener sales have more than doubled," Henry Piel, a son of one of the brewery's founders and its technical director, wrote to his wife in 1914, "and I am sure it will treble this present fine output." To be on the safe side, Henry Piel husbanded the brewery's yeast supply, in part through a "propagation apparatus." His and other American breweries did not want to have to rely on anything from Europe—and the likeliest material from Europe would have been yeast, given that America itself had amber waves of grain to provide beer's malted material.

But America would not stay out of the war forever. Woodrow Wilson cleverly won reelection in 1916 promising just that. No small marketing feat, given the rising tide in public sentiment against the kaiser and his tactics. In May 1915, a German submarine had torpedoed a British ocean liner called the *Lusitania* as it steamed from New York to Liverpool, with more than 120 Americans among the approximately 1,100 killed. US newspapers, too, from just after the war's start carried lurid details of German atrocities—some fake and exaggerated but others plenty real—in occupied areas of France and Belgium in particular. And were not those two countries as well as the United Kingdom at least nominal democracies in the same mold as the United States? Whereas Germany and Austria-Hungary, the two main spokes of the Central Powers, were more autocratic and much more militaristic. It increasingly became a matter of when the United States would enter the war, not if. It also became clear on which side the nation would enter. The congressional declaration of war that passed in April 1917 cited "repeated acts of war against the people of the United States of America [by] the Imperial German Government."

The entry of America into World War I had two immediate and profound effects on pilsner and brewing in general. First was the effect with which European brewers would have been familiar. While no conquering armies rolled through tearing up brewhouses and smelting kettles to feed the killing machine, the US government did harness its agricultural production almost entirely for the war effort. It sought to feed not only a military that the government would have to grow well beyond its size—the United States had just over three hundred thousand soldiers and guardsmen in 1917, versus Germany's eleven million—but also America's new allies. The United Kingdom, France, and Italy had been purchasing American grain in larger quantities since 1916, the fighting having disrupted their own sources. The greater demand internationally and domestically for the likes of barley and especially wheat came, too, at a time of poor crop yields. The United States was in a bind—it could not afford to expend grain in service of brewing at a time when its fighting boys and their comrades needed to eat *and* there was less grain to go around than usual. In December 1917 Woodrow Wilson would exercise powers that a wartime Congress had only recently granted him to curb the amount of foodstuffs allowed for brewing and winemaking. He cut the allowable amount for brewing by 30 percent. At the same time, the president used the same new powers to cap the legal alcoholic content at a low, low 2.75 percent, about half what most pilsners—indeed, most lagers—retailed at then. The brewing industry began to shrivel in the United States, as if a wave that had been cresting since the 1840s started to roll back.

The pressures of the war drove much of the creation of these new powers that Wilson so readily wielded. So did something else. "I am informed that there are a number of breweries in this country which are owned in part by alien enemies," Wayne Wheeler, head of the Anti-Saloon League, wrote to A. Mitchell Palmer, the former congressman now in charge of seizing the property of American citizens deemed loyal to the enemy, in May 1918. "It is reported to me that the Annhauser [*sic*] Busch Company and some of the Milwaukee Companies are largely controlled by alien Germans.... Have you made any investigation? If not would you be willing to do so if we could give you any clue that would justify your taking such action?" Wheeler had the clue, of course. The Anti-Saloon League knew of an investigation into the activities of the United States Brewers' Association in western Pennsylvania on behalf of German propaganda agents in the United States at a time when the US was officially neutral. The association had settled the charges with fines and therefore kept them quiet. Wheeler wanted them out there. He wanted everything and anything out there that would paint German American brewers as hand in hand with the dreaded kaiser.

Palmer was happy to oblige and used the subsequent investigation into supposed anti-American activities as a stepping-stone to becoming attorney general in 1919. A sensational congressional probe in the fall of 1918, when US forces were definitively turning the tide against Germany and its allies, revealed a laundry list of alleged wrongdoing on the part of German American brewers. Or at least that was the idea. Much of what the investigation and its public hearings revealed had to do with brewers' efforts to combat the temperance movement: the founding of a newspaper in support of their cause; lobbying politicians; boycotting manufacturers sympathetic to the drys; etcetera. But what Wheeler and company succeeded in doing—what they had set out to do, in fact—was soak these Americans of German descent in a cauldron of suspicion that might drown their industry entirely. "Everything in this country that is pro-German is anti-American," went a screed from the Anti-Saloon League. "Everything that is pro-German must go." Or as a Wisconsin politician sympathetic to the drys thundered, "We have German enemies in this country too. And the worst of all our German enemies, the most treacherous, the most menacing, are Pabst, Schlitz, Blatz, and Miller." It was a classic case of not letting a crisis go to waste.

It worked. Without all that much effort, the drys were able to entwine their own temperance campaign with a general—and understandable, given the carnage in Europe—anti-German sentiment in the United States. Never mind that many German American brewers threw their financial support behind the US war effort and solemnly pledged allegiance in the effort to defeat kaiser and fatherland, and that the scions of many of these brewers' families joined the US military. "By equating the brewers' defense of their product with pro-German propaganda, the temperance movement silenced its most powerful opponent, the U.S. Brewers' Association," notes Alfred McCoy, not only a Piel descendant but also a professional historian and expert on government surveillance. More than a century on, it can be easy to forget that the anti-German sentiment that the drys so deftly wielded went beyond seemingly minor acts such as municipal orchestras refusing to play Beethoven or Brahms and grocers and restaurants renaming sauerkraut "liberty cabbage." There was a real, long-term effort on the part of the government and its supporters to stamp out German identity in the United States, and that included the enlivening lagers—pilsner most prominently—that had come to be associated so much with German Americans. McCoy summarized the crackdown on his own German American brewing family and others:

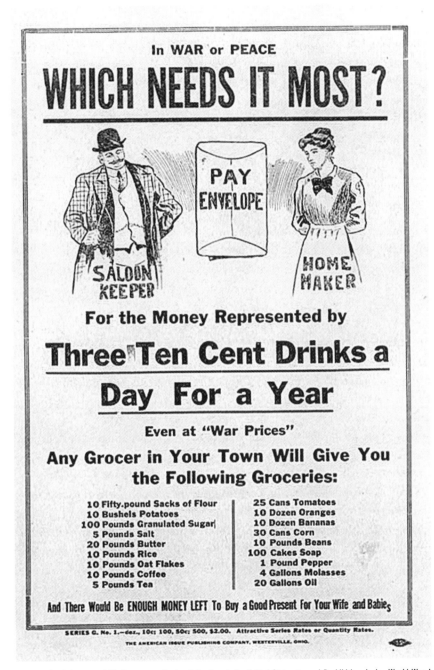

An example of the sort of "dry" propaganda that helped push the United States toward Prohibition during World War I. COURTESY OF LIBRARY OF CONGRESS

For German Americans as a whole, the forced Americanization was painful—their language outlawed, orderly lives terrorized by mob violence, community organizations banned, and their signature beverage prohibited. During the war, half of the forty-eight states restricted the teaching of the German language schools and several banned speaking the language in public. By the war's end, half the country's five hundred German-language newspapers had folded. . . . Conscription of German-Americans was relentless, with draft raids to ferret out "slackers" and no exemptions for pacifist German sects, the Mennonites and Hutterites, many of whom fled to Canada "under a barrage of patriotic oppression."

Palmer and his men also went after the fortunes of the nation's great brewing dynasties, a move that imperiled not only these families' finances but also the operations of their breweries, which still employed thousands each in many cases. The pursuits unfolded, too, despite many of these employees having been drafted into the war effort under the country's first conscription since the Civil War. In a particularly vengeful move that editors and reporters splashed across newspapers, Palmer impounded $60 million in assets belonging to Lilly Busch under a decision that any German American brewers caught in Germany by the war were "of enemy character." Lilly Busch had been vacationing in Germany with her family when the war broke out in 1914. She stayed on even after her American relatives returned home and was volunteering for the Red Cross in Germany when the United States declared war in April 1917. That made her fair game in Palmer's eyes, even though she had lived all but six months of her seventy-four years so far in America.

A constitutional amendment enacted just before the war also helped the drys toward their goal of another amendment banning the manufacture, import, and sale of alcohol. The Sixteenth Amendment—which enabled the federal government "to lay and collect taxes on incomes, from whatever source derived, without apportionment among the several States, and without regard to any census or enumeration"—opened up vast reserves of revenue to the federal government, and eventually to the states, which would quickly follow with their own income taxes. It also meant that these governments were much less reliant on taxing alcohol. Stunning as it may seem today, at times the federal government had been relying on the taxes on beer, wine, and spirits for at least one-third, if not up to half of its revenue. The United States Brewers' Association estimated that its members ponied up 40 percent of all the federal taxes levied between July 1 and November 30, 1898, to fund the

American war effort against Spain—and that was just the brewers, without the nation's similarly robust distilling and fledgling winemaking industry factored in. It would be safe to say that brewers, the vast majority of whom made lighter-colored and lighter-tasting lagers modeled after pilsner, underwrote a healthy part of America's expansionism in this era. That war with Spain, after all, allowed the United States to seize the Philippines, Cuba, and other territorial booty. As for the states, the addiction to alcohol taxation could be even more acute. New York, the most populous state in the union at the time of World War I, drew an astounding three-fourths of its revenue from taxes on alcohol. Simply put, it was all a tasty gravy train that the United States and state governments would rather not have stopped.

The Sixteenth Amendment—though originally just intended to level the economic playing field at a time of rampant income inequality—effectively weaned the government off alcohol taxes as public officials and their bureaucracies quickly realized they did not need them as much as before. It strengthened the power of the drys that much more and further watered down the bargaining power of brewers and other ethanol vendors. Even had Archduke Franz Ferdinand escaped death and Europe escaped war, national Prohibition might have come to fruition because of this alone.

It was all just too perfect a storm for the drys: a climate of anti-German hysteria mixed with thick clouds of official repression as well as that same officialdom's indifference to the economic impact of brewing. Thunder rumbled, and a righteous lightning that had seemed far off ten years ago, and improbably distant ten years before that, struck. National prohibition tumbled out of Congress in December 1917 for the states to ratify, which they began doing almost immediately, starting with Mississippi in January 1918. By the time Nebraska a year later became the decisive thirty-sixth state to ratify the Eighteenth Amendment prohibiting the manufacturing and sale of most alcohol, the Great War had been over for two months. No matter—the drys had made the most of it. Within a year, Congress would pass the amendment's enforcement mechanism, the Volstead Act, and Prohibition would be the law of the land.

24

"A GOOD TIME FOR BEER"

1919–1933 | Washington

Other countries besides the United States enacted prohibitions against alcohol and toyed with temperance. But none enacted it on the scale and with such vigor—and for such a length of time—as America.

"We are fighting Germany, Austria, and drink; and as far as I can see the greatest of these deadly foes is drink," said the United Kingdom's wartime prime minister David Lloyd George in March 1915. The following month, King George V pledged to avoid alcohol for the war's duration, and the British monarch encouraged other nobles to join him. Besides government controls on grains and some other supplies, that was as far as prohibition got in the UK—and, it should be noted, most nobles declined to join their king in setting such an abstemious example.

In Canada, then a largely independent dominion of the UK, decades of incremental prohibition at the local and provincial level ended with a short-lived stab at a national ban that barely survived the war, even if it lingered piecemeal in some provinces for years. Norway, Finland, Iceland, and Russia—and the Soviet Union that followed—tried some forms of partial or total prohibition, too, during this period. But none stuck or struck so deeply in terms of duration and enforcement as the national ban in the United States. That ban lasted into the 1930s and, as a result, all but killed off the American brewing industry and its favored style.

It did not kill individual breweries themselves—particularly the larger ones—and that would have a profound effect on American business and society in the twentieth century. "Essentially our business has always been the conversion of grain into other products," August A. Busch told his hometown newspaper, the *St. Louis Post-Dispatch*, at the outset of Prohibition. He was smiling into the storm, and he knew it. He and other major brewers would have preferred that the latest burst of temperance hysteria had blown over, but the war saw it over the finish line. And so breweries that could, such as

Anheuser-Busch, moved into the manufacture of myriad products, including malt extract for baking and syrups, ice cream, soft drinks, very low-alcohol "near beer," candies, pastas, breakfast cereals, other processed foods, and yeast. There was even talk of converting all or parts of grand breweries to entirely other, non-food-related manufacturing purposes. Could part of the Anheuser-Busch plant in St. Louis make the bodies of motor trucks?

Most breweries that could held on to making some combination of foodstuffs, though Anheuser-Busch did turn over some of its plant to packaging the flesh and by-products of slaughtered animals. The idea was simply to ride out what would surely be a short national experiment. Brewers drew particular hope in the results of the 1922 midterms, when several candidates that the drys backed got trounced at the polls. "The leading New York brewers expect the return of beer and are ready to turn out the real stuff," Jacob Ruppert, a brewer who also happened to be a former congressman, told a reporter after the elections. "They look to the Congress which assembles next year to speedily modify the Volstead Act."

That turned out to be wishful thinking. The new Congress came and went without modifications to Prohibition, and more breweries found their stopgap measures insufficient for the long term. Closings and consolidations became common. It was not unusual to see an advertisement for a failing brewery's supplies and equipment in the industry's trade journals. "Brewing on a national scale came to an end at this point," the historian Stanley Baron notes. That also meant the end of American brewing as an international force. Pabst by 1910, for instance, shipped its flagship pilsner and other beers to some thirty-eight countries and colonies beyond the continental forty-eight, including as far away as eastern Africa and the Philippines. As Prohibition took hold, the nation's second-largest brewery found virtually all those accounts disappearing. The vaunted Milwaukee brewery instead found itself, via acquisitions and other moves, pivoting to the production of malt products just to survive. Though, like other large breweries muddling through, Pabst always held a candle for the end of Prohibition.

There was reason to be hopeful. "My position may surprise you, as it will many of my friends," John D. Rockefeller Jr., one of the nation's wealthiest industrialists and a staunch proponent of Prohibition, wrote in an open letter in June 1932 to Nicholas Murray Butler, the president of Columbia University. Butler had recently come out in favor of a resolution to the Republican Party's convention platform calling for repeal of the Eighteenth Amendment. "I was born a teetotaler; all my life I have been a teetotaler on principle," Rockefeller's letter went on, winding up to what was coming.

"When the Eighteenth Amendment was passed I earnestly hoped—with a host of advocates of temperance—that it would be generally supported by public opinion and thus the day hastened when the value to society of men with minds and bodies free from undermining effects of alcohol would be generally realized." Alas, Rockefeller had to admit, "but rather that drinking has generally increased; that the speakeasy has replaced the saloon, not only unit for unit, but probably two-fold if not three-fold." What's more, according to Rockefeller, "a vast army of lawbreakers" had arisen to slake the public's illicit thirst, and Prohibition, far from temporizing society, had fomented an unhealthy disrespect for the law. It had to stop, Rockefeller wrote. America had to end the longest experimentation with prohibition any modern nation had undertaken, and those ardently opposed to alcohol had to instead trust in the good sense of their fellow citizens. "My hope," Rockefeller concluded, "is that the tremendous effort put forth in behalf of the Eighteenth Amendment by millions of earnest, consecrated people will be continued in effective support of practical measures for the promotion of genuine temperance."

With this open letter, Rockefeller joined other prominent business leaders in championing a kind of third way out of Prohibition—turning back the clock to advocating temperance. The Republican National Convention resolution that Columbia's Butler proposed, in fact, called for returning regulatory authority to the states and asking the states to basically curb consumption and trade—but not ban it. Why the change of heart? Why did anti-booze advocates go from a scorched-earth policy toward beer, spirits, and wine to one of grudging accommodation in all of a dozen years? Part of it was the lawlessness born of Prohibition that Rockefeller cited. Another was that the general public had never really come around to the idea. There was an especially big gulf between Prohibition's largely evangelical Protestant supporters, many of them clustered in the nation's vast interior, and its largely Catholic opponents, made up of recent immigrants and their immediate offspring, who tended to cluster on the coasts and in the big cities.

Nothing illustrated that more than the 1928 presidential election. New York's Manhattan-raised, multiterm Democratic governor, Al Smith, was the first Roman Catholic to headline a major-party ticket. The grandson of European immigrants who identified most strongly with his Irish roots, Smith was also a well-known "wet," and made it clear that he favored repeal. His opponent was the dour engineer and former commerce secretary Herbert Hoover, who was raised a Quaker and who lustily supported Prohibition, even if he thought its enforcement needed tweaking. The Protestant Hoover trounced the Catholic Smith in 1928, even winning southern states that usually went solidly Democratic. The divisive and decisive issue was religion—James Cannon Jr., a Methodist bishop who headed the still-powerful Anti-Saloon League at the time, supported Hoover, dismissing the Catholic Church as "the Mother of ignorance, superstition, intolerance, and sin." That issue might have been possible to overcome, but coupled with Prohibition it was just too much for even a consummate politician like Smith to maneuver around. Still, that a wet Catholic from speakeasy-heavy New York City landed a major-party presidential nomination at all—and that he got more than fifteen million votes out of nearly thirty-seven million cast—spoke volumes about the comfort level the public had for repeal of Prohibition.

This sentiment melded nicely with another reason for Rockefeller and his business-friendly ilk turning on the drys. This was a less talked about reason, but it was becoming too much for Rockefeller and company to ignore. The government's loss of tax revenue at the state and federal levels from being unable to place levies on beer, wine, etcetera, had contributed to a spike in income tax rates. To be sure, the Great Depression—which started with a legendary stock market crash in October 1929 and which worsened steadily afterward—had been the main cause of an increase in 1932 of the top marginal rate for federal income taxes to 63 percent from 25. The federal government needed money and could not readily extract it from the great masses of the American public anymore. Nearly one-fourth of the population that could work was unemployed. The government could not tax income that did not exist. So Washington in part leaned on its wealthier citizenry, who pushed back. Had not alcohol taxes once made up so much of the federal government's revenue and the revenue of some of the largest states? That was before the 1913 income tax, the Great War, Prohibition, the Volstead Act, all of that. Might the government again tap that reserve, especially at a time of such national need, when at least a couple of banks on average were failing every day and capitalism itself seemed on some kind of cosmic trial? A lot of affluent Americans, including industrialists who had not seen much benefit to the enforced sobriety of their workforces anyway, certainly thought so.

They piled up behind Rockefeller's efforts, and the Republican convention platform did adopt a call for at least limited repeal, a new constitutional amendment that would "allow the States to deal with the problem as their citizens may determine." The Democrats, for their part, called for outright repeal in their platform. In the meantime, the party wanted "immediate modification of the Volstead Act; to legalize the manufacture and sale of beer and other beverages of such alcoholic content as is permissible under the Constitution and to provide therefrom a proper and needed revenue." Their nominee, Franklin Roosevelt, won in a landslide that fall. Prohibition was doomed. In March 1933 a heavily Democratic Congress passed, and a freshly inaugurated Roosevelt signed, legislation that amended the Volstead Act to allow for the manufacture and sale of beer and wine with up to 3.2 percent alcohol by weight (4 percent by volume) in states that had already done away with prohibition laws. Officials picked the percentage arbitrarily, groping as they were for a compromise to further the legislation that many knew would hasten the death of Prohibition. Three-two beer essentially became a watered-down version of previous beers, including the pilsners that dominated the market pre-Prohibition, thinner tasting and of course weaker in alcoholic kick. More important from the federal government's point of view, the Volstead Act amendment allowed Washington to tax the revenue from the sales of three-two alcohol, including a five-dollar barrel tax on beer. Full repeal of Prohibition would have to wait until December 1933, when Utah became the thirty-sixth state to ratify the Twenty-First Amendment voiding the Eighteenth. Brewers were ready even before that happened—even before FDR signed the legislation allowing three-two beer—and so was the general public, as events would show.

The Depression, as it turned out, was at its worst in 1933. People needed cheering. Roosevelt seemed to capture the mood in a remark to guests at a private dinner in the White House on March 12, shortly before he delivered the first of his legendary fireside chats that evening—this one about closing the nation's banks temporarily to stem a wave of withdrawals—and eleven days before he would sign the three-two legislation then still pending. The thirty-second president told his dinner guests he planned to draft a message to Congress on the legislation after his date with the wireless that evening. FDR left no doubt of what the gist of his message would be. He told his guests, "I think this would be a good time for beer."

PART IV

25

THE AMERICANS' CENTURY

1933–1934 | New York City; St. Louis

On Tuesday, April 11, 1933, the *Statendam* passenger ship steamed into Hoboken, New Jersey. Across the Hudson River, the Empire State Building and the Chrysler Building, each barely more than two years old and each among the tallest structures humans had ever built, creased the sky above Manhattan. With a capacity for more than thirteen hundred travelers, the *Statendam* had departed the Netherlands' massive port of Rotterdam at the end of March with stops in Boulogne-sur-Mer in northern France and Southampton in southern England. Along with those passengers, the steamer carried another bit of cargo: several crates and barrels of pilsner. "The first legal shipment of imported beer in thirteen years arrived Tuesday in Hoboken, N.J.," the *New York Times* reported on April 14. "It was about one hundred gallons from Heineken's brewery in Rotterdam." However anticipated the shipment, it would take about a week for the crates and barrels to be lowered from the *Statendam* via giant nets. And only some of the pilsner ended up down the throats of enthusiastic Americans. Prohibition was still on the books constitutionally, and the legislation of March 1933 had allowed only for three-two beer, not anything even slightly stronger. Plus, the Hoboken Heineken ran afoul of import duties. Undoubtedly some of the pilsner was distributed and drunk, but at least some, perhaps most, had to be poured out.

Still, the gesture was a significant one for those paying attention to the death throes of Prohibition. It was not just a public relations coup for Heineken or a sign of the citizenry's appetite for decent brew. It was a signal of the relief that looming repeal brought to the commercial beer market, particularly the market for its most popular style. Foreign brewers were glad to have America back. It had entered the dark tunnel of Prohibition in 1920 as the world's largest beer market—a title it wrested from Germany, with a little help from the devastation of World War I—and it had emerged with the same potential. Yes, there were steep tariffs on beer as on many imports.

It was said that every Heineken account in the United States in the 1930s could be seen from the top of that Empire State Building as a result. But even an infinitesimal slice of the American market—foreign beer accounted for probably no more than 1 percent of the market in the 1930s—was good news for foreign brewers. And there was a chance that that slice might widen.

In the meantime, the biggest beneficiaries of Repeal in the beer world were of course American brewers. They, too, welcomed the looming change as soon as possible in 1933. Some of the biggest players—and in general only the big players had survived the lean Prohibition years—had been preparing to welcome the change for quite some time. "It's a risk, I know," Fred Pabst told a reporter in late 1930, when asked why he was terminating the leases of tenants using the space in his Milwaukee brewery that Prohibition had rendered superfluous. Why, for that matter, was the son and namesake of Frederick Pabst acquiring new storage tanks, kegs, and other brewing equipment? "Public opinion is a pretty good barometer. It is my own firm opinion that beer will return in the not so distant future, and I am willing to take the chance."

Fred Pabst turned out to be absolutely right. When the three-two beer legislation took effect on April 7, 1933, at a time when nineteen states had already ratified the repeal, there was Pabst pilsner readily available for grocers and delis to sell—and, in some instances, to deliver to private homes before breakfast that Friday morning. Police estimated that as many as two thousand Milwaukee establishments, ones ostensibly in business to move soft drinks, served beer that day at ten cents a pop for eight- or ten-ounce glasses and fifteen cents for a full twelve-ounce bottle. Pabst and other breweries commissioned brass bands to play throughout Milwaukee. Some "tooted their German tunes," the *St. Louis Post-Dispatch* told its readers back home. The newspaper did not note if anyone remarked upon the irony. Anti-German bigotry had done so much to further Prohibition. Now oompah music played at its wake.

Farther south in St. Louis, Pabst's onetime archrival Anheuser-Busch was also rolling out its wares to a grateful public. America's biggest brewer before Prohibition had started production in late March in anticipation of the April 7 start date for three-two beer sales. On its eve, crowds gathered outside the company's two St. Louis breweries, including one near the Mississippi River that had been turning out a cereal-based drink called Bevo. The assemblage there swelled to about twenty-five thousand, one of the largest gatherings ever to that point in Missouri's largest city. As midnight crept nearer, a brass band that August A. Busch had hired ripped tunes, and reporters on the scene recounted a general feeling of revelry. While the return of even watered-down

Budweiser pilsner after fourteen years undoubtedly buoyed that revelry, the brewery itself had carefully stoked public demand. In a foreshadowing of the decades to come in American brewing, Anheuser-Busch had run a million-dollar advertising campaign during the three weeks leading up to April 7. That included posters and other more traditional marketing material.

The bulk of the money was probably spent on sixteen Clydesdale horses from St. Louis's stockyards, some of which pulled an ornate four-ton wagon that two green-clad teamsters piloted through the city bearing empty cases with the Budweiser label. A train carried six of those Clydesdales to New York City, too, to do the same thing—with a twist. They also would pull a four-ton wagon through the city, but this wagon would carry a case of Budweiser to the Empire State Building to present it to former New York governor Al Smith, whose 1928 presidential campaign had proved a watershed in the march toward repeal. Smith managed the world's tallest building and was on hand to receive the case on April 7, following its journey on a specially charted Transcontinental & Western Air flight from St. Louis to Newark, New Jersey.

Adolphus Busch III, August Busch Sr., and August (Gussie) Busch Jr., smiling with good reason after Repeal. COURTESY OF

"Surely it is a happy day for all," Smith said upon receiving the case, "because it will in some measure deplete the ranks of the unemployed and promote happiness and good cheer." President Franklin Roosevelt—another former New York governor—also got a special airborne case, though it traveled its final leg to the White House via automobile. Some fifty-five additional government officials received similar attention from Anheuser-Busch on April 7, and FDR would receive other cases from other grateful brewers.

Midnight came, and blanket Prohibition went. The crowds outside Anheuser-Busch's plants erupted. Workers opened the great doors of the plants—great in a practical sense because they allowed for vast amounts of distribution but also in an aesthetic sense, looking especially grand on this night—and dozens of trucks poured forth stacked with pilsner for deliveries. Anheuser-Busch would ship a remarkable forty-five thousand cases of bottles of pilsner and an additional three thousand thirty-one-gallon barrels in just the first few hours of April 7. The company was one of only three in all Missouri with the wherewithal to do so when three-two beer became legal. Dozens of others had either not survived the lean years or did not have the means to restart so powerfully. Anheuser-Busch did, and it intended from the outset to dominate the brave new world of brewing.

August A. Busch would have it no other way. He had inherited America's largest brewery in 1913 upon the death of his father, when the younger Busch was already nearly fifty and when the horizons seemed particularly bright and infinite. He saw the looming threat of the drys but like nearly every other brewer in America assumed their ultimate triumph was either improbable or a ways off. When it came early because of the war, Busch saw to it that his brewery diversified into other products, including cereal-based nonalcoholic beverages and malt syrup, and he prepared it for the coming day of repeal. Fleshy and rotund, August A. Busch was nevertheless more comfortable with the public spotlight than his father had been. But while his father had carried his expanding carriage in an aristocratic way, his son, despite the best tailoring and barbering that money could buy in the Midwest, looked like an exhausted salesman on the commercial front lines, not a cosseted CEO, his thin mustache scruffy and his head erupting from his collar in multiple chin folds. Maybe that was what he was at that time—an exhausted hawker of his late father's product. He had to be. All the second- and third-generation American brewers had to be—and many, it should be noted, shared the younger Busch's frumpiness, with many looking like thoroughly beefier, fatigued iterations of their immediate forebears. Sumptuous habits—nearly all of them smoked, and all of them drank—and the fear of the regulators' knock would do that.

Their companies' spectacular rise during the past eighty or so years behind the sweeping appeal of pilsner had been against the odds and remarkable in its achievement. As an American beverage, beer went from an also-ran to the nation's number-one tipple. Then it was nearly wiped out forever.

That would not happen again. August A. Busch took to the radio a few minutes before midnight on April 6, 1933, through a special hookup that St. Louis's KMOX was able to provide. It allowed him to address the entire nation as if he were President Roosevelt himself. "Happy days are here again," he declared in an obvious nod to the looming sale of three-two beer and to a popular tune that FDR had embraced on the campaign trail the year before. Busch also cleverly wrapped not only the success of the brewing industry but "the permanency of personal liberty" in the need to pass the Twenty-First Amendment. Yes, three-two beer would soon flow and some nineteen states were then no longer enforcing their own prohibitionary statutes. But the only way to slay the beast once and for all, Busch told his millions of listeners, was to ratify an amendment to the Constitution. That would surely cause, Busch told his listeners somewhat too hopefully, "for all time, divorce of the liquor business completely from politics." After the amendment came in December 1933, the brewing industry truly quaked to life.

Sales surged so much in some areas—in and around big cities and in the still heavily Germanic regions of the upper Midwest—that brewers initially simply ran out of beer to sell, or came awfully close. So brisk were initial post-Prohibition sales of Budweiser that August Busch asked buyers to hold their orders while the brewery got up to full speed. He even felt the need to issue a public explanation. "The reason the supply is so limited is that beer must be thoroughly aged," Busch explained. "This process takes more than three months, and cannot be hurried even under the present exceptional conditions." Other breweries experienced similar runs on their products in late 1933 and 1934, and the effects of brewers meeting this pent-up demand of course rippled through distribution and sales networks. Brewing put tens of thousands of Americans back to work. But this initial surge and the general merriment and relief that attended the end of the longest experimentation with prohibition of any modern nation masked some hard truths.

The thirteen-year ban had changed the way Americans viewed alcohol, including pilsner. A wine historian once wrote that wine emerged from Prohibition as "an article formerly contraband, in the bastard category of things legally allowed but morally reprehensible." The same could be said of beer. It was as if it had been run through a decontextualization machine, with the conviviality of the German beer gardens and the sincere belief that beer was much better for a drinker than whiskey and other harder stuff forgotten under the crush of year upon year of news about illicit speakeasies and the associated crime. Also, while Prohibition may not have fully ended the trade in alcohol, it did spur a dramatic decline in consumption. This decline was not codified in any polls or surveys but rather showed up in sharp drops in alcoholic cirrhosis and other maladies tied to overconsumption. Part of this surely stemmed from the fact that beer, wine, and so on were not as readily available. A shift in attitude, though, likely had something to do with it too. The brewing industry in the United States, including foreigners seeking a share of the market, would struggle with this shift in the public's perception for the next few decades. Brewers would chase every gimmick, play, and ploy they could conceive and crib to claim as much as they could of what analysts in the late twentieth century would call "share of throat." Indeed, so much of pilsner's second one hundred years—for it would click over the century mark in 1942—would be about what happened to it *after* it left the brewery, for brewers had settled how it was made long ago. In the breweries they would only continue to refine their approaches to the point where pilsner the style became more and more homogenized, stripped of its individuality in order to appeal to plurality. This pilsner approach spread to American beer in general.

Then there was the competition from just beyond beer to well beyond it. The soft drinks industry—which had benefited from some of the same innovations that spurred brewing, and that brewing spurred, including refrigeration—went from being an industrial flyspeck at the start of Prohibition to one valued at $175 million in 1931 and almost $750 million sixteen years later, with no end in sight to its growth. And American winemaking—which had entered Prohibition much less technologically advanced than brewing and which still did much of its trade in jugs of sweet, fortified plonk of unsurprisingly uneven quality—was poised for one of the great, if not greatest, gastronomic rises of the twentieth century. Even bourbon, which had stormed out of the upper South several decades before pilsner stormed out of Bohemia and then had declined precipitously, would enjoy a resurgence in post-Prohibition America. Then there were tipples that many Americans had either never tasted or never even heard of by the 1930s. These included the English and Dutch mainstay gin and the Russian legend vodka, the latter of which would swamp American shores.

But at least within beer itself, American brewers knew which style they would use to combat the wariness of consumers whose ranks had been thinned and altered by Prohibition and the advances of soda pop and chardonnay. The style would be mildly bitter, lower in alcohol, lighter in color and mouthfeel, and with a bubbly effervescence—it would be pilsner. As history's cumulus enveloped Prohibition, brewers from Australia to South Africa to eastern China to northern Europe were turning out this most popular of alcoholic beverages. It would be what happened to it in America, though, just as had been the case in the decades up to 1920, that would dictate pilsner's newest chapters.

26

CRUSHING IT

1934–1946 | Richmond, Virginia; Newark

On January 24, 1935, a Thursday, shops and grocers throughout Richmond, Virginia, put out cans of cream ale and pilsner from the Gottfried Krueger Brewing Company of Newark, New Jersey. American Can Company of southern Ohio, the largest such manufacturer in the United States and one of the nation's fifty largest companies then, had constructed the cans from heavy-gauged steel coated with a thin exterior layer of tin to prevent rusting and a similarly thin interior lining designed to mimic that of a conventional keg. They were relatively heavy, each about four ounces. But that was because of the steel, which was necessary to tame the carbonation. They were skinny, too, and green and red—the cream ale in the green and what the company called its Krueger's Finest, a light, lower-alcohol lager resembling pilsner, in red—and held twelve ounces, SAME AS BOTTLE, as lettering at the top made clear. Drinkers had to puncture a triangular-shaped hole in the top with a church-key opener to get at the beer. But that was all part of the novelty, as the whole Richmond setup was novel: Krueger beers were the first anywhere to be commercially sold in cans.

The brewery behind the milestone was as boilerplate as they came. Fifteen-year-old Gottfried Krueger had immigrated to the United States in early 1853 from a small town in a small Germanic state near the Rhine River. A maternal uncle ran a small wood-framed brewery in Newark and promised the boy's parents opportunity in the New World. And so "in wooden shoes and leather apron," young Gottfried labored in his uncle's concern for five dollars a month, plus board. Following the script so many young German Americans followed, Krueger gained full control of his uncle's brewery by 1865, and soon sold it to a syndicate, which in turn retained him to manage it. That same syndicate, though, sold in 1908 to another consortium—one that included Gottfried Krueger. The earnest-looking immigrant with trimmed brown hair and goatee in the middle of a fleshy face had grown into a major investor whose partnership controlled a number of northeastern breweries, including the one that once belonged to him. It was a testament to his own work as well as to the rise in popularity of the lighter lager that powered it all. When Krueger died amid Prohibition, his son William took over management of the Gottfried Krueger Brewing Company in Newark. It was William Krueger who would pull the proverbial trigger on canned beer.

It was a technology that had been in the works since at least 1909 through American Can Company, and one that Prohibition interrupted. Pabst in particular had led the way, with a laboratory the brewery had set up on its home turf of Milwaukee to develop better manufacturing, aging, and shipping methods. One such method the laboratory zeroed in on was developing a metal barrel to supplant wooden ones. The single biggest hurdle had been coming up with a lining to prevent the beer from coming into contact with the metal. An early attempt just as Prohibition ended to coat steel and black-iron barrels with the same pitch as those used in metal barrels had failed—the pitch wore off, the beer and the vessel met, and the drinker could taste the metallic difference. The Pabst researchers found salvation in a heated synthetic resin that successfully held between steel and beer. With this leap and the development of the beer can, "the brewing industry was on its way to emancipation from the age-old sway of glass and wood shipping containers," according to a chronicler of Pabst.

However, Pabst's trial-and-error experience with linings for metal barrels had apparently made the brewery skittish about testing their vaunted product in cans. American Can Company, which had restarted its own research coming out of Prohibition, dispatched its president to a private meeting with Harris Perlstein, Pabst's bespectacled, balding chairman, to try to convince him to let American Can use Pabst as its testing ground. It would be a fantastic get for the manufacturer—one of the largest breweries in the world's largest beer market—but it was not to be. American Can's president poured bottled and canned beer samples for Perlstein and dared him to tell the difference. Perlstein did. Three times. He cautioned his visitor to slow American Can's research.

There was a certain urgency coming out of Prohibition about packaging beer, pilsner invariably, as tightly and soundly as possible for shipment. Everyone in the industry knew that cans could likely do that better, as they would protect the beer inside more thoroughly from air and especially light than glass. But if there was metallic seepage, that would ruin the taste and eventually ruin a brewery's sales. Pabst was not interested in American Can's research—probably in part because it was still looking into its own linings at the Milwaukee lab, but also because canned beer had not been tested yet on a large commercial scale.

That was where William Krueger and his brewery came in—albeit cautiously. Most beer was still sold via draft, and if not draft, via bottle, whatever the concerns about damage from too much light. Bottling had revolutionized the industry sixty years before, and breweries and their customers had grown accustomed to it. So Krueger started with its own canning test run in June 1934 in Richmond, where it already had a presence and where an unusually large share of all the beer sold was sold in bottles—drinkers in the Virginia capital were comfortable with beer not from the tap. One thousand Richmond households, picked because the brewery had identified them as existing customers, received four cans of Krueger's along with a questionnaire that sought feedback on the novelty at their doorstep. Nearly all the respondents said they would drink the canned Krueger's again. "The results surprised even Krueger," historian Maureen Ogle noted. The brewery quickly moved ahead with wider production and distribution, striking a deal with American Can Company to install the necessary apparatus in Newark under an arrangement that left all the onus on the canning concern. American Can would eat the cost of the installation and material if the wider distribution proved a flop.

Within a month of that late-January 1935 citywide debut, following the test run, more than 80 percent of Richmond's beer distributors were selling Krueger's Finest and cream ale in cans. It was enough to get the attention of competitors, who lost sales in Richmond to this newfangled technology and who therefore chased it into a new era for the millennia-old craft of brewing.

One of the defining characteristics of pilsner's rise to global ubiquity was that new technologies seemed to come along at just the right times to further that ascent. The methods and means either helped brew a better pilsner or unspool pilsner farther and farther from the breweries doing the brewing. Canning was one of those technologies. Pilsner sales would have surged coming out of Prohibition even if Krueger and American Can never joined forces, never dipped their tin-coated toe in the Richmond market, never returned with gusto in January 1935. But canning ensured that more pilsner would reach farther than ever before, would arrive where it was going pretty much as it had left the brewery, and would therefore alter the very trajectory of the business of brewing.

What had changed? Efforts at canning beer had been going on since that first decade of the twentieth century, after all. A few conditions came together in the mid-1930s, however. On the practical side, American Can Company found its lining in a product from the Union Carbide and Carbon Corporation of New York. The lining's brand name was Vinylite, a plastic made from material impervious to the sort of seepage that preyed upon earlier linings. Vinylite worked so well it was used not only to line canned drinks and foods but also to coat everything from phonograph records to suspenders to floor tiles. Second, the heavy-gauged steel cans themselves could withstand the pressure that carbonation caused. Leaky and explosive cans had also hindered those earlier pre-Prohibition pushes. Third, as an early brochure advertising Krueger's pioneering cans made clear, such packaging offered the consumer all sorts of supposed benefits. Literal bullet points highlighted cans' advantages over bottles: "No deposit," "No breakage," "No returns," "Less storage space," "Better taste." These points offered clues to the other conditions that came together in the 1930s to revolutionize pilsner packaging.

The returnable bottle system that had arisen in the United States since the nineteenth century obligated tipplers to return the glass vessels to the retailer—pub, tavern, hotel, etcetera—or the brewery for refilling. The bottles themselves were clearly marked as the property of said source with firm reminders such as "This bottle not to be sold" or "This bottle to be washed and returned." This de facto honor system rarely worked as it was supposed to work. Individuals simply forgot to return the bottles, or were too lazy, or traded them for cheap, or appropriated the containers altogether. "That period of the year when the good housewife begins to bottle her ketchup and make her preserves is at hand, and it is also the season when the Pennsylvania Bottlers' Protective Association makes its greatest efforts to prevent the bottles of its members from being utilized for purposes that necessitate hiding them in cellars and closets until gentle spring comes around again," went one anonymous report in 1902. The husbanding of bottles could spark dramatic turns as fed-up producers came to take what was legally theirs. Legislation that several states passed around the turn of the century aided in their crackdowns. In 1921, four months after state lawmakers created fines for dealing in used bottles, "the Massachusetts Bottlers' Exchange took more than sixty thousand bottles in raids and prosecuted thirty bottlers for illegally using registered bottles." The growth of a bottle deposit system to complement the return system cut down on a lot of this lawlessness. Retailers and breweries charged cents on the bottle, and consumers could get back those cents if they returned the bottles. Still, it could be a chore for the unmotivated drinker.

Enter cans, and all the drama associated with bottling and bottles could be brushed aside. And—given that the technology, let alone the civic and moral imperative, for large-scale recycling was decades off—cans could simply be discarded. Advertisements into the mid-twentieth century advised drinkers to do just that: down the beer and toss the can, whether from a fishing boat, a car window, or a neighbor's yard—never mind the litter. So when Krueger and other breweries advertised "no returns" and "no deposits," early adapters of the beer can knew exactly what they were talking about. "No breakage," too, was a no-brainer.

As for "Less storage space" and "Better taste," those phrases spoke to another condition that arose in the 1930s and that would change people's relationship with food and drink. Mechanical, artificial refrigeration had leaped forward into widespread industrial use after Carl Linde's tinkering at Gabriel Sedlmayr's Spaten brewery in the early 1870s, humankind finishing its pivot from centuries of ice harvesting in a matter of years. As for personal or domestic refrigeration, ice reigned a little longer in the form of regular deliveries of blocks of the material, to be deposited for a week at most in snug kitchen boxes lined with zinc or tin. Then, in the second decade of the twentieth century, home refrigerators emerged as a replacement for the ice-box. General Electric's so-called Monitor Top model—a steel cabinet on four legs that combined the air compressor with the cold-storage box—proved an especially big hit in 1927. It and other home refrigerators, though, relied for effectiveness on ammonia, methyl chloride, and sulfur dioxide. These gases were flammable as well as deadly, every last one of them, if handled the wrong way or ingested. Indeed, there were fatalities in the 1920s, prompting most Americans to cling to their iceboxes. It was not until the straight-to-market development in 1928 of Freon from General Motors subsidiary Frigidaire that the home refrigeration industry heated up. Seen as a "miracle compound" that was colorless, odorless, nonflammable, and noncorrosive, Freon allowed for greater and safer mass production and usage of home refrigerators.

The United States ended up leading the world in such usage. Even in the crucible of the Great Depression—and even with the costs per unit reaching upward of one hundred dollars—the sales numbers were astounding. At the start of the 1930s, not even two years after the development of Freon, just 8 percent of American households owned a refrigerator. By the end of the decade, 44 percent would. "The refrigerator came to be one of the most important symbols of middle class living in the United States," one historian of the trend has noted. And one of the most important inhabitants of these new electric, Freon-cooled, invariably gleaming-white gizmos became canned beer. The slender, lighter-weight cans rolled out of breweries and into people's fridges with increasing regularity—despite prices for canned beer generally being the same as for bottled. As the Krueger brochure bragged, Americans really did like the convenience. And breweries, as they had learned to do, responded. Dozens of breweries by the end of 1935 had rolled out canned releases. These included Pabst Export Lager, one of the world's bestselling pilsners. Anheuser-Busch's Budweiser pilsner would follow in 1936 (as would the first canned beer outside the United States, from a small brewery called Felinfoel in Wales, then one of the world's great sources of tin).

Soon—very soon—American Can Company had competition in the supply game, with the National Can Company and the Continental Can Company introducing their own tin vessels, the former's with a cone-shaped cap that made it look like a can-bottle hybrid. Breweries were chasing growth in the brave, new post-Prohibition marketplace. Nothing illustrated the commercial allure of the tin can more than the success of its first risker. Krueger, which did not even rank among perhaps the twenty largest US breweries coming out of Prohibition, saw its production quintuple shortly after its canning test run started in 1934. Much of this newly canned beer, from Krueger and elsewhere, was pilsner or based on pilsner. The style had entered Prohibition as the most popular in the nation and probably the world, and there was little indication that that popularity would not pick up where it had left off. Plus, pilsner's comfortability with travel, proven with the bottle, made it a natural for the can, which because of its lighter weight would become brewers' preferred shipping vessel.

In 1934—the first full year after Repeal and the year the immigrant Gottfried Krueger's progeny started testing canned beer in Richmond—three in four beers sold in the United States still came from a tap. As their parents would have done, or their great-grandparents, or some far-off ancestor in the brutishly curtailed world of feudal Europe, Americans of the third decade of the twentieth century drank beer mostly filled from kegs or barrels, served in glasses almost exclusively, but at times in a mug or a stein. That would end in well under a decade, part of a larger seismic shift in food and drink. The exact year that packaged beer overtook draft, in fact, would prove portentous for the whole world.

27

SHARE OF THROAT

1939 | Queens, New York

Leo van Munching was a tall, gregarious ship's steward in his early thirties from a small town in the Netherlands. His main job aboard Holland America Line steamers traveling between Europe and North America was to chat up customers and keep their glasses full. Heineken pilsner—the bestselling beer in the Netherlands—invariably filled many of those glasses. Gradually, Van Munching developed a deeper understanding of beer and brewing, and also of New York City. The megalopolis was the disembarkation and embarkation point for so many Holland America runs, and Van Munching would use his time in between to explore, to build up contacts with others in the hospitality industry, and to simply practice his English. The knowledge of beer and Gotham, combined with his outgoing personality and his position, enabled Van Munching to seize a life-changing moment when it arrived.

Van Munching happened to be working the *Statendam* when it steamed from Rotterdam to Hoboken in April 1933 with those first post-Prohibition crates of Heineken. On board was Heineken export manager Pieter Feith, who had already engineered the pilsner's inroads into East Asia, including the establishment of a brewery in the Dutch East Indies in present-day Indonesia. Feith, of course, was doing what so many European brewery executives were doing in the early 1930s: trying to get a handle on an American market that had entered Prohibition thirteen years before as the world's biggest beer market and that held the potential to quickly become so again. But high tariffs meant a high barrier to entry for foreign beer. And what did get in had to go quickly, lest it waste away to spoilage unsold. Feith knew Heineken needed somebody on the ground. Maybe not in every American market—the continental empire was too vast for that—but at least in major ones, especially New York. It was during his April 1933 transatlantic trek, with all this on his mind, that Feith ran into Leo van Munching.

Feith knew Van Munching from the latter's visits to Heineken's Rotterdam outpost. The ship's steward would regularly try to convince the brewery to hire him as its point man in the New World. The brewery would decline or would put Van Munching off. Then Prohibition started to recede into history's rearview, and events sped up. Heineken needed a well-connected English speaker on the ground in New York, and Van Munching was on board the *Statendam* with one last sales pitch to Feith. This one was successful, and he would spend the next several decades leading the rise of pilsner-driven Heineken into becoming the bestselling foreign beer in the United States and several other countries.

Van Munching focused on New York. While his main approach was simple shoe-leather salesmanship from one potential account to another— and the odd contact with organized labor or organized crime to get a foot in the door—Van Munching did have a taste for the theatrical when peddling the Dutch pilsner. One of his favorite tactics was to stride into a bar or a restaurant and demand a Heineken in a loud voice. Inevitably, given the Dutch brand's small footprint, the establishment would not carry the pilsner. Van Munching would look aghast and stride fussily back out. One of his contracted salesmen would then show up at the bar or the restaurant later, a crate or more of the stuff in tow to ensure that such a scene never ensued again. Another tactic had Van Munching and his wife dine at tonier places such as the Waldorf-Astoria hotel and the New York Athletic Club that did carry Heineken. He would order it—loudly—with all the care and celebration one usually reserved for champagne. Van Munching wanted the other diners to see the performance. "Snob appeal is much stronger in the United States than anywhere else," Van Munching would explain. "When they wanted to show off, they needed something that was imported."

And when Heineken wanted to move product in the United States, it relied increasingly on the lanky, exceedingly amiable ex-steward. Van Munching would form his own import company and focus almost entirely on spreading Heineken pilsner and other beers in the brewery's stable beyond the big cities and into the deepest corners of the nation. That, of course, meant going well beyond old-fashioned salesmanship and stunts at bars in Manhattan. Van Munching began thinking bigger—all the more aggressive breweries did—and one of his coups was a float at the 1939 World's Fair in Queens, New York.

Such grand expositions had long lost their power to hold the world in their thrall like they did in the late nineteenth century. But the fair that took place from April 1939 to October 1940 on twelve hundred acres of a repurposed ash heap that F. Scott Fitzgerald had immortalized in *The Great Gatsby* still drew fantastic crowds to the New York City borough. Some forty-four million visitors—the equivalent of nearly one-third of the US population at the time—visited the myriad exhibits at the fair whose motto was "The World of Tomorrow," many of them streaming over the Bronx-Whitestone Bridge between upstate New York and Long Island, which had gone up specifically for the festival. Van Munching saw to it that Heineken was the brewery represented most prominently. He arranged for a pavilion on the stream that ran through the fair. Dubbed "Heineken on the Zuider Zee," it was a replica of a quintessential Dutch village, complete with a full-sized windmill, the famed blue-and-white ceramics from the South Holland town of Delft, and actors in traditional Dutch garb, clogs included. More important for the brewery's bottom line, the faux village included a ground-floor bar that ended up serving more than 264 gallons of beer, most of it pilsner, to the thirsty crowd. It was golden exposure for the still smallish brand.

For all the grandiosity, though, Van Munching's pilsner-powered pavilion would have been a gambit familiar to Adolphus Busch or Frederick Pabst. Ostentatious displays of the beer's origins and intricacies were old hat by the end of the 1930s. So was the door-to-door—or bar-to-bar—salesmanship of Van Munching and his agents. The same went for newspaper and magazine advertisements and, increasingly, for signage, including the illuminated kind. Conventional approaches to spreading the word about a beer reached only so far anymore.

It was one of the reasons why the number of American breweries had failed to grow as fast as post-Repeal demand suggested it might. By 1940, the number of breweries would not equal even half of the fifteen hundred operating in 1910, when the braying incantations of the drys seemed a nuisance rather than a threat. Many breweries simply never reopened after Prohibition, and others withered amid increased competition as imports started to drip into the country again and national concerns such as Anheuser-Busch and Pabst gobbled market share. A half-dozen breweries—including those two—would be selling at least one million barrels each by 1940. None attained that milestone simply through upping production. It was instead because of increased reach due to myriad reasons, including the necessary equipment and distribution channels coming out of Prohibition and the introduction of canned beer. At the same time, though, the US population was booming—the country would slap on some twenty million residents between 1920 and 1940—meaning that per capita beer consumption stayed basically flat. The competition, then, for beer drinkers was growing fiercer by the year as increasingly larger—and fewer—breweries muscled each other for share of throat. Any edge counted.

The sharpest edge emerged at that 1939 World's Fair, though it would be years before anyone connected to brewing realized it. RCA Corporation, a New York City–based electronics consortium best known by the 1930s for its work in radio, had its own pavilion at the expo. The centerpiece of the pavilion—which, from an aerial view, looked not unlike a rocket readying for takeoff—was a collection of bulky wooden boxes with screens no larger than 5.5 by 7.25 inches showing grainy black-and-white broadcasts of radio shows that RCA did through its National Broadcasting Company, or NBC. "A preview of television, newest contribution to home entertainment," read a brochure accompanying the boxes at the pavilion. Such television sets had been around for at least a few months by April 1939, picking up signals from RCA's NBC antennae atop the Empire State Building, the world's tallest tower. But they were few and far between and—because of that signal—only found in the New York region. A fairgoer could be forgiven for considering television a much lesser technology than radio. Television was seen mostly as a complement to radio, not a usurper. Nylon stockings—which got their biggest public airing yet at the fair—might have been seen as more revolutionary.

Yet tucked away in that RCA brochure were signs of the company's ambition and of the coming influence of the small screen. A question-and-answer section included this exchange:

Will Television programs be sponsored?
At present, there have not been any commercial licenses issued for Television programs, and until such time as there are, programs cannot be sponsored commercially. However, in the event that such licenses are issued, and if there are sufficient receivers in an area, it is quite likely that sponsors will be found.

This promise of monetizing television lay in the future. In the present, RCA and others in the fledgling industry could take hope from a checklist of milestones, one of which was ticked at the World's Fair. On April 30, 1939, Franklin Roosevelt became the first US president to be televised as he delivered remarks to open the expo. Clad in a three-piece suit and displaying the cockeyed grin that had helped shepherd a nervous nation through the Great Depression, FDR "with great happiness" kicked off the festivities before a vast seating area dubbed the Court of Peace—but not before he hinted at something else entirely in remarks about rising tensions in Europe. "Often I think," Roosevelt said, "we Americans offer up a silent prayer [that] the years to come will break down many barriers to intercourse between nations, barriers which may be historic but which so greatly through all the centuries have led to strife and have hindered friendship and normal intercourse."

Any prayers to this effect would, of course, go unanswered. Barely four months after FDR's opening remarks at the fair, the Polish government would shroud that nation's pavilion there in black. Germany and the Soviet Union had invaded Poland in September, sparking the second major war in Europe in twenty years.

28

A DIFFERENT WAR

1940–1950 | Pilsen

World War I had been bad for beer. The four-year conflict that ended in a stalemate in November 1918 disrupted supply and distribution chains, and fueled prohibition movements, most notably in the United States, which was just becoming the world's leading beer nation. Pilsner in particular had marched out of central Europe in the late nineteenth century to become the world's most popular and imitated beer style, only to see its advance cut off because of the Great War that started near its own birthplace.

The roots of World War II also lay in central Europe—near Pilsen itself, in fact—but that conflict would not disrupt beer and its most popular style nearly as much. Pilsen was in a Bohemia that was by 1939 in the far western reaches of the nation of Czechoslovakia, which had emerged from the carcass of Austria-Hungary during the last days of World War I. That was important, for just beyond Bohemia's borders lay a part of Czechoslovakia that was home to hundreds of thousands of ethnic Germans. Adolf Hitler craved the annexation of that German-infused Sudetenland, and to placate him the great powers—in particular France and the United Kingdom—handed it over in the notorious appeasement pact of September 1938. With the handover, Czechoslovakia lost much of its industrial power, including two-thirds of its supply of coal, and became by mid-1939 a vassal of the Nazi regime. Its collapse months before the invasion of Poland showed the world the hand this new German menace intended to play. It was conquest and barbarism all the way, and one of its very minor casualties early on—at least in the grand, grim scheme of things—was pilsner. The takeover of Czechoslovakia disrupted the flow of Saaz hops from Bohemia that undergirded so many of the world's pilsners.

Breweries the world over adjusted for the scarcity of Saaz hops, which imparted an aromatic scent and taste to different pilsners. Many breweries switched to "less robust domestic varieties" of hops, as one American account put it, and lost some of the quality associated with their releases. It was an adjustment—and, more important, a *willingness* to adjust—that would have far-reaching effects on beer after the war. The same was true for a barley shortage that came later. In early 1943, the US government mandated that brewers cut their barley usage 7 percent because the grain was needed for industrial alcohol for the production of weaponry. "To make up for the deficiency," the *New York Times* reported, "brewers turned to corn and rice." Some brewers had long used both as adjuncts to make their lagers clearer and cleaner. Now they used them more than ever—and would not be able to stop after the war.

As for during the war, the effects were not as acutely felt. In fact, the terrible conflagration turned out to be good for business. Even with the rationing of grain and packaging materials such as tin and even with disruptions to distribution and supplies—never mind the drafting of so many brewery workers—production numbers remained steady or better throughout the conflict. Even in Germany under the Nazis, all-sacred beer, much of it lighter lager meant to compete with pilsner, remained a domestic priority. Production figures did not slip until merciless Allied bombing runs in 1944 and 1945 halted much of the Third Reich's industrial muscle, brewing included. In the United States, production went from about fifty-three million barrels in 1940, just before the nation entered the war, to a record eighty million in 1945, the year the Allies emerged triumphant.

Part of this was that with exports drying up, domestic players had more of the sandbox to themselves. What's more, regional breweries in particular—those whose reach was wide but not national or international—discovered greater demand as the rationing of supplies and matériel hit the national companies harder because of their greater output. Another big part was simply that 1941 was not 1918 in terms of a temperance movement and the anti-German bigotry that the former had seized on twenty-some years before. Despite early public sympathy for Hitler's regime from German Americans—some twenty thousand members of the Bund, a German American booster group, had filled Madison Square Garden in 1939 for a pro-Nazi rally—and despite early German success against US forces, including the sinking of dozens of vessels just off the East Coast, the ethnic panic was nowhere near where it had been during World War I. The United States—its government and its people—appeared to reserve such prejudice this time for Americans of Japanese descent, who faced internment by the hundreds of thousands and confiscation of goods. German Americans on the other hand had assimilated so thoroughly that there could be little doubt as to their loyalty. And if there was, then German Americans would do their best to dispel it. "The Germans leave mankind no other choice—they only learn the hard way—perhaps not even then!" Paul Piel wrote in a letter to a relative in 1944. His family controlled one of those regional breweries that did so well during the war. Piel's first cousin had died during the last conflict fighting for the kaiser. This time, the family—and other German American ones like it across the brewing industry and the land at large—wanted it known where they stood. "Sooner or later, the Germans too will have to come round to see that humanity is far more precious than any [German race]."

Piel's industry had also been fairly clever in how it approached the conflict, which Americans had the benefit of seeing coming for years, as the war was nearly two years old before a US soldier or airman fired a shot. "We must, perhaps, first of all recognize that we are definitely in a military economy and shall continue to be for many years irrespective of the fortunes and the progress of the war," Rudolph J. Schaefer Jr., president of the United States Brewers' Association, said in early 1941, months before the United States entered the war. Schaefer's grandfather, a German immigrant, had cofounded the F. & M. Schaefer Brewing Company, by then based in Brooklyn and on its way to becoming one of the nation's largest breweries behind a signature offering that it called "America's oldest lager beer"—and that ticked every box associated with the pilsner style in its bubbliness, mild bitterness, and golden clarity. The brewing industry, which the Brewers' Association by and large represented, got out of the way of government efforts to mobilize for the war effort in Europe and the South Pacific. It acceded to the rationing and other measures, and found itself rewarded. An early effort to ban alcohol sales at military bases and to military personnel collapsed. "It would be harmful to the men in the service to direct a prohibition against them that did not apply to other citizens," General George Marshall, chief of staff of the US Army, wrote in a memo in 1941. "To do so would inevitably lead to intemperance."

It seemed that the military brass had imbibed the lessons of Prohibition quite well, and any notions that such a blanket ban would ever return to the world's leading beer nation disappeared, probably forever. Alcohol, including and especially pilsner, found a place throughout the growing Allied military complex that waged global war on fascism in the early 1940s. So much so that when brewery workers went on strike in Minneapolis in January 1945, the National War Labor Board ordered it stopped. The rationale? That brewing was "an essential industry" for the duration of the conflict—it was too important for morale and for the hundreds of millions of dollars in tax revenue it provided annually. This attitude toward beer and brewing would have far-reaching effects after the war, on pilsner in particular, even more so than the recipe changes that the hops and grain shortages necessitated.

In the end, as far as obscenely violent and degrading wars go, the second global one of the first fifty years of the twentieth century was not that damaging for the brewing industry. Particularly in its already most successful location, America, it became that much more successful. The United States Brewers Foundation, a successor to the United States Brewers' Association, themed its 1946 national convention rather blandly but accurately as "a greatly improved financial position." A general manager at one of the regional breweries that had seen a sales bounce during the war would later describe the industry as having "flourished" during the conflict. Most important, though, was the support that the US government and its military threw behind the industry. With it, beer and its most popular style were able to spread that much further and farther, collecting future consumers and testing new markets. The spread during and after the war came, too, as the habits of consumers and the approaches to markets changed. As was so often the case with pilsner since Josef Groll birthed it during that Bohemian autumn 103 years before the surrender of the Axis powers, it found itself in the right place at the right time.

29

BEYOND THE BREWERY

1946–1950 | St. Louis; Milwaukee; New York City

O n Thursday, August 29, 1946, Adolphus Busch III, grandson and namesake of
Adolphus Busch, died of a cerebral hemorrhage at a hospital in St. Louis.
He had been ill for a while with stomach cancer and other maladies, including what was likely alcoholism. The fifty-five-year-old left behind a wife and
two daughters. Since a woman was not seen as suitable for taking the helm
of one of America's largest industrial operations, Busch's younger brother,
August Busch Jr., took over.

Both brothers were old enough to have seen their paternal grandfather at
the height of his powers. They knew the source of those powers: the wealth
from the manufacture and distribution of pilsner, in particular the Budweiser
that their grandfather had spirited from St. Louis to just about all corners of
the globe. Budweiser and Anheuser-Busch products before World War I were
available in North America, South America, Europe, parts of southern Africa,
and the Far East. Along with Pabst's own pilsner flagship and a handful of
other beer brands, Budweiser dominated the American market, which before
Archduke Franz Ferdinand's assassination in June 1914 was on its way to
becoming the world's biggest. Both Adolphus III and August Jr., then, were
also old enough to have seen it all come to a near screeching halt during the
war and certainly after. Prohibition gutted the family business and sullied
the family name with accusations of anti-American sympathies.

The clawback that began after Repeal in 1933 was not inevitable, though
Anheuser-Busch started off better than most. The brewery had diversified
even before Prohibition and certainly during—the brothers' father, August
Sr., had admonished them and other executives to see that the brewery was
never "caught with all its eggs in one basket." Adolphus III personally led the
company's branch into yeast manufacturing for breads and other foodstuffs
during Prohibition. And when he died suddenly in 1946, the *New York Times*
obituary rattled off a web of connections that spoke to Anheuser-Busch's

diversification, including signs of the vertical integration approach the brewery had helped pioneer: president of the Dallas Hotel Company (also known as Hotel Adolphus); chairman of the Manufacturers Bank and Trust Company of St. Louis, the Busch-Sulzer Brothers Diesel Engine Company, the Manufacturers Railway Company, and the St. Louis & O'Fallon Railway Company; and a trustee of the St. Louis Refrigerator Car Company. And his interest in the brewery alone included the manufacturing capacity not only for beer but also for bottle manufacturing and filling. The Busches controlled or outright owned the links in the long chain that took grain, rice, water, hops, and yeast from their breweries to their consumers. August Busch Jr.—Gussie to family and friends—intended to maintain that.

The *New York Times* once headlined a section of an article about the five-foot-ten, 164-pound Gussie Busch as MEDIUM STATURE, LOUD VOICE. He was indeed unassuming to look at, with short, slicked-back brown hair and a fleshy face with eyes that either squinted or twinkled. If he looked like just another harried salesman seizing a share of booming postwar America, that was fine with Busch. For that was how he saw himself, even before the deaths of his father and brother—the former from suicide during a gruesome battle with cancer—cleared the way for his ascension as a consummate salesman, "possibly the most brilliant beer salesman who ever lived," according to one biographer, and a "master showman and irrepressible salesman," per the *New York Times*. As such, Busch was volatile and brash, imposing and imperious, yet also fiercely fun loving and tirelessly loyal to the family firm and those who would advance its fortunes. "My name is Gussie Busch, and I'd like to buy you a Budweiser," was a favorite opening sales pitch when he strode into a bar or a restaurant on a personal call. He delivered the line in a booming Midwestern twang, with that twinkle in the eyes and a wide grin shooting side to side across that fleshy face.

Anheuser-Busch needed such a presence at the top in 1946. The brewery was largest by production and sales in the United States, and one of the largest in the world. Its signature pilsner was available in bottles and cans, and often on draft, just about everywhere beer was sold globally, a reach similar to what it had enjoyed before Prohibition. But the brewery was losing ground domestically. Its foe there would have been very familiar to Gussie Busch's grandfather. The Pabst Brewing Company had ended up coming out of Prohibition particularly strong, thanks to a merger that closed a year before Repeal in 1932. Harris Perlstein, who had cofounded a company that became Premier Malt Products and that specialized in just what the name implied, had approached his good friend Fred Pabst Jr., son of Frederick Pabst

himself, about a merger during brewing's darkest days so far. The rechristened Premier-Pabst Corporation emerged from Prohibition with its finger in
many grain-based pies, including beer and cereal. In the case of the former,
it barreled forward behind its Pabst Export Lager—which most consumers
probably knew as Pabst Blue Ribbon, the pilsner that had performed so well
at the World's Columbian Expo in Chicago way back in 1893. By the time
World War II ended, the re-rechristened Pabst Brewing Company—for it had
changed its name again in 1938, though Perlstein remained at the helm—was
emerging as the bestselling brewery in the United States.

Meanwhile, other breweries that led with pilsner were undergoing their
own changes in leadership and fortune. Fred C. Miller started the second act
of a storied life in 1947, when he took over as president of the Miller Brewing
Company from a younger first cousin who had briefly led the operation
that their grandfather, Frederick Miller (né Friedrich Müller), had nurtured
starting in the 1850s. As "a swarthy skinned lad of medium height"—in the
words of a *Milwaukee Journal* reporter—Miller had been elected captain of the
Notre Dame football team for the 1928 season. This was the era of legendary
coach Knute Rockne and his popularization of the forward pass, and that
meant that Miller, a tenacious tackle with a ready smile and outgoing personality, attained a modicum of athletic fame, including back in Milwaukee.
His family was one of the most prominent in that city, of course, but the
brewery they controlled had yet to break out nationally in the same way as
the likes of Anheuser-Busch and Pabst. Miller Brewing exited World War II
not even among the top fifteen breweries domestically, and had virtually no
international footprint. Fred C. Miller—forty-one years old when he took
over—would see that that changed. Like Gussie Busch, to whom he was often
compared and contrasted, Miller loathed second place. The rivalry between
Miller and Busch, and their companies, would define much of pilsner and
of international brewing in the late twentieth century.

Another brewery founder's grandson was also coming up in the 1940s.
Alfred Heineken looked the part of the Dutch aristocrat he was literally born
to be. Tall and handsome, with a high forehead and broad nose, Freddy
Heineken, as he was known, was courtly and reserved where Gussie Busch
might be profane and brash. Heineken started working at the family concern
as a teenager during the German occupation of the Netherlands, when even
the Nazis saw the necessity of a steady beer supply versus seizing and smelting
the brewery's equipment. It was after the war, though, that Freddy Heineken
really came into his own and set his family's eponymous brewery on course to
become the biggest pilsner producer outside the United States. With Leo van

Munching to make introductions, the young Heineken plodded the streets of New York City for two years in the late 1940s, introducing himself to bartenders and other vendors, and, most important, imbibing American advertising and marketing. He would later say that he discovered that the best way to sell beer in the late twentieth century was to sell the lifestyle or the perception around particular brands. "I don't sell beer," Freddy Heineken would say, "I sell warmth." Gussie Busch probably would not have put it the same way, but he would have likely understood the sentiment immediately.

Busch, though, would not have given the budding Dutchman much thought upon his ascension in St. Louis in 1946. He did not have to. Heineken and other imports were still mere blips on the periphery of the world's biggest beer market. Instead, Busch was focused on the fact that as the 1950s approached, Anheuser-Busch was running neck-and-neck with Pabst. For Busch, that was unacceptable. And it was personal. He was keenly aware of his grandfather's rivalry with Frederick Pabst, and how the two of them raced each other, and others, to develop the cleanest, crispest pilsner on the planet.

Freddy Heineken became perhaps pilsner's most consummate salesman after Gussie Busch. COURTESY OF HEINEKEN USA

The race had made both clans rich, and, with Prohibition well in the rearview and a world economic order up ahead in which America dominated, it seemed entirely possible that manifold more riches were possible. But a brewery had to be bigger, bolder, and better than the next to ensure that. Consolidation on the production side and marketing on the sales side were both about to define the industry for the rest of the twentieth century. "Being second isn't worth shit," Gussie Busch told a reporter when asked about Pabst's success (the reporter dutifully cleaned up the quotation to "Being second isn't worth anything" for publication).

A force such as Busch taking the reins of Anheuser-Busch just after the Second World War ended ushered in what might be called brewing's "Great Man Era," after the historical school of thought that ascribes major changes more to personality and personal ability than anything else. Busch epitomized the direction of American—and thereby global—brewing after the war, as the third and fourth generations stepped in to lead what were still essentially family firms. From 1946 onward, pilsner found itself in the beefy, twitchy hands of Gussie Busch and contemporaries such as Fred C. Miller and Freddy Heineken. By then, much of what made the style had been settled. Science and innovation had seen to that. What happened after 1946, then, had more to do with what happened to pilsner after it left the brewery. Marketing and advertising—the salesmanship that Busch glorified—became so much more important.

That was because the nature of how pilsner was consumed was changing dramatically. Packaged beer in the United States had begun to outsell draft in 1941—barely, with an oft-cited estimate pegging the shares at nearly 52 percent to around 48 percent that year. The difference grew, though, every year afterward. That meant that a beverage once entirely consumed outside the home—in pubs and restaurants, bars and speakeasies, ballgames and political rallies—became something consumed mostly in the home, or at least at private events. Part of this had to do with the rise in the refrigerator and with the introduction of the beer can. More of it had to do with simply how Americans—and increasingly others in the developed world such as Canadians and Western Europeans—lived.

That television technology on display at the 1939 World's Fair became more ubiquitous, cheaper to buy for viewers, and lucrative to advertise on for companies, never mind to sell for the likes of RCA. Indeed, movie attendance in America would peak in 1946 and drop ever after as the silver screen lost share to the small screen at home. Innovations such as the twin rises of frozen and fast foods facilitated easier cooking and eating in those homes too.

Preparation that might have consumed the better part of an evening fell by the wayside during the 1940s and 1950s, especially as Americans just grabbed and went, or defrosted. That defrosting might happen, too, in a new technology born of radar research during World War II: the microwave, which weapons manufacturer Raytheon introduced in 1947 and that within ten years was within financial reach of millions of households. In a grand stroke that combined the twin trends in television and frozen food, New Jersey–based C. A. Swanson & Sons introduced what it called a "TV Dinner" in 1953. The company would be selling thirteen million amalgams of frozen turkey, vegetables, and potatoes a year by 1956. The global frozen food industry in general, an industry that did not really exist before the war, would be a multibillion-dollar one by the end of that decade. As far as fast food, once that was loosed upon America and the world, it never stopped spreading. There were instances of it as far back as the 1920s with White Castle burger joints, but the true, inexorable spread began after the war with the launches of the likes of McDonald's and Kentucky Fried Chicken. It was the former that really revolutionized things. McDonald's used an assembly-line approach to put together meals quickly and acquired different steps in the production process to ensure steady supplies. These were moves that would have been familiar to pilsner producers, with their stakes in bottle-producing plants and distributorships and their assembly-line approach to brewing and lagering.

Canned and bottled pilsner fitted in with these trends. Brewers such as Gussie Busch were not passive actors, though. "In the days of draught beer, the customer never saw or examined the barrel, and so there was no need to make it distinctive or dress it up," as one observer noted. "But the bottle and the can were quite different." People saw those. They examined those. They collected them and displayed them. Brands and breweries became more recognizable and omnipresent than ever before—the Budweiser and Miller eagles, Pabst's blue ribbon, even the fonts on labels—and the need to "dress it up" became all the more important. Enter advertising and marketing on a world-changing scale.

30

NEVER BREAK THE CHAIN

1950–1959 | Omaha; New Orleans; Los Angeles

B eer was a staple for United States military personnel stationed in Japan in
the early 1950s, during that nation's occupation after its defeat in World
War II the decade before. US and European brands were in abundant supply, including in particular the Danish pilsner Tuborg and the Dutch pilsner
Heineken. They tasted pretty much as they tasted back home, a homogeneity
that the tens of thousands of marines, airmen, and sailors may not have realized but that would come to define beer in the rest of the twentieth century.

This was no accident. Brewers of pilsner—who for the most part had
become the biggest brewers on the planet by 1950—made sure their brands
tasted the same no matter where they were shipped. That had been holy writ
as far back as innovations such as pasteurization and artificial refrigeration
in the late nineteenth century. The post–World War II expansion that many
breweries underwent, however, made such homogeneity all the more sacred.
Breweries, especially in the United States, met that challenge through buying
up competitors in different, often far-flung locales—what would come to be
called chain brewing.

Falstaff Brewing Corporation, a St. Louis operation with origins in the
1860s and with two plants in that Missouri city, pioneered chain brewing.
Falstaff's flagship was a golden-hued lager clearly based on pilsner, and the
brewery's reigning Griesedieck clan originated from a small German village near the Rhine River, where the family had also run a brewery. Like
other breweries that participated in the postwar consolidation wave, Falstaff
did so well coming out of Prohibition that it needed to expand beyond its
St. Louis capacity. It was either unable or unwilling to do so, however, and
so decided to look farther afield. It found its first opportunity in the flailing
Krug Brewing Company of Omaha in Nebraska, a state that had embraced
prohibitionary measures longer than most and therefore had left its alcohol
vendors struggling more than others after Repeal. Plus, the Griesediecks had

a connection with the owners, and were able to arrange an acquisition in early 1935. Falstaff beer started flowing from the old Krug plant in Omaha, and within two years, it needed even more capacity to meet demand. Enter another struggling brewery in New Orleans. The National Brewing Company was one of the largest producers in the American South. Its early 1937 acquisition enormously expanded Falstaff's footprint to more than twenty states and put it well on the way to becoming one of the ten, then five, largest breweries in America.

It also gave Falstaff a headache. Although "Falstaff was literally the talk of the town" as it rolled out in New Orleans—thanks in large part to a massive advertising campaign—complaints started trickling in about the beers from this St. Louis usurper. Alvin Griesedieck, who ran Falstaff with his father, began to worry. What if the family had made a terrible mistake in becoming the first American brewery to own plants under the same name in more than one state? Would it have been better to work within the confines of St. Louis to increase capacity and compete with the likes of Pabst and Anheuser-Busch? It was too late for second-guessing. The younger Griesedieck knew that too. "Gradually the talk about 'bad beer' spread, however, and by the time we had located the trouble, we had taken quite a beating," Griesedieck later wrote. Falstaff risked losing its base in New Orleans and its influence in the southern market. "Naturally, our competitors took every advantage of the situation." Griesedieck and the brewery sprang into action, replacing as much of the New Orleans equipment as possible and adjusting recipes to make the pilsner and other Falstaff beers made there taste the same as those that had come famously out of St. Louis. "All of this was in 1937," Griesedieck wrote after the crisis had long passed, "and it took us the better part of ten years to come back in the New Orleans market." Falstaff found itself switching things around in Omaha, too, to make the beer brewed there taste close to identical to the beer made in Missouri's largest city.

Other breweries watched Falstaff expand through chain brewing in the late 1930s and through the 1940s. By the early 1950s, major competitors were embracing the trend. The decade would carry headlines of regional and local breweries collapsing into debt or into infighting among the third or fourth generations of a family, first and second cousins unable to come to terms with ownership or management of a firm their grandparents or great-grandparents had started. There had always been some churn in the brewing industry in America and elsewhere. Big players in the mid-twentieth century such as Anheuser-Busch, Miller, and Pabst had been born out of mergers, acquisitions, and partnerships, often of the familial sort, in the mid-nineteenth century. Falstaff itself sprang from mergers and acquisitions beginning before Prohibition, including of a brewery that traced its history to Civil War–era Missouri. But the sheer scope of the consolidation that amped up in the 1950s set it apart from earlier eras. When America entered World War II in 1941, there were around 860 breweries nationwide. By the end of the 1950s, there would be fewer than 200.

All the major players, including Pabst and Anheuser-Busch, acquired existing plants and not only rebranded them as their own but rejiggered the equipment, the supply channels, and the recipes so that these new acquisitions produced not the beers they *had* produced—those brands went to a kind of commercial graveyard for collectors to pick over like so many bibulous baseball cards—but the beers of their new owners. This scaling-up through acquisitions presented challenges, as Alvin Griesedieck and other brewery owners discovered. The water had to be the same, the ingredients similar if not identical, the training of the brewers steeped in the methods and traditions of the parent brewery. After all, one historian noted, "in the years following the Second World War, when the operation of subsidiary plants in various parts of the country became common practice among the national brewers, the beer manufactured in California, the Midwest, and New York, under one label, was sold as being identical in every respect."

This led to an almost fanatical devotion not necessarily to innovation—as in the past, when breweries cottoned to the latest in making their pilsners clearer and more uniform—but to engineering. As Falstaff's Alvin Griesedieck noted years later, when his brewery had settled comfortably (fleetingly, it would turn out) into the upper echelons of American brewing, making the beer taste the same no matter where it was brewed and no matter how far it was shipped was paramount. He wanted future brewers to understand that and to know that he had learned it the hard way in New Orleans and Omaha. "I cannot emphasize too strongly however, the necessity of continuous and regular taste tests by the chief executives of our company, in addition to the daily tests made by our own technical and production staff." Experimentation was for a different era, not the current one.

The current one was all about science and engineering. That was reflected in some of the plants that went up during this era or that breweries retrofitted upon acquisition. The most prominent was Anheuser-Busch's Newark facility, which it built on fifty acres that Gussie Busch had acquired at the turn of the decade. The company spent up to $34 million, an incredible sum at midcentury, on its first new outpost since the St. Louis expansions before and during Prohibition. Everything about it was gleaming and capacious, the equipment new and the technology the most recent available, including bottling and canning lines that could package hundreds of vessels a minute and giant brewing vats that adjusted easily and quickly to specific temperatures. As the scion of a competing brewing dynasty put it, the new Anheuser-Busch plant had "a crushing capacity" of 1.6 million barrels—more than most breweries in the world produced in a year. "Nothing said more about brewing's future than this announcement," the historian Maureen Ogle wrote of Anheuser-Busch's northern Jersey foray. "Nothing did more to enable the industry's largest beer maker to grow still larger." Anheuser-Busch would follow the July 1951 opening in Newark—which drew thousands of applicants for hundreds of jobs—with breweries in Los Angeles and Tampa before the end of the decade. Competitors such as Pabst, Schlitz, and Miller would also build new breweries or retrofit acquisitions during the decade to spread their brands that much farther and to thereby cut distribution costs. Many of these new and improved breweries were on the West Coast—both Schlitz and Pabst joined Anheuser-Busch in Los Angeles alone—as that portion of the American empire boomed. California's population by itself would jump more than 48 percent in the 1950s.

These new breweries by and large produced pilsner brands to the specifications of the mother companies. And since there were ever fewer such companies—around 185 American breweries either closed or sold out from 1949 to 1958—that meant that the crisp, clear, slightly bitter, reliably effervescent likes of Budweiser and Pabst Blue Ribbon seeped further and farther into the world's largest beer market. It was not necessarily that these brands became more popular than so many other competitors, but that they simply became the only beers available in many places. The biggest US breweries basically shrank the field in which they competed, and then turned on each other, wielding advertising and marketing as weapons. It was a trend playing out in myriad industries at the time, from accounting firms to automobile companies to snack-food vendors to toy manufacturers.

The brewing industry did hold out more than most. The top fifteen companies controlled a relatively small 55 percent of the business by the end of the decade. Compare that with other industries well known to consumers. "It is not uncommon in other brand name consumer goods industries to find one brand achieving something like that percentage [55 percent] of the total volume, and to find three or four together doing 80 per cent is commonplace," wrote one analyst toward the end of 1959. But consolidation nevertheless came to the US brewing industry and then to the world. Pilsner ended the 1950s concentrated in fewer and fewer hands. That these were largely American hands was no accident, because pilsner after World War II was largely a product of that science and engineering, the breakthroughs in crafting it on a large scale long in the style's rearview. Its brewers in America had the advantage of having escaped the conflict of the early 1940s physically unscathed, while breweries and their surrounding cities in areas such as central and northern Europe were literally bombed out.

Nothing illustrated this point more than what happened to the original pilsner producer: the Burghers' Brewery in Pilsen. The Germans had occupied Pilsen and surrounding Bohemia since March 1939. Among other indignities and hassles, the occupiers required billeting of as many as eighty military police personnel at the brewery and the use of much of its vehicular fleet. Liberation would come in early May 1945, when the American Third Army under General George S. Patton rolled into western Czechoslovakia. That was not before Allied bombers softened up the area quite a bit. Major air raids on western Czechoslovakia beginning in October 1944 not only killed several brewery employees but also disrupted operations for weeks. The most severe bombing run came on the night of April 17, 1945, as the American army closed in on a shattered Third Reich. Some 111 bombs landed on the Burghers' Brewery complex, including the water treatment plant, the cooperage, the malt house, and the power station. Though the people of Pilsen would

What Pilsner Urquell today calls its Old Brewhouse dates from 1930, about a decade before the outbreak of World War II, which would do major damage to the surrounding Burghers' Brewery complex. COURTESY OF ARCHIVE OF PLZEŇSKÝ PRAZDROJ, A.S.

have pilsner to toast their liberators the following May, it would be months before the brewery attained some semblance of its pre-1944 self. Other pilsner breweries in Europe would struggle through the same postwar mist, giving the Americans that much more of a head start.

Americans also gained a head start through an investment and a dedication to science and technology education that was unprecedented in the nation's history. The country had quickly replaced the Axis powers as enemies with the Soviet Union and its allies. The Cold War had started in the late 1940s and raged through the 1950s through all sorts of proxies, including races to put satellites and humans into space and to develop new technologies to further streamline industrial production. The Cold War, as US leaders saw it, would be won in the classrooms and the factories. It was a kind of militaristic motive for education, with a desire on the part of the governing classes to translate gains in knowledge to gains in industry and defense. To that end, Congress proposed and funded—and President Harry Truman's administration formed—the National Science Foundation in 1950 "to promote the progress of science; to advance the national health, prosperity, and welfare; to secure the national defense." The federal government also sunk millions of dollars into technical education and research, particularly when it came to agriculture, which of course benefited breweries, major customers for grains and hops. The nation's citizens felt this elevation of science in tangible ways. "Here I was, a black kid in a segregated school that was under-resourced—Sputnik kind of crossed the barrier," a student in Birmingham, Alabama, would recall of those days after the Soviets launched the first artificial satellite into Earth's orbit in October 1957, beating the United States into space. "All of a sudden, everybody was talking about it, and science was above the fold in the newspaper, and my teachers went to institutes and really got us engaged. It was just a time of incredible intensity and attention to science."

American brewers felt it too. The largest breweries created veritable farm systems for training brewers, plucking promising prospects early and sending them for training, which usually meant the Siebel Institute. That Chicago school, which dated from the 1860s and was the leading training program for brewers by World War II, moved to spacious, modern digs in 1952. Falstaff's Alvin Griesedieck explained it this way, especially when his brewery began peppering the country with new plants making the same pilsner and other beers. "In effect, under our present system, we literally raise our brewmasters, taking likely prospects from among journeyman brewers, or laboratory technicians, first sending them to an accredited Brewers School. After graduation, they come back to work in our plants, as assistant brewmasters and continue their practical training in the actual production of Falstaff." Such a setup did all the more to ensure consistency in American-made pilsners. American winemaking was still largely an art in the 1950s—with famously uneven results—but American brewing no longer was in this era of science as king.

The reverence for science in the middle of the twentieth century appeared to be a distinctly American phenomenon too. It was that Cold War climate that saw science and technology education as a wing of national defense. It was that emergence from the war years relatively physically unscathed. And it was something else. The United Kingdom had been the United States' greatest ally in defeating fascism. The two nations came out of the war continuing to share common strands of law, governance, culture, ethnicity, and religion—and they would be said to have a "special relationship" into the twenty-first century when it came to diplomacy. But when it came to science and industry, the United States left its top ally in the dust. While the UK had birthed the initial Industrial Revolution that gave the world innovations such as steam power and the railroad, it "generally sat out the 'Second Industrial Revolution' of the late nineteenth and early twentieth centuries, built around oil, chemicals, metals, electricity, electronics, and light machinery, such as automobiles," historian Thomas E. Ricks noted. It was not just that the United States blew by its old friend and mother country. The former saw a value in science—even if the Cold War framed much of that value—that the latter simply did not. As Ricks and others have pointed out, Winston Churchill, the greatest Brit of the twentieth and maybe any century, barely mentioned scientists in his Nobel Prize–winning writings on the UK and Western civilization. The statesmen and generals counted; the engineers and chemists barely rated. This attitude toward science could go a long way in explaining why the UK and neighboring Ireland, which was a British dominion until 1949, remained the most prominent holdouts against pilsner into the late 1900s.

Little wonder, then, that there were really only two foreign pilsner producers with sizable presences in the United States in the 1950s: the decades-old Dutch concern Heineken, which had largely escaped the Allied bombings of the Netherlands and whose reach would come to include one million case sales annually in the United States in 1960, and a newcomer called Carling. The Canadian brewer got its first beachhead in the United States through a deal with the Peerless Motor Car Corporation in the early 1930s, which allowed what was then called the Brewing Corporation of Canada to convert a defunct automobile factory in Cleveland into a brewery. This American subsidiary adopted the name the Carling Brewing Company in 1954—scrapping the rather dry Brewing Corporation of Canada in favor of one after the surname of an early executive—and then promptly acquired or built six breweries "to saturate all regions of the country with Red Cap Ale and Black Label Beer." The latter was a pilsner clone, golden in color, light in taste, and ceaselessly effervescent. Black Label powered much of Carling's meteoric rise in the United States—a rise so steep that by 1959 the company was telling *Fortune* magazine that it intended to top the American market as the "two hundred or so [breweries] now operating will be winnowed down to ten or twelve."

PART V

31

THE SOFT SELL

1953–1960 | St. Louis; New York City

In February 1953 a group of St. Louis businessmen, including members of the Anheuser-Busch board of directors, approached Gussie Busch with a proposition: buy the St. Louis Cardinals, the city's longtime Major League Baseball franchise. "Gussie didn't give a good goddamn about baseball or the Cardinals," according to a biographer. But he recognized what the businessmen were on to. The team was one of the most popular attractions in the St. Louis area, and because of the scope of professional baseball then, one of the most popular attractions in all the United States. "As the farthest west and farthest south major league franchise, [the Cardinals] were the home team of more Americans than any other ball club." The team had won the World Series in 1946—its sixth such title so far—and its first baseman and occasional outfielder Stan Musial was in the midst of one of the greatest sports careers of the twentieth century. People flocked to fill most if not all of the more than thirty thousand seats at the Cardinals' Sportsman's Park home, a captive audience for advertisers and vendors alike. Radio and television often carried the games—another marketing opportunity. Besides, the Cardinals' current owner had pleaded guilty the month before to tax evasion and really needed to sell. Either that, or the team might have to move to Milwaukee.

Busch and his company acquired the Cardinals in a $3.725 million deal. He quickly became a hands-on owner in a sport that he barely knew anything about. During a spring training visit to the Cardinals' camp in Florida early on, Busch stood awkwardly at home plate with a baseball cap and a frozen smile, and proceeded to whiff some half-dozen softball pitches from the mound. He finally connected on "a couple of dribblers and called it a day," as one sportswriter put it.

What he lacked in athletic prowess, Busch more than made up for in marketing ability. He turned the Cardinals virtually overnight into a promotional juggernaut for Anheuser-Busch. "This is one of the finest moves in the history of Anheuser-Busch," he had told a stockholders' meeting in March 1953, and he turned out to be right. Sportsman's Park, which Busch also bought and then refurbished, became Busch Stadium. Major League executives and his own people had talked Gussie out of trying to name it Budweiser Stadium after the company's signature pilsner—Major League Baseball then forbade corporate sponsorship. He was only able to slap "Busch" on the name because he said it was after his immediate ancestors and not his company. Either way, Budweiser did flow like mighty rivers through the newly renamed ballpark, transforming it into "a giant outdoor tavern." The ubiquity of Anheuser-Busch at Busch Stadium helped force the Griesedieck Brothers Brewery, a company associated with the same clan behind Falstaff, to sell the television and radio rights to Cardinals games to the franchise's new owner. Griesedieck apparently had no intention of promoting its St. Louis rival's beer throughout a sizable chunk of the United States.

Gussie Busch's acquisition of the Cardinals and his moves afterward cemented a bond between beer and professional sports that would continue uncracked into the twenty-first century. Brewers had dabbled in sponsorships, even ownerships—brewer Jacob Ruppert had helped turn around the Yankees in the early twentieth century as the New York team's owner—but none had wrapped a team so tightly with a brewery before. The Cardinals became a de facto extension of Anheuser-Busch, like the Busch Gardens amusement and animal parks the brewery would begin opening in 1959. Ownership of the team helped Anheuser-Busch move that much more of its pilsner and less popular brews to that many more people—and it showed the way for rivals to do the same. Before the end of the century, other breweries would not only buy other pro sports franchises but would also become some of the largest sponsors of pro and college sports in the United States, not to mention the Olympics and foreign sports.

Around the same time that Gussie Busch was turning the St. Louis Cardinals into one of the biggest promoters of pilsner in the style's 110-year history, the much smaller Piels Brewery in Brooklyn was opening an even bigger venue for breweries. Brewers had been marketing on television for years by the mid-1950s. Anheuser-Busch in 1950 had become the first brewery to straight-up sponsor a program. *The Ken Murray Show* ran during the "Budweiser Hour" every Saturday evening on fifty-one CBS stations. The variety number not only carried Budweiser ads, but the namesake host and his guests were seen to quaff the pilsner live from tall, tapered glasses filled from bottles with the labels turned carefully toward the camera. The whole production paid dividends for Anheuser-Busch. Its sales of Budweiser in those fifty-one markets were double those in other US cities. An entire show on a major network, even during the salad days of television, was not something every brewery could afford. What Piels Brewery did, though, other breweries could readily copy.

The third generation now controlled the family-owned firm, which, like many regional breweries, was struggling to keep up with more rapidly expanding nationals such as Pabst, Anheuser-Busch, and Miller as well as imports such as Heineken. In a divide that was becoming increasingly typical, Piels, the regional, was earning $0.73 on every barrel it produced by 1952, a sharp drop from just after the war, while Anheuser-Busch, the national, was pulling in $1.80. An attempt at joining the chain brewing trend with acquisitions and revamps in Staten Island and another part of Brooklyn failed spectacularly. Piels was on the ropes.

Enter Ed Graham, a junior copywriter at the Young & Rubicam advertising agency barely past his twenty-fifth birthday. The Manhattan-based firm handled Piels' advertising, which revolved around incredibly dry and straightforward approaches about the beer's lower caloric content—or, as the ads put it, the fact that Piels had "less N.F.S.," the abbreviation standing for nonfermented sugar. Dismissing the less-than-scintillating concept as "pretty horrible," Graham partnered with a cartoon artist named Jack Sidebotham to come up with a lighter approach. This was an era of the hard sell, when advertisers and their clients preferred to lean on approaches such as repetition and ubiquity. A brewery—or an automobile maker or a toaster manufacturer or any company with a product to trade—made sure the name of its brand was said or shown as often as possible, usually in the most straightforward of ways. Anheuser-Busch's *The Ken Murray Show*, which ran until 1953, was a case in point, with the "Budweiser Hour" behind it and the brewery's product as the veritable star, enjoying as much airtime as the show's human characters.

Graham went for something different, and his idea reverberated well beyond Piels and pilsner. Working with Sidebotham, he developed two cartoon characters. They were balding brothers from Brooklyn, graduates of P.S. 3 and Samuel J. Tilden High in the Flatbush neighborhood. One—the short, blustery Bert—worked in car sales. The other—the tall, urbane Harry—was a chemist. They loved Piels beer, of course, and they had strong opinions about it, opinions they shared through one hundred television commercials over five years beginning in the summer of 1955 with test runs on stations in Binghamton, New York, and Harrisburg, Pennsylvania. Young & Rubicam did not think such a soft sell—two aesthetically unappealing characters, one quite acerbic and the other kind of a snob—would work. Where was the hard sell, the repetition, the product placement? One of the brothers, usually Harry, might pour a golden-colored, foamy Piels into a pilsner glass during the commercial, and the siblings might comment about it throughout. But the characters were the clear stars, not the product—and it worked nevertheless.

The cartoons, which New York comedy duo Bob Elliott and Ray Goulding voiced, worked so well that Bert and Harry fan clubs sprang up, and viewers actually wrote real letters to the fake characters, addressing them to the Piels plant in Brooklyn. Newspapers began listing the times when Bert and Harry commercials were likely to air, and people stayed home or stayed put to watch. "One of the most effective hucksters on eastern TV is a bashful botcher who muffs his lines, meanders off-camera, even mumbles his apologies for intruding on TV viewers' time," *Time* magazine reported in May 1956.

> His name: Harry Piel. Since January, when Harry and Brother Bert made their debut in a series of cartoon commercials plugging Brooklyn's Piel Brothers' beer, they have won such fame that even the most blurb-worn viewers are changing their ways: instead of ducking out when the commercial goes on, Easterners are now turning on their sets to catch the Piel cartoons.

The popularity changed Madison Avenue forever. Characters and backstories would count prominently in advertising from then on, the influence of Ed Graham's decision fanning out first in the United States and then the rest of the world, altering how companies and individuals pitched themselves to the public. "Encouraged by the success of the entertaining Piel skits," a *New York Daily News* editor wrote in January 1957, "more and more admen who once believed solely in the hard sell are venturing into a field where only Bert and Harry dared tread a long time ago."

Pity this popularity did not help the real Piel brothers. The brewery saw an initial sales bounce in the late 1950s, which executives attributed to the commercials, enough to keep Piels among the twenty largest breweries in the nation. But, ultimately, Bert and Harry sowed the seeds of Piels' destruction. The pair convinced a lot of people to try a pilsner that was not all that good. "The big mistake with that campaign," Jerry Della Femina, an advertising executive and chronicler of the industry wrote later, "was that it got people to taste Piel's Beer. A guy would take a sip of it and say, 'Screw Bert and Harry, they were a lot of fun and I like to look at them on the late news, but they're not going to make me drink this stuff.'" Or as *Sports Illustrated* later put it, "Unfortunately, the beer itself was not very good. Because of the

Bert and Harry mania grew to include other marketing material beyond the commercials, including coasters. COURTESY OF ALFRED W. MCCOY, FROM HIS BOOK *BEER OF BROADWAY FAME*

great ads, all kinds of people bought it for the first time, hated it, and spread the news everywhere about how awful it was." Piels, a brewery that like so many Germanic brethren traced its genesis to the immigration boom of the mid-1800s, was out of business within a decade of the first Bert and Harry ads.

As for the fictional duo, the brewery's declining fortunes—coupled with pay and planning disputes involving Young & Rubicam, the brewery, and Ed Graham's production company—croaked Bert and Harry in 1960. Aside from the fan fallout—angry viewers inundated the CBS flagship in New York City with one and a half million letters after the commercials stopped running—the duo's demise presented a big issue for the industry behind the ads. "The question now is whether a good part of humorous advertising will pass with Bert and Harry," the *New York Times* asked in a December 1960 article headlined CURTAINS FOR BERT AND HARRY. "Because Bert and Harry were in their way symbolic of the whole off-beat approach to advertising," the newspaper went on, "it is now feared that their demise may signal a general retreat from the humorous approach and a consequent return to the hard sell."

That did not happen. Whatever the fate of the fictional siblings and the brewery behind them, the selling of pilsner had changed advertising and marketing forever. That was true because of the Bert and Harry commercials, and it was also true because of Anheuser-Busch's acquisition of the St. Louis Cardinals. The twin moves in the mid-1950s advanced the fortunes of pilsner—and of its largest producers. Neither move could have come at a better time.

32

THE CUSTOMER IS ALWAYS RIGHT

1950–1960 | Rochester, New York

"I think we have a winner here." Clarence Geminn had just sampled the fruits of the labor of his fellow brewery workers at the Genesee Brewing Company in Rochester, New York. The forty-six-year-old Geminn, whose father had immigrated from Germany and who had also been a brewer, had been with Genesee since 1951, first as an assistant brewer and then as its brewmaster since 1959. The brewery's reach barely extended beyond the Northeast but it had a loyal enough customer base to make Genesee one of the twenty largest breweries in the nation. Still, the trend in American and global brewing was toward consolidation. Relatively small fry such as Genesee, with its annual barrelage of around one million or a little more by the time of Geminn's brewery-floor declaration in 1960, could not afford too many stumbles against the likes of an expanding Anheuser-Busch.

So Geminn's tinkering from 1959 into 1960 had been a risk. He had been trying to develop a happy medium between two earlier Genesee offerings: a so-called dry ale that had a short run in the 1950s—it was too dry, even for consumers increasingly used to crisp, mildly bitter pilsners—and a heavier-tasting ale that seemed increasingly out of place. What Geminn came up with was a version of cream ale. The style was one of only a few beer styles born in the United States—born outside northern and central Europe, for that matter—and was characterized by a lighter body and mouthfeel than more conventional ales. Cream ale had grown up in the United States in part as a response to the rise in popularity of pilsner. Some considered it the American version of kölsch, the light German style that enjoyed a resurgence in the late nineteenth century, also because of the rise of pilsner. The version of cream ale that Geminn developed for Genesee was light-tasting and lighter-looking than most ales on the market, with a frothy head and both a mild alcoholic kick and a mild bitterness.

Not that there were many ales on the market. Like much of the beer-drinking world by 1960, the United State was lager country—pilsner country to be specific. That Genesee Cream Ale, in its signature green-and-white cans and squat bottles with similarly green-and-white labels, became the best-selling ale in the United States with just one million barrels sold annually in the early 1960s says a lot about the beer market at the time. Each one of Anheuser-Busch's newer plants could produce several more times that of pilsner annually. And the company could count on selling most if not all of it, as its footprint was global. Genesee and the other regionals plodded along with their more modest output. One million barrels? That was a drop in the beer bucket.

Though the bucket was not as deep as it used to be. In the United States and Europe, the larger breweries were finding a changing marketplace as the calendar clicked over from the 1950s into the 1960s. The resurgence through and out of the war years, a resurgence that had benefited larger American breweries in particular because they could scale up more easily, was teetering as demographic trends shifted and competition for share of throat arose from new corridors. As so often had happened over its lifetime, though, pilsner stood to gain from the shifts. The style fitted with the times in a way that more esoteric ones such as cream ale and kölsch could not. Pilsner had already ushered so many beer styles to the historical rafters, where their practitioners and fans could only watch in dismay as the Bohemian upstart gobbled ever more of the spotlight. The late twentieth century would see the style reach its zenith. At the same time, it would face its greatest challenge since Prohibition, one that came from inside the beer world that it thought it dominated and that Genesee Cream Ale's relative success foreshadowed.

For now, though, the most immediate threat to pilsner came from outside the brewing industry. Simply put, the number of likely beer drinkers was shrinking in the world's leading beer market. There were a number of factors to blame. For one thing, the birth rate in the United States shrank markedly between the 1920s and the 1940s. The demographic shift really manifested itself in the 1950s, with the number of Americans between the ages of twenty and forty—the target demographic for beer sellers—sliding to historic lows.

At the same time, a surge in the consumption of spirits ate into beer sales. The spirit leading this advance was that old American standby, bourbon. In 1950 the corn-based whiskey born in Kentucky nearly two hundred years before accounted for nearly one-fourth of the bottled whiskey sold in the United States; much of the rest were lighter-colored and lighter-tasting whiskey blends from Canada and Scotland. By 1961, though, bourbon accounted for half the whiskey sold in the United States. More important, the brownest of the brown spirits ballasted a rising baby-boomer subculture that gravitated toward bourbon-based cocktails such as Manhattans, old fashioneds, Singapore slings, and Rob Roys. No one was quite sure the reasons for this gravitation. It might have been a generational backlash against the boomers' parents' affinity for those lighter blends and for that juniper-infused Dutch spirit gin. Then again, maybe the spirit's popularity had something to do with bourbon producers, most notably the outfit behind Jim Beam, making the spirit available near and sometimes on US military bases in the 1940s. Returning GIs tended to carry a torch for bourbon once back stateside.

Joining bourbon at the crest of the spirits wave—and eating that much more into beer's share of throat—was a colorless, odorless, largely flavorless spirit that was virtually unheard of in North America as recently as the early 1930s. Vodka was born in either present-day Scandinavia, Poland, or Russia, and, much like pilsner in the previous century, the spirit distilled from grains or potatoes leapfrogged to America by way of revolutionary tumult in Europe. In this case, it was the Russian Revolution, which drove a branch of the Smirnoff family to sell the rights to its vodka brand to an enterprising Ukrainian American who in turn in 1934 opened the first vodka distillery in the United States since Prohibition in Connecticut. Smirnoff and lesser vodka labels soon stormed into American dining rooms and American pop culture. The first James Bond film, 1962's *Dr. No*, has Sean Connery's 007 ordering a vodka martini—"shaken, not stirred"—and vodka cocktails, including the Bloody Mary, the Moscow mule, and the screwdriver, became particular favorites of Hollywood stars. Vodka's success was perhaps easier to explain than that of bourbon; unlike other spirits, never mind beer, it did not leave a telltale odor on the breath.

On top of the competing alcoholic beverages, a shift in consumer taste upset the market. The explosion in processed foods in the US marketplace led to a blander diet for many if not most Americans. That was because food and drink lost more natural flavor the more it was processed, a truism that turned out to suit consumers just fine. Nuance was out, sameness was in. Part of that was the postwar rise of television and the way it kept people home more—a shift that also aided the rise of canned pilsner—but probably a bigger part was a pivot toward convenience above all else. "One of the most important changes of the first half of the twentieth century was the way in which Americans associated modernity with convenience," the historian Maureen Ogle has noted. Americans old enough to remember the stove-bound hours that went into food preparation turned away from that in droves at midcentury in favor of foodstuffs that they could zap to edibility in microwaves or that they could more quickly prepare because it came largely ready from a can or a package. Soups, fruits, vegetables, meats, potatoes, and more, and versions of the same, could be consumed more quickly and conveniently than ever before.

The evolution of the American kitchen, including the proliferation of microwaves and refrigerators, helped this trend toward convenience along, as did the boom in plastic after World War II. Efforts at creating and mass-producing the synthetic material dated from the late nineteenth century at least, but the conflict in the early 1940s spurred a tripling in plastic production in the United States, as everything from airplane windows to goggles to parts of the atomic bomb utilized plastic. After the war, the industrial forces behind plastic found it easy to fit the material in with this jones for domestic convenience. As one plastics executive put it at the time, "Virtually nothing was made of plastic and anything could be"—including those newer American kitchens. A plastic that industrial giant Westinghouse developed before World War I proliferated in kitchens beginning after World War II under the name Formica. Easy to clean and quick to shine, Formica covered countless countertops and tables by 1960.

The processed foods served from these countertops and on these tables invariably tasted the same no matter where they were reheated, and that was the point. The foods were designed to appeal to the masses. Little surprise that they were most widely available at supermarkets, which dotted the American landscape by the late 1950s and spurred imitations all over the world. The number of supermarkets in the United States doubled to more than twenty-five hundred in the ten years ending in 1958. Although post-Prohibition regulations threw up barriers between breweries and consumers—most restrictively through the so-called three-tiered system, which required beers to go through a distributor in the first place—most states by 1960 allowed beer to be sold in supermarkets. Theoretically shoppers could pick up a six-pack of pilsner on the way home, along with plastic-wrapped chicken and canned green beans.

But would they? Beer's share of throat—which essentially meant pilsner's share of throat—was receding in the 1950s, a decade during which America bestrode the world like a colossus. Industrial output increased 54 percent, the gross national product zoomed more than 200 percent, and per capita income increased 35 percent. Yet beer sales started to stagnate and then slide. The post-Repeal bounce had faded, and per capita consumption slid too—from nearly seventeen gallons annually in 1951 to below fifteen in 1961. America was clearly booming economically, but the success of other alcoholic beverages in the market and the population's fetish for what was modern, convenient, and bland were affecting beer sales. And, as the fate of Piels Brewery in Brooklyn highlighted, the industry could not necessarily advertise itself out of its sales hole. It needed to adapt to the changing marketplace.

Luckily, pilsner was just the type of beer that could do so. It was already convenient: packaged in cans that traveled easily and that fit just as easily into refrigerators—and that were just as easy to crush and toss. Plus, the style already had a well-earned reputation as modern. Pilsner had been and still was the brightest, crispest, clearest, bubbliest style of them all, a fact that those studying the drinking public had recognized for decades by the 1950s. "A careful and impartial student would not have far to seek in order to explain the universal popularity of modern beers," the United Kingdom's *Brewers' Journal* pointed out in October 1898. "It is their quality, brilliancy, wholesomeness, and pleasant refreshing flavors that have made the beer-trade what it is now."

The trick became to marry that modernity won in the late nineteenth century and that convenience achieved in the early twentieth with the blander diet many Americans were adopting. Breweries did this through leaning more on adjuncts such as corn and rice—and, eventually, corn syrup, a concentrate derived from the former—when it came to pilsner. The additions essentially dried out the style. It undercut the hoppy bitterness and made signature pilsners such as Budweiser and Pabst more watery—turning them from more distinct interpretations of the great Bohemian export into "alcoholic soda pop," as one later critic put it. There was a lot of truth to that critique, a critique that would become deafening by the end of the century. The bigger pilsner producers really did increase the amounts of rice and corn in their beers, and they really did cut back on the hops, that great definer of beer style and the bringer of beer's distinctive bitterness. American brewers overall halved the amount of hops they used from 1948 to 1969, according to one study. That hop makeup would drop even further after 1969, as US and then world brewers chased beers that could appeal to mass audiences. The head of the Master Brewers Association of the Americas, a trade group with roots in the heyday of pilsner's rise in the 1870s and 1880s, urged members to brew "streamlined," "modernized" beers free of "bitter aftertaste" and with a more "agreeable, mild hop flavor."

American pilsners were especially poised to absorb this change, thanks to the boom in science in a United States keen then to one-up its Cold War rival, the Soviet Union. So what was essentially another scientific and engineering pivot came more easily to bigger US brewers, who had the technology and the talent to adapt—never mind the material. The 1950s and 1960s were when

US corn production took off—a by-product of that scientific revolution—with the number of bushels per acre shooting from around forty to around sixty, and then double that before the 1990s.

Finally, American pilsner was the exact sort of beer that rewarded streamlining. The very style shed more of its distinction more easily. Ales were thicker and richer to begin with. So was every other lager style besides pilsner available in the United States. It was difficult to shear these beers of what made them special. That was not the case with pilsner. Pilsner was already the epitome of the modern beer and conveniently available, too, in a way that the likes of cream ale from Genesee could never hope to match. Making pilsner all the more accessible meant tweaks, not a reboot, and the largest pilsner producers already had decades of experience with the style at their backs. "Indeed, what consumers understood as modern beer came to its most coherent expression in the globalization of a singular, unique style in the spread of the golden lager and its related scientific and technological innovations," an academic study of pilsner put it.

Pilsner emerged from the 1950s ready to spend the last decades of the twentieth century doing battle with the forces that would curb its appeal and the fortunes of its biggest producers. It proved an especially durable weapon. Theories as to how it succeeded during these decades despite the blandness became a kind of parlor game among academics, critics, and consumers. One theory held that pilsner's lower alcohol content had made it a favorite among temperance advocates and therefore helped its rise. Another was that the grain and other material shortages during World War II spurred recipe adjustments that produced a thinner, weaker style. Another theory out of the war had it that GIs became acclimated to thinner beers and took that taste with them stateside much as they might have the richer taste of bourbon.

None of these were true. The temperance advocates played for keeps, and steadied the same lethal aim at pilsner producers as they did at whiskey distillers and winemakers. Prohibition almost wiped out brewing in the United States, and that was exactly what temperance advocates wanted. Also, the recipe changes came *after* World War II, and the pilsners that soldiers, sailors, and airmen tasted *before* the 1950s would have been made with smaller proportions of adjuncts.

In the end, what appears to have birthed the iteration of pilsner that would ride out the twentieth century was something simpler, even boring: customer demand. The brewing burghers in 1830s Bohemia had banged on about the need for a more appealing local beer because they were losing money to the Bavarian upstarts. That financial need had sparked the style in the first place. A few decades later, German American brewers tweaked their recipes based on the materials they had at hand in their adopted country. As the style caught commercial fire, they used new techniques and technologies to make more of it and to ship it farther. After Prohibition, these same approaches held—for a while. As the ground shifted again under brewers, they steadied themselves with recipe adjustments and they fired up a marketing machine that changed the world. By the 1960s, too, it helped that few in living memory could remember a time when pilsner did not dominate the beer marketplace. The relatively piddling success of other styles such as cream ale only highlighted the depth of this memory hole.

Yet some did remember.

33

A GNAT AT AN ELEPHANT

1960–1970 | San Francisco; Milwaukee

It would turn out that Fred Kuh had picked the perfect time to open his Old Spaghetti Factory Café and Excelsior Coffee House in San Francisco's North Beach neighborhood. The year was 1956, and the Chicago stockbroker's son and World War II veteran had converted a former pasta factory into what the *San Francisco Chronicle* described as the city's "first camp-decor cabaret restaurant." Kuh, who called himself a "bohemian businessman," festooned the capacious space with décor, some of it secondhand from a local brothel, that included beaded lampshades and upside-down chairs on the ceiling. The Old Spaghetti Factory quickly became a magnet for San Francisco's beatniks and left-leaning activists. It served as a kind of unofficial local headquarters for Democrat Adlai Stevenson II's 1956 presidential run and later attracted the hippies that seemed to swarm the Bay Area during the following decade. The vicissitudes of Northern California's largest city were kind to Kuh's café, then, in the early part of the late twentieth century.

Kuh tried to be kind in turn. For one thing, he carried local products when he could. That included his only beer on draft, which was called Anchor Steam and which came from a San Francisco brewery that dated from the 1890s. It had survived the city's epic 1906 earthquake and the changing fortunes and misfortunes of several owners up to the 1960s, and by that time was hanging on by a thread financially.

Anchor Brewing occupied a cramped space on San Francisco's east side, where a lone employee unenthusiastically produced small batches of a style called steam beer. No one was quite sure where the style came from or why it was still made. It might have had something to do with the California gold rush in the 1840s. So many newcomers flooded California that brewers met demand by creating an entirely new beer style with the material at hand—and that new style turned out to be a kind of ale-lager hybrid that gave off a lot of carbonation and a puff of steam when drinkers opened bottles. Another theory held that in these pre-refrigeration times brewers cooled the unfermented beer on San Francisco rooftops and the Pacific breeze blew steam off the liquid. However it came to be, steam beer was a style native to the United States—one of only a handful that also included cream ale—and Anchor was the only brewery making it. And, like a dying language, Anchor Steam had only a few people left to keep it alive. One of those people was Fred Kuh, who ordered a steady supply of kegs of the stuff for his Old Spaghetti Factory.

Some of his regulars, after all, preferred the bubbly, slightly bitter, color-of-dried-honey Anchor Steam to the much more widely available pilsner imitations that, like in other areas of the United States, routinely flooded San Francisco's bars, restaurants, and grocery stores. One of those regulars was a trim twenty-five-year-old Midwestern transplant named Fritz Maytag. An heir to the vast home appliance empire that carried his surname and a Stanford graduate with a degree in American literature, he had pursued graduate studies in Japanese through the same university before dropping out after John F. Kennedy's assassination in November 1963 rattled his views of the world and of his future. Maytag was in San Francisco essentially to figure out what he wanted to do with his life. A particular visit to Fred Kuh's Old Spaghetti Factory in August 1965 would provide the answer and change the course of twentieth-century food and drink.

"Fritz, have you ever been to the brewery?" Kuh asked Maytag as the bar owner placed a glass of Anchor Steam in front of him.

"No," his regular replied.

"You ought to see it," Kuh said. "It's closing in a day or two, and you ought to see it. You'd like it."

Maytag did have a soft spot for local foodstuffs. His father—a grandson of the German immigrant who founded the Maytag Washing Machine Company around the start of the century—had developed a famous blue cheese back on the homestead in Iowa. Maytag blue cheese was made from milk from a herd of Holstein cows and aged in artificial caves, with an initial researching assist from the dairy science department at Iowa State. The younger Maytag had seen with pride how his father reacted when people asked him, "Have you anything to do with that blue cheese?" The idea of a small, independent brewery churning out an esoteric style for a small handful of clients such as Fred Kuh struck a chord with Maytag. The day after his conversation with Kuh, he walked the short distance between his apartment and Anchor Brewery, then at Eighth and Brannan Streets, and bought a majority stake for what he later described as "less than the price of a used car."

Fritz Maytag's rescue of the Anchor Brewing Company in the late summer of 1965 marked the start of what came to be called craft beer or microbrewing. His decision to keep the brewery small, to keep it turning out that somewhat arcane style rather than an iteration of the pilsner style that dominated the marketplace, and his decision to do so in a more hands-on, less mechanized way set the parameters for all other craft brewers to come. They would look to Maytag's example—particularly his use of all-malt, no-adjunct recipes—for their own work. His toils took on the stuff of legend.

The wider beer world at the time hardly noticed, however. Why would it? Anchor's reach barely extended beyond the brewery, and the quality control for its steam beer—all of it kegged, none of it bottled, much less canned—was spotty at best. "We were doing a hundred kegs a month," Maytag would recall, "and if the Old Spaghetti Factory weren't taking ten each week, we'd have been in trouble. I always say Frank Kuh was the one who really saved Anchor Steam." Improbable as it might have seemed, a self-described "bohemian businessman" turning on a home appliance heir to the idea of owning a small brewery that ran on a nearly extinct style would not end up as all that unusual a backstory for microbrewing. That was how craft beer would be—coming from the fringes, a puny pugilist up against Goliath.

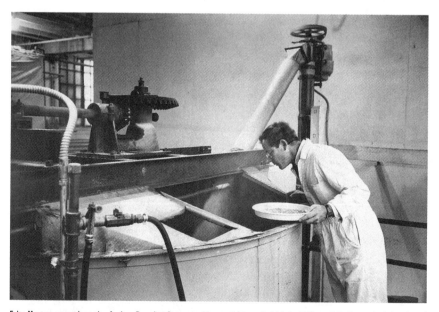

Fritz Maytag at work at the Anchor Brewing Company, his acquisition of which in 1965 unwittingly sparked the rise of what came to be called craft beer. COURTESY OF ANCHOR BREWING COMPANY

The wider beer world had settled long ago on pilsner, and it had no time for the likes of steam beer or cream ale or India pale ale, the last of which was dying a slow commercial death as the once-mighty P. Ballantine & Sons in Newark, New Jersey, faded. The brewery had started the 1960s as one of the ten largest breweries in the United States, with an annual output of more than four million barrels. What's more, Ballantine did that from a single plant—the only company among the top ten breweries to not have embraced chain brewing. Even more remarkable, Ballantine owed much of its success to an ale in the IPA genre—a bitter, rich offering so unlike the pilsners that dominated the market. The 1960s would not be kind to that offering or to its brewery. The decade would be unkind to a lot of breweries as the consolidation wave that had been building since Prohibition broke against a general mania for mergers. "When an industry starts to consolidate, you either get consolidated or you consolidate," Bill Coors would tell a Colorado newspaper years after the dust of the decade settled. Coors, a Princeton-trained chemical engineer who later chaired the Colorado brewery that his grandfather founded, had helped along the consolidation by spearheading the development in 1959 of the seven-ounce aluminum can. It made it that much easier and cheaper to package and transport pilsner, including the golden-crisp signature beer of the Coors Brewing Company, which clearly labeled that beer a "pilsner." The introduction of the pull-tab opening in 1963 helped aluminum supplant tin as the preferred metal in beer packaging, a preference that spread to other canned drinks as well.

Despite his pivotal role in these developments, it was the consolidation that Bill Coors would remember. It was what everyone noticed: the big got bigger. The sky seemed the limit behind the new packaging, the fresh advertising approaches, and the recipe tweaks. It was time to do battle for shares of throat in the United States and beyond. And battle the breweries did, with the ones that were biggest already emerging from the 1960s that much bigger. The number of brewing companies went from an already low 188 in 1960 to 138 in 1970. Most of the exits were thanks to mergers and acquisitions, and many were because breweries simply gave up the ghost in a time of frenetic competition. There were some surprising casualties. The Narragansett Brewing Company of Cranston, Rhode Island, took over the Krueger brewery out of Newark, which only thirty years before seemed destined for great things behind its landmark decision to can its beer. The Falstaff Brewing Company absorbed Ballantine, though its IPA would lumber on a bit longer like a dinosaur in the days after the meteor struck. "Since 1937, Ballantine has been consistently among the top ten brewers in the country," went one approving take on the Newark operation in 1962. Things changed very quickly. In Europe, a growing Heineken—the biggest competitor internationally to the American brewers—acquired its Dutch archrival Amstel in 1968, and soon launched its first television commercials.

The biggest casualty of the period was Pabst Brewing Company, though no one would really know it until the following decade. Like many of the older American breweries that German immigrants had started in, and shepherded out of, the late 1800s, Pabst was now in the hands of people not named Pabst. A corporate structure, seen as necessary to compete in such a competitive and geographically diffuse marketplace, had arisen. And it was floundering. Pabst's share of the marketplace, one that perhaps only Anheuser-Busch could match, sank. It went from the nation's third-largest brewery to its seventh before the 1960s even started, and the phalanxes of sales and marketing executives could not seem to come up with a plan to reverse the slide. Lower prices for its signature pilsner did not work, nor did odd gimmicks such as coupons redeemable for salt shakers and barbecue tools. Pabst spent the late 1950s and 1960s trying to merge and acquire its way out of terminal decline, including an ultimately futile attempt to sell itself to soft drinks giant PepsiCo.

The Jos. Schlitz Brewing Company was also starting what would become in the 1970s a spectacular flameout. Its original owners, the Uihlein family, still ran things, and in the 1960s that meant Erwin Uihlein and his nephew Robert Uihlein. Their Milwaukee-based brewery played in the same commercial playground as Anheuser-Busch and Pabst in terms of market share, but that began to change in the 1960s. Schlitz's signature pilsner had been known as "the beer that made Milwaukee famous," as one advertisement tagline went, but with the addition of more additives, especially corn syrup, customers were undoubtedly turned off and Schlitz's reputation was hurt. That reputation was increasingly built on advertising and marketing anyway. Robert Uihlein, a tall, square-jawed man fond of big-game hunting and championship polo, wrested most of the control of the brewery from his uncle in 1961, and promptly turned over most of its direction to executives outside the family. Schlitz expanded with acquisitions as diverse as a glass factory in Pakistan and breweries in Puerto Rico, Belgium, and Turkey. In the end, these moves would assist in overextending Schlitz to the breaking point, but the admen that Robert Uihlein brought in clouded the picture during the 1960s, and the brewery merely felt its way along toward disaster.

The soft sell that Piels had pioneered the decade before was near-sacrosanct in the brewing industry in the 1960s. That it had not saved the Brooklyn brewery seemed to be collectively forgotten. The sales pitch was the thing. Surely it would move bottles, kegs, and cans. Salvation was always one marketing move away. "Beer to us is a product to be marketed—like soap, corn flakes, or facial tissues," a top executive at Schlitz put it to a reporter in October 1964. Drinkers should "imbibe the image" in an advertisement as much as they should actually imbibe the beer. The breweries that were left in the 1960s were fixated on selling pilsner as a lifestyle choice or accoutrement—the drink of the workingman after work or the perfect side to an all-American meal such as burgers and fries or, better yet, the best refreshment for an afternoon at the ballpark. F. & M. Schaefer Brewing Company, which could trace its origins to the early 1840s and two brothers from Prussia, summed up this approach perhaps better than anyone with a 1961 advertising jingle that reminded drinkers, "Schaefer is the one beer to have when you're having more than one." Like with Piels before and like with Schlitz, the marketing helped boost Schaefer in the short term, though, like Schlitz, it would barely limp out of the 1970s.

So many breweries, in fact, had unwittingly set themselves up to fail in the 1960s, for if the positioning of pilsner as a lifestyle choice did not work, then there was little to fall back on in the modern beer world. "The beer consumer is a very unforgiving animal," one financial analyst explained to the *New York Times*. "Once a brand has lost its luster, it's hard to shine it up again."

This reality would leave only two operations to carve up much of the beer world after the 1960s: Anheuser-Busch and Miller. Those operations spent the 1960s building upon growth and changes from the 1950s. Miller was especially fertile, despite the death in a December 1954 plane crash of Fred C. Miller and the family squabbling that followed. Its production and sales footprints grew during both decades as it ascended first into the ranks of the ten largest US breweries and then the five largest. Though its production figures paled against those of Anheuser-Busch, Pabst, and Schlitz, the steady success of Miller brands such as High Life—an unusually pale and dry iteration of an earlier pilsner—helped the brewery weather the uncertainties of the 1950s and positioned it well for the century's second half. That, and Miller was the first major brewery to gear its advertising toward women. It took out full-page ads in magazines such as *Vogue* and *McCall's*, and sold Miller pilsners in supposedly more female-friendly six-ounce bottles. This expansive view of what the market for pilsner could be presaged just how big Miller and its looming archrival Anheuser-Busch intended to get.

As for that eventual archrival, it would exit the 1960s as indisputably the world's largest brewer. By 1973 Anheuser-Busch would be producing nearly thirty million barrels annually, most of it Budweiser pilsner. The only three breweries that approached it in production were Schlitz, Pabst, and Heineken—though the first two were in a long twilight. Nothing perhaps illustrated Anheuser-Busch's growth heading into the 1970s better than its latest plant in Merrimack, New Hampshire, which launched just as the decade started. The approximately one million-square-foot brewery on nearly three hundred acres could produce up to six hundred million twelve-ounce bottles annually—it would add cans later—and cost $40 million to outfit. The Merrimack opening followed on the heels of new Anheuser-Busch breweries in Jacksonville, Florida, in 1969 and Columbus, Ohio, in 1968. That same year, Anheuser-Busch successfully filed to trademark a new slogan that seemed to reflect the ambitions of the company and its chairman, a position Gussie Busch would hold with an iron grip until 1977.

The beer coming out of Bohemia in the Austrian Empire in the late 1800s had at some point earned the sobriquet "the beer of kings." One theory went that the golden, crisp pilsner invented in this region had won the hearts and mouths of the royal court in Vienna, and perhaps other royal courts around beer-drinking Europe. Another held that it was the specific unofficial slogan for the specific pilsner coming out of that small Bohemian city of České Budějovice—or Budweis in German—the same city from which Carl Conrad and Adolphus Busch had taken the name for their Budweiser pilsner in the United States. Whatever its origin, the phrase "the beer of kings"

This postcard shows the Anheuser-Busch bottling operation in St. Louis around the turn of the twentieth century. Courtesy of and used with permission of Anheuser-Busch. All rights reserved

came into the twentieth century describing, in some circles at least, some of the pilsner from Bohemia. Adolphus Busch himself likely knew this. In the 1890s his brewery adopted the phrase "the king of bottled beers" to describe Anheuser-Busch's increasing dominance of that then-newfangled packaging. The brewery did not, however, start using its 1968 slogan until after that year's trademarking. The slogan, though, was a clear reference to the old country and its wondrous contribution to the world of beer, a contribution that was still peaking as the twentieth century commenced its closing run. For that slogan for Budweiser was "the King of Beers."

34

"YECCCH"

1970–1975 | Chicago

Mike Royko was one of the most read newspaper columnists in America at a time when most people got their news from newspapers. He was one of the most prolific too. The forty-year-old with bushy brown hair and eyebrows on a thin face propping up thick glasses wrote five columns a week for the *Chicago Daily News*, and those columns found their ways into other newspapers through syndication. Mostly, Royko wrote about dirty politics and dirty politicians—Chicago provided a veritable buffet of both—but in early 1973 the recently minted Pulitzer Prize winner in the commentary category turned his scope on another subject entirely: beer. Specifically, Royko went after his home country's beer, for his home country produced most of the world's most famous beer. And, to Royko, it all tasted awful.

"I have tried them all," Royko wrote in a column published May 22, 1973. "I've grabbed for all the gusto I can get. I've said it all when I've said Bud." Royko was referencing two popular taglines for Schlitz and Budweiser, respectively. And, as an air force veteran and a denizen of what was then America's second-most populous city, Royko probably had had good access to an enormous variety of the most popular beers since World War II. The problem for Royko was that this variety was one of brand, not palate. The beers looked different and they had different marketing jingles helping along their soft sells, but they all tasted to him rather similar. They were light, in color and in taste, and relentlessly bubbly and barely bitter. To the astute newspaperman, it was as if the dwindling number of American breweries had settled upon a single formula but cleverly poured it into different packages. Or, as Royko memorably put it in that same column, "regardless of what label or slogan you use, it all tastes as if the secret brewing process involved running it through a horse."

Readers did not receive Royko's pronouncement gingerly. "Go to hell, if you don't like this country's beer," one reader wrote in. "Maybe you'll like what you are served there." Another suggested, "Love it or leave it," perhaps referring to America at large and not just its beer.

That Royko's column struck a nerve was not a surprise. Beer, especially the most popular brands based on pilsner, was everywhere in a way that no other alcoholic beverage could match. The bourbon boom had drastically subsided by 1973. There was even talk of the once-vaunted American spirit becoming virtually extinct by century's end. Also, vodka was still yet to peak, with the American debut of the Swedish brand Absolut more than five years off. Neither advertised as much as beer, and neither was as readily available from as many retailers.

The only beverage that came close was wine. The vast majority of it in the United States was as cheap and unremarkable as much of the beer, another by-product in part of the general American pivot to blandness after the war. It was an era before fine wine, too, with all its myriad varietals and descriptors, when most of the fruit of the vine was fortified hooch in screw-top bottles and the adjective "oaky" might still refer only to trees. About six months before Royko's column, in fact, *Time* magazine had celebrated the success of brothers Ernest and Julio Gallo with a cover story praising their California wine juggernaut, which leaned heavily on wines sold mostly in jugs and with little to nothing on the label to tell consumers where the grapes came from or when they were harvested. Still, this plonk proved remarkably resilient—"the Gallo Winery sold one hundred million gallons last year," *Time* raved—and wine in general probably vied with beer in the early 1970s as America's most popular alcoholic beverage.

But beer had an edge wine did not. It had that ubiquity. It was on billboards and on television and radio, in sports stadiums and arenas, in magazines and newspapers, on coasters and on the sides of trucks and on the sides of buildings. Breweries contracted out clothing—T-shirts, swimsuits, hats, sweatshirts, and more—and sold various gadgetries for making drinking that much easier, including bottle openers, can cozies, and glassware. "Beer is the star of the summer season," the *New York Times* declared of an upcoming TV season in the 1970s. The article underscored yet another sign of beer's omnipresence: for the first time in the United States, beer enjoyed copious press coverage.

There had been articles on beer and brewing going back to at least the German migratory infusion of the 1840s, but by the early 1970s a week did not seem to pass without the large or midsize dailies or weeklies dissecting aspects of the beer business. Usually the coverage focused on marketing or production moves—rarely, if ever, on styles. A long *New York Times* piece in

December 1975 on the popularity of Colorado-brewed Coors in the eastern United States, where it was not yet distributed, did not mention pilsner at all, though Coors itself threw the style name across its cans, bottles, and other packaging. "Coors is a light-bodied beer, meaning it is brewed with less malt, fewer hops, and more rice than beers with tangy taste," was about as close as the *Times* writer was willing to get stylistically—that and, "Coors does seem almost flavorless, and it is this quality that could account for its popularity among young people just starting to get acquainted with the pleasures of beer drinking."

This was generous. Most of the articles on the business of beer then barely touched on style. Pilsner had so taken over that it and its iterations were synonymous with beer. Beer was light and bright, barely bitter, and very dry. And, to an increasing multitude, it was indeed "almost flavorless." Following the backlash to his May 1973 newspaper column, Mike Royko arranged what was likely the first blind beer taste test in a major English-language outlet. It was done partly tongue in cheek, but its results were telling and devastating. Royko had eleven men and women sample twenty-two domestically available beers, and rate them on a 1-to-5 point system with 1 "barely drinkable" and 5 "great." The *Chicago Daily News* published the results in July. A pilsner from a brewery near Frankfurt, West Germany, finished first, with the Burton-upon-Trent classic Bass Ale finishing second and a pilsner from a Wisconsin regional brewery called Stevens Point finishing third. Heineken was fourth. Pilsner Urquell, the signature beer from the Burghers' Brewery in pilsner's Bohemian birthplace, finished toward the middle. Budweiser, perhaps the most popular pilsner of all time, finished dead last. Regarding Bud, the judges were merciless: "a picnic beer smell," "lousy," "Alka Seltzer," "yeccch."

Very well. But such dismissals mattered little to the business side of pilsner. Most of the style's biography since World War II had had to do with what happened outside the brewery anyway. The latest tweaks in the 1950s were a response to shifting consumer demand, not to any seismic changes in beer or brewing. Those had all come a long time ago and appeared to be permanently in pilsner's rearview. So at a time when public rebukes such as those from America's top newspaper columnist or from the *New York Times* might have led the world's largest pilsner producers to pivot in terms of taste, they instead doubled down.

35

LITE AND EVERYTHING AFTER

1975–1982 | Munich; Milwaukee

George Weissman and John Murphy were on a business trip in Munich in what was then West Germany in 1972 when Murphy suggested they have beer with one of their dinners. It was not an unusual suggestion at all, for the two Bronx natives together controlled the destiny of what would turn out to be the decade's fastest-growing brewery. Weissman was chairman of tobacco giant Philip Morris, which over the past few years had acquired full control of the Miller Brewing Company from a company that had bought it in the late 1960s from the descendants of Frederick Miller himself. Weissman was a navy veteran—he had enlisted the day after Pearl Harbor and spent World War II chasing submarines and bombing beachheads. He liked to say that he embodied the Marlboro Man, the iconic Philip Morris cigarette soft sell that he had done a lot to further. "I'm no cowboy and I don't ride horseback, but I like to think I have the freedom the Marlboro man exemplifies." That braggadocio reflected the craggy-faced Weissman's background as a journalist, Hollywood publicist, and advertising man before joining Philip Morris in the early 1950s and working his way to the top position.

His dinner companion for the evening was the six-foot-three, 250-pound Murphy, a lawyer who had been with Philip Morris since 1962 and had been president and chief executive of Miller Brewing since just after the tobacco giant took it over. Murphy liked to joke that it was the dream of any good Irishman to run a brewery. So his suggestion of beers with dinner that evening in Munich was doubly unsurprising.

Yet Weissman was on a diet. Might the waiter recommend a beer that was not too heavy? The waiter recommended a diät pilsner. Despite the name—*diät* is "diet" in German—this pilsner iteration had nothing to do with conventional dieting. It had emerged out of northern Germany after World War II as a pilsner for diabetics, with especially thorough fermentations draining much of the residual sugars from the beer and leaving

211

behind an exceptionally dry, pale body. However, those thorough fermentations meant generally high alcohol contents—especially for a pilsner—and that meant more calories. So perhaps the waiter's recommendation was lost in translation, and Weissman took him very literally. Whatever the reason, Weissman and Murphy ordered the diät pilsner. The waiter brought it, the two sipped it, and Murphy had an idea: "There's room for something like this in America."

The epiphany would change not only brewing and the life of beer's most popular style but a sizable chunk of popular culture, too. Murphy exhibited a keen knack for marketing that Weissman, the former Hollywood PR and Manhattan adman, supported. It was not necessarily, then, that Murphy saw room for another bone-dry pilsner with little bitterness and lots of bubbles. Mergers and acquisitions were the meta-trend in the industry, after all, something that Philip Morris' blockbuster deal for Miller—which involved out-maneuvering fellow suitor PepsiCo—exemplified. Instead, Murphy saw the potential in "diät" or "diet" as he and most people understood it: something lighter in calories and not just appearance or taste. And that understanding planted the seed that bloomed into nearly half the American beer market before the decade's end and came to dominate sales internationally, to boot.

Breweries had poked at the idea of light beer before, almost invariably playing off a pilsner already in a brewery's stable. Just add water—that seemed to be the animating approach. Not surprisingly perhaps, none met with sustained success until advances in the late 1960s. The most notable example before then was from Piels. That Brooklyn brewery had a light beer offering going back to at least just after World War II, and produced another called Trommers Red Letter via the Brooklyn plant of a competitor it had acquired in the 1950s. Liebmann Breweries—later called Rheingold after its most popular brand and acquired by Pepsi-Cola United Bottlers in 1964—had bought Trommers' other plant, in New Jersey's Essex County. Piels Light and Trommers Red Letter did not move the commercial needle much. Any lightness was due more to that wateriness than to any low calorie count. It was not until Rheingold took a more ground-up approach that light beer's fortunes began to change.

With the Trommers attempt perhaps as inspiration, a biochemist at Rheingold named Joseph Owades discovered a way to isolate an enzyme that could break down higher-calorie starches and make them easier for yeast to devour. The result was a lower-calorie beer with some semblance of beery taste left over. What Rheingold called Gablinger's Diet Beer should have been a breakthrough, but the brewery gummed up the marketing upon its December

1966 debut in upstate New York and Connecticut. The name itself was clunky, and the advertisements had none of the smooth soft sell of beer ads then. One early commercial had an obese man scarfing spaghetti with one hand while drinking a Gablinger's with the other. The ad was not subtle, and it did not make sense—beer was not going to be the man's answer for losing weight, no matter how low in calories. "Not only did no one want to try the beer," Owades remembered, "they couldn't even stand to look at this guy!" Further appeals to Gablinger's dietary lightness, including a somewhat stern-looking anonymous doctor staring out from its cans, flopped too. It just seemed that nobody thought of beer as a way to lose weight or keep off the pounds.

Federal government pushback and a lawsuit from a German brewery compounded Rheingold's troubles in rolling out Gablinger's. Regulators claimed that the brewery misled consumers into thinking the beer was indeed a dietary product. The government—perturbed in particular that Rheingold did not list the calorie count on Gablinger's packaging, as the law required of any foodstuffs sold for "special dietary uses"—went so far as to seize shipments of the light beer in December 1967. Rheingold eventually agreed to alter its labeling to make sure people knew the beer inside was not for dieting or dieters necessarily. The same month as that seizure, though, the US importer for a Hamburg brewery that had pioneered the spread of diät pilsner sued Rheingold for false advertising and for falsely claiming to be a diet beer in the German tradition. Rheingold would countersue. All this—the advertising misfires, the government crackdown, the lawsuit and countersuit—combined to doom Gablinger's in the marketplace and to eventually help croak Rheingold itself in the mid-1970s.

Light beer might have finally died there or at least never have broken through were it not for a competitor in the Second City. Rheingold either gave Joseph Owades permission or the biochemist took it upon himself—the impetus would never be clear—to share his recipe with a friend from a Chicago brewery called Meister Bräu, which a Prussian immigrant named Peter Hand had started the previous century and which prominently advertised its signature Meister Bräu beer as of the "genuine pilsner type" on cans and other packaging. Meister Bräu would try out Owades's recipe on that signature beer, releasing a Meister Bräu Lite in May 1967, a few months after the Gablinger's rollout. The misspelling of "light" appeared deliberate, a way to catch consumers' attention, though usage of "lite" likely stretched back to the nineteenth century, when it meant exactly what these marketers in the late twentieth wanted it to mean: not heavy. Meister Bräu Lite even slapped things such as "non-filling" and "one-third less calories than our regular beer" in black letters on the blue-and-white cans, and enlisted a lithe twenty-one-year-old woman to be the exceedingly fit face of the beer.

But the brewery was also careful to note that the beer was "full strength" and "non-dietetic." "Meister Bräu gives you more of what you drink beer for," ran one print ad. It was as if the Chicago brewery was trying to have it both ways, and for a time it did. Meister Bräu Lite proved an initial success locally and then nationally—thanks in part to a licensing agreement that saw the P. Ballantine & Sons brewery of Newark producing it for the East Coast—but it could not save the brewery from the fate of so many others. It faced legal pushback of its own from Rheingold, which in 1968 scored a patent on its low-calorie beer approach, and began to wobble financially. The recently acquired Miller itself acquired Meister Bräu in 1972, and with it the Meister Bräu Lite brand and formula.

So the glory for this latest iteration of pilsner, an iteration that would prove as influential as or even more so than American brewers' embrace of rice and corn in the late nineteenth century, ended up belonging not to Owades, Rheingold, or Meister Bräu but to Miller and its parent, Phillip Morris. Under the direction of master brewer and Miller vice president Clement Meyn, Meister Bräu Lite's new keeper tweaked the recipe to create—in Miller's own official words—"a low-calorie brew that tasted like beer." The brewery then began test-marketing what it called Miller Lite, instead of Meister Bräu Lite, in August 1973 in Providence, Rhode Island, Knoxville, Tennessee, San Diego, and Decatur, Illinois. Crucially, Miller ran as far away from dieting as it could when it came to hawking this new beer. Instead, at John Murphy's urging and with the help of Manhattan-based advertising giant McCann Erickson, Miller went the soft sell route, hiring professional athletes to tout Miller Lite's supposed drinkability. The beer would run behind tags such as "Great taste, less filling" and "Everything you always wanted in a beer. And less." These were decidedly more rugged and direct than the even softer sell behind Miller's other major offering at the time, the bubbly, crisp Miller High Life, which the brewery since the early part of the century had been calling "the champagne of beers."

By early 1975 Miller was confident enough to uncork the biggest attempt yet to sell light beer to a mass market. Miller began rolling out white-and-blue cans and bottles of Miller Lite just after New Year's Day. Smack in the middle of the largely white labels—in a seal wreathed in gold and hemmed by barley stalks and surrounding a sheaf of the same—were the words "a fine pilsner beer." Given the success that Miller Lite would enjoy, this would likely be the term's greatest exposure. The only thing that likely came close was Heineken's earlier regular use of "pilsener" on its labels and packaging. For Miller Lite did become unusually ubiquitous unusually fast.

Miller's 1975 introduction of Miller Lite, which it labeled from the start "a fine pilsner beer," upended the brewing industry and profoundly affected popular culture. Courtesy of MillerCoors Archives

Part of that was the modern brewing industry and the place of American breweries in it—the distribution reach, the production capacity, the advertising muscle—but another part was just that this particular twist in the story of pilsner clicked. Miller Lite did have a drinkability to it at a time when consumers were returning to the fold following that alarming drop in consumption in the 1950s. It was only mildly bitter, even slightly sweet, and foamed like high tide. And it was lower in calories than other bigger brands, however Miller Lite's maker tried to mute that fact in the marketing. America was just entering the throes of a diet craze in the late 1970s that would flower in the next fifteen years with hundreds of exercise videos for newfangled VCRs, a boom in home exercise equipment, and gym chains such as Crunch, Planet Fitness, Bally Total Fitness, and Equinox launching. John Murphy and the Miller Brewing Company might not have wanted consumers to think of Miller Lite as a diet beer, but almost certainly many people did. Finally, the brewery wrapped its new offering in that great American obsession: sports. It spent some of its nearly $250 million ad budget for Miller Lite's first seven years on exclusive rights to commercials on *Monday Night Football*—probably the most watched regular television show on the globe—and the *College Football Game of the Week.*

The pilsner itself and the marketing behind it paid off spectacularly for Miller. The brewery went from the eighth largest in the nation in 1970 to the third largest within twenty-four months of the release of Miller Lite—"a meteoric and unprecedented rise," according to the *New York Times.* Miller's production levels bounced 43 percent as the rest of the domestic brewing industry's increased barely 2 percent. It was assumed that Miller would soon once and for all nudge Schlitz or Pabst or whatever other dowager from the number-two spot and set up its long-awaited showdown with number one Anheuser-Busch. The pair were already gobbling up smaller competitors and expanding distribution deeper into more and more markets. The *New York Times* predicted in August 1977 that Anheuser-Busch and Miller could capture half the beer sales in the United States by the end of the decade, and then turn their respective forces on the globe, where each already had an expanding footprint. Pilsner was reaching farther and further than ever before behind this mounting rivalry.

Anheuser-Busch answered the success of Miller Lite with its Natural Light in 1977, its Michelob Light in 1978, and what it originally called Budweiser Light in 1982—each at a different price point to capture that much more of the burgeoning light beer market. Andrew Steinhubl, Anheuser-Busch's vice president of brewing, oversaw these creations. "We're looking for consistency and control, and especially to maintain quality," Steinhubl, whose eyebrows on his ruddy face arched in seemingly perpetual amusement beneath a bald pate, described it to a reporter the year after Budweiser Light's introduction. That consistency involved regular taste tests among Steinhubl and several other professional brewers and others in a climate-controlled room atop Anheuser-Busch's St. Louis hub, the atmosphere pin-drop quiet and the beer cooled to a precise forty-two degrees. "It's hard work, but it's enjoyable," Steinhubl would say.

Other larger breweries, both foreign and domestic, would introduce their own versions of lower-calorie, thinner pilsners during the decade after Miller Lite's 1975 commercial earthquake. None would overtake it in terms of influence. For what John Murphy and Miller had unlocked in the early 1970s "took on a life of its own," according to the *New York Times.* Light, or lite, became synonymous not only with lower-calorie fare—more than 350 new products adopted the adjective during the first half of the 1980s, according to one estimate—but with the idea of lightness in terms of "diminishing substance:

relationships, entertainment, politics, work, health," as one chronicler put it. The marketing twist that Miller pioneered for its new pilsner would therefore end up clanging around the commercial marketplace and popular culture for decades—"Murphy was right beyond anything he could have imagined," as the *New York Times* put it after John Murphy died in 2002—proving a remarkably influential twist in this most influential of beer styles.

It could have also served as an ending to the story of pilsner. The rest of the tale might have been merely recounting how Miller, which did rise to the number-two spot in America behind its Miller Lite, and Anheuser-Busch sorted out the world beer market with advertising, marketing, and carefully screened new products. For that was what was destined to happen by and large. At least on the business side of pilsner. On the style side, it was a different story.

36

A FINAL TWIST

1976–1996 | Boulder, Colorado; Sonoma, California; Louvain, Belgium

For five hours in the late afternoon and early evening of Friday, June 4, 1982, some 850 paying guests strolled through and stopped at twenty-two spots within the five-thousand-square-foot ballroom of the Hilton Harvest House in downtown Boulder, Colorado. At each spot, the guests at the first Great American Beer Festival could sample a different brewery's beer, including those from larger concerns such as pilsner-fueled Coors, which was based nearby in Golden, Colorado, and the Rochester, New York, operation Genesee, which still clung to commercial relevance behind its cream ale. Then there were much smaller operations that few had ever heard of, such as an operation out of the then-remote northern California city of Chico called the Sierra Nevada Brewing Company. The brewers poured samples for the guests, who included not only brewing suppliers and the event's organizers but also members of a new field of American letters: beer critics. Fred Eckhardt was among the bunch.

Eckhardt was a former marine who had developed a preference for the Danish pilsner Tuborg during service as a radio operator in the Korean War, bringing the taste for it home to Portland, Oregon, where he worked as a photographer, among other trades. Tuborg was not as readily available stateside, but recognition that there was a wider beer world out there led Eckhardt to immerse himself in brewing. The move put the compact Eckhardt—balding in his postmilitary days and sporting a carefully curated handlebar mustache—in the vanguard of the few people paying attention to what Fritz Maytag had started in 1965 with his financial rescue of the Anchor Brewing Company in San Francisco. Eckhardt had visited Maytag and Anchor in 1968 and had photographed and written about what would come to be called the last craft brewery in the world's biggest beer market—an independently owned brewery that made its beers in more traditional methods from recipes free of adjuncts such as corn and rice.

Another member of the vanguard was one of the organizers of the June 4 event at the Boulder Hilton. Charlie Papazian had studied nuclear engineering at the University of Virginia, before heading to Colorado after graduation in 1972 to bunk with a friend's brother while Papazian figured out what to do with his life. Wiry thin and woolly bearded, Papazian found work as a preschool teacher by day. At night, he taught homebrewing, a hobby he had picked up through a neighbor of a friend back in Charlottesville.

The hobby was technically illegal. Through a quirk of oversight, the federal government had legalized—or relegalized—home winemaking after the repeal of Prohibition in 1933. Homebrewing was left in limbo. People took it up—often out of desperation because so much available beer tasted like the same few spins on pilsner—but they took it up quietly, sharing supplies and recipes surreptitiously and sometimes wondering when it all might crash. Papazian himself thought that if the feds raided one of his evening homebrewing classes it would be good publicity. He did not seem to give much thought to up to five years in prison and a $10,000 fine, both possibilities under the law. As it turned out, the federal government did not prosecute anyone for homebrewing from 1933 onward, though state governments were known to crack down. In probably the most famous instance, Kentucky authorities charged a couple in 1962 with "illegal possession of alcoholic beverage." Such stories and the federal warnings fostered a climate of mild fear. "Nobody wanted to be a test case" for the federal government, according to Byron Burch, another homebrewing instructor who was at that first Great American Beer Festival. When Burch toured Anchor Brewing with Fritz Maytag for research for a homebrewing guide in the early 1970s, Maytag politely asked Burch not to mention him by name in the subsequent book.

As it was, though, in the shadows of the law and of the increasing predominance of Budweiser, Miller Lite, and other bigger pilsner producers, these homebrewers grew in number and skill. Homebrewing clubs popped up, starting with the Maltose Falcons out of Los Angeles in 1974, and the underground movement coalesced in a major way through the American Homebrewers Association, which Charlie Papazian and a friend founded in 1978. It was less a formal organization than an informal network, a method for more readily sharing information about a hobby that many would liken to a passion. Plus, not a few of these homebrewers had dreams of turning professional. One finally did.

In late 1976, a former navy mechanic named Jack McAuliffe cobbled together financing and secondhand dairy equipment to launch what he called the New Albion Brewing Company in Sonoma, California. He had learned to homebrew while stationed in Scotland, having fallen in love with the richer brews available in that part of the United Kingdom, which had not fallen under pilsner's sway as fully as had places farther south and on the Continent. The beers that McAuliffe made in New Albion's makeshift brewery in one-half of a grape warehouse in California wine country were all ales—richer, darker, and stronger in alcohol than the pilsners so widely available then. He did not have many sales accounts, and the whole thing was hands-on, door-to-door, an all-around arduous and unprofitable affair. A federal excise tax cut on smaller breweries in 1976—which larger breweries pushed for in a bid to boost beer consumption overall—helped by lowering operating costs and would have an outsized effect on aiding other smaller breweries in opening. But for McAuliffe the help came too late, and people were simply unfamiliar with what he was trying to do with these often complex-tasting ales, so dominant was pilsner at the time.

"The people who sit at a bar and drink eight or nine bottles of Budweiser are not going to be the people who drink New Albion," Suzy Stern, an investor in New Albion who also helped McAuliffe at the brewery, told *Newsweek* for a September 1978 article on the battle for marketplace dominance between Anheuser-Busch and Miller. *Newsweek* called New Albion "America's small-est brewery," and that would be how it passed into lore, for Jack McAuliffe's stab at small-batch, traditional, independent brewing died the same year as that first Great American Beer Festival in Boulder.

It was not before New Albion, though, like the rescued Anchor, served as a living classroom for others interested in standing athwart pilsner and yelling stop. One visitor to both New Albion before it closed and to Anchor was a rumpled, plump Englishman with bushy brown hair and a bushy brown mus-tache, who favored screaming ties and sported oval, owlish glasses. Michael Jackson—the name sprung from the anglicization of his Lithuanian Jewish surname—had worked as a journalist since dropping out of high school in northern England in the late 1950s. He had worked for the broadsheets and tabloids of Fleet Street, getting side work in production and writing for British television. But his career took a final and momentous turn in the mid-1970s when a publisher hired him to pick up another writer's dropped contract for a tome on that great staple of English life: the pub. That book on the history and culture of the pub led to another work, published in the United Kingdom in 1977 and later in the United States, that became the most influential book on beer of the twentieth century.

Jackson's *World Guide to Beer* functioned as a kind of excavation site for styles and approaches that pilsner's rise over more than a century and a half had all but chucked into the ash heap of history. It also served as a roadmap for the burgeoning numbers of homebrewers and other enthusiasts for any style that was not pilsner. Jackson highlighted pilsner's dominance in his *World Guide* chapter on the United States, which he noted "produces a greater volume of beer, by far, than any other country." But that did not necessarily mean the United States led in terms of taste. "The big brewers of the United States lead the world in the production of light-bodied and exceptionally mild-tasting beers in a very distant derivation of the Pilsener (or, to be more general, Bohemian) style of lager." Jackson plunged on with a backhanded compliment that perfectly encapsulated what pilsner had become by then and how it was perceived.

> These mass-market beers are made to the highest standards of quality control, but they are more notable for their consistency than for their individuality. They are the beer world's answer to a generic Chablis rather than a Chardonnay from Burgundy. Their first intention is to win widespread acceptance. They seek to offend no one, and therefore offer little to excite anyone. Should any drinker nonetheless become excited, there's always the option of an even lighter-bodied version of the same style. This is identified, with breathtaking understatement, as "light beer." (The world's precursor to "light wine"; what else?)
>
> These mass-market products are advertised so heavily that many Americans are unaware of any others. Foreigners can be forgiven for a similar ignorance.

This decidedly low opinion of American beer probably fueled Jackson's supposed answer when Charlie Papazian told him of his plans to launch the Great American Beer Festival: "That's a great idea, Charlie. Only what will you serve for beer?" Papazian had solicited Jackson's reaction at another national gathering that seemed a little too big for its britches: the Great British Beer Festival. That festival had grown out of the Campaign for Real Ale, or CAMRA, a volunteer group that four men from northwest England formed one day in a pub in the far western Ireland town of Dunquin in 1971. CAMRA was a direct reaction to the members' belief that the beer in the British Isles was becoming entirely too homogenized and industrialized, not least because of the importation of foreign-brewed pilsners. Heineken in particular had permeated pubs and markets. Believing that the Brits preferred less of a punch in their lagers, Heineken in the 1970s introduced a lower-alcohol version of its famed pilsner specifically for the British market. The Dutch company that Freddy Heineken led used catchy marketing to sell the special pilsner—"In the early 1970s, Heineken was only 3.5 percent alcohol, but 96.5 percent advertising," one wag put it—and it worked. Heineken pilsner dominated the British lager market for the last three decades of the twentieth century.

So along came CAMRA to try to counter that with an almost fanatic devotion to the sort of traditional English pub that Michael Jackson wrote about and to what was known as cask ale or real ale. That was ale—*not* lager—made traditionally and served as fresh as possible, preferably from the last vessel used to ferment it, without the aid of extra carbon dioxide to help form a foamy head. CAMRA launched the first Great British Beer Festival in celebration of real ale in late September 1977 in London's Alexandra Palace. Seven hundred volunteers poured more than two hundred thousand pints of more than one hundred different ales for an estimated five thousand attendees.

Like that of the American Homebrewers Association and despite the numbers at that first beer fest, CAMRA's reach was initially small and niche. Its membership long seemed confined to "middle-aged men with beards and sandals," according to one chronicler. And the American Homebrewers Association's membership was so small that that first Great American Beer Festival in 1982 had just about every prominent member of the group or ally right there in the Boulder Hilton ballroom, including Michael Jackson, who must surely have been impressed that the Yanks had at least seen the thing through. The Homebrewers Association and CAMRA members also shared a realization that each organization arrived at independently: the old ways were in danger of being lost for good and somebody better do something about it. CAMRA's short-lived original name—the Campaign for the Revitalization of Ale—spoke to that directly. Beer was a millennia-old beverage once made in a kaleidoscope of styles in usually hands-on ways and with as much precision and care as human patience could muster. The meteoric rise of pilsner during the past 150 years—not really that long a time in the life span of beer—had drowned or nearly drowned so many of those styles with its popularity and had threatened so many of those ways with its industrialized engineering. These sapling movements were the direct reactions to that and would become globally influential in their own rights, not least through inspiring and aiding the likes of Jack McAuliffe to start breweries and rejuvenate styles such as India pale ale and porter.

For except for Guinness and its sweet, dark stout, all the world's largest brewing companies leaned on pilsner. It was what sold. Consumer demand had decided that decades before, not the breweries. This was true even if an individual brewing company's host nation also hosted a particularly rich brewing history. Belgium was probably the best example in the 1980s. "No other nation has a more colorful, individualistic, or idiosyncratic assortment of beers," Michael Jackson wrote of the Maryland-sized kingdom in his *World Guide to Beer*. "Many towns and breweries like to think of their style of beer as being exclusively their own." Yet Belgium's largest brewer by the 1980s was Interbrew, a conglomerate based out of Louvain, east of Brussels, that was best known for Stella Artois, a pilsner it had been making since 1923. By the 1980s Interbrew was aggressively positioning Stella Artois as a premium brand globally to compete with Heineken's flagship pilsner, including through print advertisements introduced in the United Kingdom in 1982 and the later carefully curated placement of the beer in trendsetting bars and restaurants in the United States. This was despite the fact that, like Heineken in the Netherlands, Stella Artois in Belgium was considered an everyday cheap beer.

At the same time as it was pushing its leading pilsner to a wider audience, Interbrew also started gobbling up breweries and brands throughout the world, amassing a stable that included Canada's Labatt, America's Rolling Rock, and, perhaps most momentously for the story of pilsner, Spaten in Germany. Heineken itself was on a shopping spree, adding the Dreher breweries that had originated with Anton Dreher's family the century before, and boasting an international footprint in terms of production and sales second only to Anheuser-Busch, with brands such as Amstel and Cobra and production holdings in places as varied as Ghana and Indonesia. Heineken's humble origins in 1860s Amsterdam seemed as distant as Anheuser-Busch's origins in St. Louis during the same decade. It was said that Interbrew had developed Stella Artois as a special Christmastime beer for the Brussels-area market. That, too, seemed quaint several decades on.

As would the beginnings of craft beer, eventually. It would grow from its own almost laughably humble origins via events such as the first few Great American Beer Festivals and breweries such as Anchor and New Albion to heights unimaginable to people like Michael Jackson and those who knew enough to read him. Simple demand would drive much of that growth, the same as had driven the rise of the likes of Heineken and Anheuser-Busch. The two—macro and micro brewing—would run parallel to one another throughout the 1980s and into the 1990s, though one a bull elephant and the other a gnat at its tail in zigzag flight. One would stick to a particular kind of lager, pilsner, that had served it so amazingly, and the other would stick largely to ales, though with a few lagers. It was only in the mid-1990s that micro and macro beer began to converge in a meaningful way, and, in doing so, to provide the latest—and, so far, last—twist in the story of pilsner.

37

SNOW AND REIGN

1982–2018 | Downingtown, Pennsylvania; Shenyang, China; Pilsen

In the early 1990s Ron Barchet and Bill Covaleski were working on the production sides at breweries in Virginia and Maryland. These breweries had been part of a wave of openings over the past ten years as what came to be called craft brewing toddled forth from Northern California and Colorado and spread across the nation and then the world. The legalization of homebrewing at the federal level in early 1978 had helped, as had that excise tax cut on barrels of beer in 1976. The former brought the hobbyists out of the legal shadows to better share information and material, and the latter made start-up and operating costs for smaller breweries that much cheaper. Moreover, various older craft operations, especially Anchor Brewing in San Francisco, had provided inspiration and, in some cases, guidance for younger breweries.

The commercial success of two craft brands in particular had shown just how brightly a reaction to the wares of Anheuser-Busch and Miller could burn. Jim Koch, a management consultant in Boston whose family had worked in brewing, launched with a partner and several investors what he called the Boston Beer Company in 1984, with a flagship called Samuel Adams Boston Lager. Koch, working with Joseph Owades, the biochemist behind light beer, patterned it after the Vienna lager style that Anton Dreher had pioneered. Maltier and darker than almost any domestic beer on the market, Samuel Adams spread to near-national distribution before the end of the 1980s. Pete Slosberg, a computer engineer in Silicon Valley who homebrewed on the side, enjoyed similar success with his Pete's Brewing Company, which started around the same time as Boston Beer. Its flagship was Pete's Wicked, a brown ale. It was also unlike much of what was on the market—an old English style amid the Czech-inspired pilsner iterations—but it too proved successful enough to achieve near-national distribution. Neither Koch nor Slosberg owned breweries, however. Other breweries with excess capacity made their Samuel Adams and Pete's Wicked under contract, which freed Koch and

Slosberg to shovel money into marketing. Still, the success of their brands in the late 1980s helped lift craft brewing to the eye level of consumers.

The number of US breweries grew behind this and other successes from fewer than one hundred in 1982, the year of that first Great American Beer Festival, to just over six hundred in 1994. That was the year—it was on New Year's Eve 1993, in fact, over bottles of the Belgian ale Chimay in Covaleski's Baltimore home—that Ron Barchet and Bill Covaleski started sketching plans for their own brewery. That brewery would come to fruition in early 1996 in the small Pennsylvania borough of Downingtown, about thirty-five miles west of Philadelphia. Barchet and Covaleski, friends since childhood, called it the Victory Brewing Company, and led with three beers: a märzen beer (that might have been familiar to Gabriel Sedlmayr, the style's progenitor), a strong lager in another German tradition (both men had studied brewing in Germany), and an India pale ale.

That last style had had an interesting shelf life after pilsner pushed it aside in the marketplace. The largest IPA producer in the United States and maybe the Western Hemisphere, P. Ballantine & Sons, had staggered into the 1970s amid slumping sales and other financial losses. This was due almost entirely to that pivot in the marketplace in the 1950s and 1960s. "The housewife doing the supermarket shopping also picked up the beer," the *New York Times* explained, "and the American taste turned to lighter and lighter brews. Ballantine officials decided their product was too heavy, but by the time they changed it in 1965, the company was on its way to a $6.5 million losing year in 1966 on sales of $90 million." Brief ownership of the NBA's Boston Celtics in the late 1960s could not spur a turnaround, and an entity called the Investors Funding Corporation bought Ballantine in 1969. That company closed Ballantine's Newark plant in 1972, and another owner, St. Louis–based Falstaff, announced it would keep brewing Ballantine IPA and other brands at its own breweries elsewhere. But Ballantine IPA basically petered out commercially. Pabst bought Falstaff in 1985 and moved IPA production to its Milwaukee brewery. But when Pabst shuttered that brewery in 1996, Ballantine IPA essentially died.

By then, though, craft beer was well on its way to resurrecting IPA stylistically and commercially, which it did by the time the slim, spectacled Bill Covaleski, who sported a near buzz cut, fired up Victory's small brewhouse around the start of 1996. It was an interesting handoff in a way between macro and micro brewing, one that would have been unfathomable only a short while before.

Craft breweries from coast to coast, particularly in Northern California, started offering IPAs. Often riotously bitter with a sizable alcoholic kick and a citrusy and chewy mouthfeel, these IPAs were as far as one might get from pilsner in the 1990s, and that was kind of the point. What became the style most associated with American craft beer was a direct reaction to pilsner's hegemony. "Anheuser-Busch's quality—if quality is consistency—is second to none," Sam Calagione, the muscular, square-jawed founder of Dogfish Head Craft Brewery, and one of the biggest popularizers of IPA in the 1990s, told a reporter. "But I'm frustrated that one beer has been hammered down people's throats." Calagione's Delaware operation would put a fine point on its opinion of contemporary pilsner with an annual summer event, opened to the public, that involved literally catapulting dozens of cans of the bigger producers' brands hundreds of yards into a sculpture of a giant toilet.

The watershed for IPA's resurrection was likely the success of Sierra Nevada Pale Ale, which the Sierra Nevada Brewing Company in Northern California started selling at the start of the 1980s. Like with pilsners, IPAs did not always adopt the name on the packaging and marketing. But Sierra Nevada's offering was citrusy and bitter, a full-bodied beer that was as honey colored as pilsners were golden hued. Besides, Sierra Nevada cofounder Ken Grossman would tell people he had been a big fan of Ballantine's IPA, and rumors would circulate that the yeast for his pale ale came from scraping off some from that much older beer. Sierra Nevada Pale Ale was one of the most recognized craft brands in the country by the time the Lagunitas Brewing Company, also of Northern California, became in 1995 the first US brewery to lead with an IPA. There was no going back commercially after that.

So it was not surprising that Victory Brewing itself led in large part with an IPA in 1996. What was surprising was that later that same year the infant company decided to release a pilsner as one of its first packaged beers (rather than draft)—and to label it as such. Covaleski himself had his doubts. "Miller Lite was parading around as the true taste of pilsner beer," he thought. Victory's distributors reminded him of that as a warning. "You're walking into the biggest battle ever," one told Covaleski. "Everything's a pilsner beer, and none of them taste like yours. This is not going to be easy." None would taste like Victory's because Covaleski would brew with all malted barley and no adjuncts (as well as hops cultivated in Germany and Czechia). In many ways, what he and Barchet called Prima Pils would be a throwback to pilsner as it arrived in America in the 1840s and 1850s: pre-rice and pre-corn, before any additives and adjuncts to ease and speed brewing and to ensure a pilsner produced a head when it was poured hundreds, if not thousands, of miles from its brewery. It was a turn in the story of pilsner that would have been hard to see coming only a couple of decades before.

There it was, though. Victory Prima Pils debuted in 1996, first on draft and then packaged in the form of twelve-ounce bottles. There had been other smaller pilsner offerings from craft brewers, but Victory Prima Pils out of Downingtown would prove the most enduring with other craft brewers and their fans.

In 2005 and 2009, Prima Pils topped a taste test that *New York Times* wine critic Eric Asimov organized. It bested American comers as well as selections from Europe, including Pilsner Urquell from the Burghers' Brewery in Pilsen. "Our top beer, the Prima Pils from the Victory Brewing Company, sounded a clear chord with its vivacity and assertive bitterness," Asimov wrote in 2005. That the pilsner earned in the national newspaper of record the sort of adjectival nods normally reserved for wine—Asimov and his fellow judges also called Prima Pils "alive in the mouth, with citrus aromas and a fine bitterness"—said a lot not only about Covaleski and Barchet's particular offering but about the critical evolution of pilsner. Asimov and company's raves in

VICTORY PRIMA PILS

The stylized hop on the label is appropriate for this very bitter Pilsner made in Downingtown, Pennsylvania, by the Victory brewery and pub. It has a "fresh sea air" aroma of Saaz hops; almost gritty hop flavors; a lean malt background; and a firm, bitter finish. This Pilsner was inspired by the very hoppy example of the style made by the Vogelbräu brewery and pub in Karlsruhe, Germany.

Region of origin Northeast US

Style Pilsner

Alc. content 4.3 abw (5.4 abv)

Ideal serving temperature 48° F (9 °C)

Pennsylvania prime
The state of William Penn was once the heart of German brewing in the US. It bids to be so again.

Victory Prima Pils as described in Michael Jackson's 1998 guide *Ultimate Beer*. Among other things, craft beer's rise—and Jackson himself—ushered in the sorts of descriptors that critics normally reserved for wine. COURTESY OF BILL COVALESKI the *New York Times* were a far cry from Mike Royko's "brewed through a horse" column and follow-up in the *Chicago Daily News* three decades before.

Pilsner was regaining an evaluative footing it appeared to have lost forever coming out of Prohibition. People cared about how it looked and tasted beyond whether it looked and tasted the same wherever it was shipped or whether it was low in calories. Mass production was now presented as anathema to a style that critics and craft brewers, and craft brew fans, now celebrated as the height of the brewing arts. "It's a beer of great finesse," Garrett Oliver, brewmaster at Brooklyn Brewery in New York and one of the great raconteurs of the craft brewing age, wrote of pilsner at the start of the twenty-first century. "Brewers sometimes refer to pilsner, with some trepidation, as 'naked,' meaning that there's nowhere for imperfect flavors to hide." Beers that had become "more notable for their consistency than for their individuality," as Michael Jackson wrote of pilsners in 1977, were now assessed precisely for that individuality.

Or at least some were. While those craft creations such as Victory Prima Pils showed up in the *New York Times*, other newspapers, food magazines, or the multiplying number of beer blogs and review sites, most pilsners on earth remained and would remain the domain of Anheuser-Busch, Miller, Heineken, and Interbrew, or some partnership or venture that included one of them. Heineken had long ago planted beachheads in East Asia for its pilsners through breweries in onetime Dutch colonies, particularly Indonesia. But thanks in part to the growth of larger breweries such as Heineken and Anheuser-Busch and to growth in global and globalized trade, pilsner would flower in the 1990s and 2000s in East Asia to the point at which that region of the world became the most promising pilsner market.

China by itself emerged in the 1990s as the world's second-largest market for beer, period. It was a trend that both astounded and titillated executives at American- and European-based breweries. "When you travel around there, you find cities of ten million people that you've never heard of," said the international chief executive of Belgium's Interbrew after one jaunt through the world's most populous nation. Breweries from the United States and Europe acquired partnerships with Chinese breweries or, in most cases, built breweries there themselves. The same went for other nations in East Asia, including Thailand and Japan, and by the end of the century, pilsner-inspired or pilsner-based brands such as Tiger, Kirin, and Singha were more ubiquitous than ever, as was Tsingtao, the pilsner born of a European colonial incursion on the Chinese coast a century before. Like their macro counterparts in the United States and Europe, these offerings were "more toward the bland side, exhibiting less bitterness and character than true pilsners," as the *New York Times* put it. Still, pilsners they were, flowing down the throats every day of tens of millions of customers.

No East Asian beer did as well as Snow, a practically translucent, thin pilsner-inspired lager born in 1993 via a state-controlled enterprise at a brewery in the northeastern Chinese city of Shenyang. A deal with Johannesburg-based South African Breweries (SAB) in 1994 boosted production and distribution significantly, and within ten years, Snow was on its way to becoming the world's bestselling beer—despite its unavailability beyond the Chinese mainland. Snow was even scarce in Hong Kong. The brand eventually came to account for more than 5 percent of beer sold globally, twice as much as Budweiser and Bud Light, the bestselling American brands. The success of Snow and the sheer size of the Chinese market—it overtook America in 2002 as the world's biggest beer market—sparked a scramble for market dominance similar to what befell North America and Europe earlier, complete with all the consolidations and acquisitions that come with it. By the second decade of the twenty-first century, five entities, including the ventures behind Snow and Tsingtao, would make up 75 percent of the Chinese beer market.

One of those ventures was Anheuser-Busch InBev. The humble St. Louis outfit that had emerged out of the American Civil War and had grown to such heights under the Busch family's stewardship passed decisively out of that family in July 2008, as Miller, Pabst, and myriad other breweries had passed from their clans. August Busch IV, the sixth member of his family to head the brewery, was in his early forties with dark hair, dark eyes, and a penchant for narcotics, fast cars, and women who were not his wife. Just as "each of his predecessors had left an indelible imprint, not just on the company but on American commerce as well," this latest Busch was destined to leave his mark too—just not in the way he might have wanted.

During a May 2008 speech to around five hundred Anheuser-Busch distributors, Busch declared that, despite takeover rumors, the brewery that his great-great-grandfather had founded would never trade "on my watch." But during a speech a month later to an even larger group of distributors at a Hyatt hotel on Washington's Capitol Hill, a sweaty, stammering, clearly stoned Busch seemed to embody perfectly a shaky corporation. For the winds of further competition were buffeting in the twenty-first century what had been the world's largest brewery as the business side of pilsner convulsed yet again. The company's stock price was stagnant amid a recession, it faced investigations from several state attorneys general for supposedly trafficking caffeinated alcoholic drinks to minors, and there was the competition.

Anheuser-Busch had the same old competition, from similarly large rivals, but also from the now thousands of craft beer upstarts, who nibbled away at its market share despite the company's efforts to co-opt their tastes and marketing and, in an escalating number of cases, to outright acquire them.

So it was little surprise when on July 13, 2008, August Busch IV conceded the sale of Anheuser-Busch to InBev, a conglomerate that included the massive Belgium-based outfit Interbrew and owners from Brazil. The $46.5 billion deal that created Anheuser-Busch InBev was the largest cash acquisition in the history of business. But what came next dwarfed that sum. In September 2016, shareholders of SABMiller, which was created out of a 2002 deal between Phillip Morris and SAB, approved Anheuser-Busch InBev's more than $107 billion takeover of SABMiller. It was the third-largest business acquisition in history—behind only Verizon Communications' takeover of Verizon Wireless and Dow Chemical's of Dupont—and the largest consumer goods merger ever. The combined Anheuser-Busch InBev would have one-third of the global beer market to itself, with significant inroads into Africa, where pilsners such as the aptly named St. Louis Lager out of Botswana and Castle Lager out of South Africa sold particularly well, and South America, where a pilsner called Skol was the bestselling beer in Brazil, that continent's most populous nation.

One of the side effects of the deal that joined the conglomerative remnants of Adolphus Busch's and Frederick Miller's breweries were sell-offs of certain brands to satisfy regulators in various countries. And one of those deals was for Pilsner Urquell in Czechia. In an alphabet-soup-like blur of mergers and subsidiaries, the sort that came to define the business side of the industry, SAB had acquired the company behind Pilsner Urquell, as well as another Czech brewery, in late 1999. Then Miller and SAB merged three years later, and so when Anheuser-Busch InBev took over SABMiller, it inherited Pilsner Urquell in the deal. However, to satisfy regulators, AB InBev quickly sold Pilsner Urquell and a handful of other European holdings to Japan's Asahi in December 2016 for $7.8 billion. Asahi also acquired Italy's Peroni in a separate deal that year that was also the result of the Anheuser-Busch InBev–SABMiller agreement. Major media worldwide covered these financial chess moves almost entirely from a business perspective, with little mention of the history or the styles of the beers involved. "The jewel in the sale is Plzeňský Prazdroj, the number-one Czech brewer and owner of the Pilsner Urquell brand," was about as far as London's *Financial Times* went in referencing the Pilsen brewery that had birthed what became the world's regnant alcoholic beverage.

The Pilsner Urquell complex—this is the courtyard outside the Old Brewhouse—is a major tourist attraction in Bohemia. Courtesy of Archive of Plzeňský Prazdroj, a.s.

It was inevitable. Pilsner had so long ago become so dominant in beer that for most consumers the two were simply synonymous. Pilsner was beer, beer was pilsner. Any explication beyond that seemed superfluous or maybe stuffily academic. Michael Jackson seemed to acknowledge this in his definition of "pilsener/pilsner/pils" for a 1988 pocket guide to beer: "Loosely, any golden colored, dry, bottom-fermenting beer of conventional strength might be described as being of this style (in its various spellings and abbreviations), though this most famous designation properly belongs only to a product of 'super-premium' quality. Too many brewers take it lightly, in more senses than one." Another guide eleven years earlier—*The Complete Idiot's Guide to Beer*, which came out just as American craft beer began to tip the entire industry and culture—was, perhaps predictably, even more direct. It described the Pilsen original as "the most imitated beer on the planet." That was indeed the case. Though it might go by different names—continental lager, Czech pilsner, German pilsner, Bohemian pilsner, adjunct lager, American light lager, pils, pale lager—it was all still descended and related to the style born, during a time of great change and innovation, in the small European town of Pilsen.

To mark the 175th anniversary of that birth in 2017, Pilsner Urquell underwrote the production of a film called *Brewmaster* celebrating beer and beer culture. The movie—which New York filmmaker Douglas Tirola wrote and directed and which went into wide release in the United States and parts of Europe in early 2018—focused mostly on the American craft beer that was changing the industry. But toward the middle, it nodded to the influence of pilsner on these upstarts and on brewing in general since Josef Groll put flame to kettle in October 1842. "Pilsner was the killer app of its time" was how Garrett Oliver tried to explain it on camera to the newest generations of beer drinkers. He then harked back to those first pours from the barrel in Pilsen in November 1842. "When people saw for the first time a beer that was clear and golden rather than dark and murky," Oliver went on, "people lost their minds. 'We've never seen anything that beautiful in our entire lives.' And the thing was over, right then and there. 'That's the one we want, it looks like gold.'"

Epilogue

HISTORY REPEATED

2018–2019 | Denver; Golden, Colorado

Every late summer or early fall, the Colorado Convention Center in downtown Denver hosts the Great American Beer Festival. The one in late September 2018 marked the thirty-sixth iteration of the world's largest beer tasting, with more than sixty-two thousand paying guests sampling four thousand beers from eight hundred breweries. Meanwhile, over in Golden, Colorado, stood Coors, the world's largest brewery, a fifty-five-acre complex where more than fourteen hundred employees worked, including eight hundred in the brewhouse, and boasting its own train depot for receiving and shipping material and products. Not even twenty miles separated these two sides of beer, one a celebration of often idiosyncratic styles made in relatively small batches and the other a triumph of engineered mass production of one style in particular.

On the Saturday of the Great American Beer Festival, as attendees sweltered and swayed on the sidewalk outside the convention center on what everyone seemed to agree was an unusually sultry late summer day for the Colorado capital, the Coors brewhouse was cool and largely empty. Automation and a smattering of workers allowed its vast plain of kettles and tuns, which seemed to stretch over the horizon, to churn away regardless on the weekends. Most were producing a pilsner that had its origins in the great German migration to America in the mid-1800s. Adolph Kohrs, who trained as a brewer in what became northern Germany, stowed away on a steamer to New York City, changed his name to Coors, and then pushed westward, first to Chicago and then to the mining boomtowns of what was then the territory of Colorado. The wide-faced, brown-haired German immigrant with big oval eyes and fleshy jowls worked odd jobs—as a bricklayer, a stonecutter, a fireman, and again as a brewer—before cofounding a modest brewery in 1873 on the site of a former tannery near the banks of a pristine waterway in the Rocky Mountains called Clear Creek.

Adolph Coors's creation would become a quiet sensation over the next one hundred years in part because Coors did not distribute nationwide until the 1980s. Because of that, its signature pilsner achieved a kind of mystique, becoming, as the *New York Times* described it in 1975, "a prize to be smuggled into the East the way Americans abroad used to smuggle in contraband copies of Henry Miller's novels." Secretary of State Henry Kissinger was a fan, as was his boss, President Gerald Ford. So was actor Paul Newman. By 2018, though, the mystique had long worn off and Coors was just another part of a larger operation, Molson Coors, one that Adolph Coors's descendants did not control. Still, its pilsner (now called Coors Banquet) and the Coors Light version of it remained two of the world's most ubiquitous brands. The Coors brewery in Golden by itself could produce up to ten million barrels annually, much of that pilsner or modeled on pilsner. The combined output of America's several thousand craft breweries in 2018 was about twenty-six million, much of that anything but pilsner.

The beer style guidelines for the 2019 Great American Beer Festival, which judges would use that fall to award medals to beers from all over the United States, included more than 150 entries, each often atomized and with its own nuanced descriptors. As in 2018, pilsner accounted for five of these entries, including "American-style pilsener" and "contemporary American-style pilsener"—the former a nod to how pilsners were made in the United States before Prohibition, with rice and corn, and the latter to the varieties that came afterward, which might rely less on those adjuncts. For the most part, though, these entries ran the gamut, entry after entry indicative of styles that pilsner had all but killed off before American craft beer rescued them, ones only a beer aficionado or brewer could appreciate, some barely produced in any sizable commercial quantities: grodziskie, adambier, kuit, gose, leichtbier, chili pepper beer, and on and on. Of course, there were also many entries for India pale ale and its iterations. That style nearly died in the late twentieth century as the light-beer versions of pilsner swept American and then foreign marketplaces. IPA has come roaring back since the early 1990s as consistently the bestselling style of craft beer in the world, a style that, though born of England's imperial lust, consumers now most identify with America.

But it is still pilsner above all in terms of volume and sales. Anheuser-Busch InBev post-SABMiller acquisition still accounts for perhaps one in three beers sold in the world, and the company's two leading brands remained Budweiser and Bud Light heading into the end of 2019. Its nearest competitors, including the Carlsberg Group, Heineken, and China's CR Snow, account for perhaps a further 20 percent of the market. The share of this big four seems to be growing, too, as the twenty-first century barrels onward. It is telling, in fact, that even after nearly sixty years—if Fritz Maytag's 1965 rescue of Anchor Brewing in San Francisco is used as the starting point—craft beer represents maybe only 15 percent of the US market, and small-batch, independently owned breweries claim much smaller market shares in other countries such as the United Kingdom, Belgium, Spain, France, Germany, and Japan. Part of this is surely because of the head starts and the capital behind these bigger players. And they continue to play the marketing game with a much sharper edge and a heftier treasure chest than their smaller competitors, whatever the medium of the day. Budweiser, for instance, was the most talked-about brand on social and digital media during the 2018 World Cup in Russia—which Anheuser-Busch InBev helped sponsor—with an estimated five billion impressions on sites such as Facebook and Twitter. Finally, the bigger brewing concerns are simply gobbling up the smaller fry, as they've done for decades. Anheuser-Busch InBev owns several breweries that started out as craft—the company bought ten from 2011 through 2018— and, in perhaps the most prominent deal in this trend, Heineken acquired Lagunitas, a once-scrappy purveyor of IPAs that grew from its Northern California roots to national prominence, for $1 billion in separate stake sales in 2015 and 2017.

Really, though, it comes down to preference. For all the ink spilled on behalf of craft beer and in criticism of the homogeneity of what pilsner has become in the hands of these bigger breweries, the numbers do not lie. It would appear that pilsner has a lock on marketplace dominance as the mid-century mark approaches. It is a dominance that the smaller players are paying more attention to as well. During the writing of this book in 2018 and 2019, I created a Google alert for "pilsner." Every afternoon, the Internet search behemoth deposited a handful of articles and reports about the style in my inbox. Most of the reports highlighted pilsner's dominance. Most of the articles highlighted new releases from craft breweries. One of the more creative, I thought, was Pizza Rat Pilsner, a limited release in spring 2019 from a brewery on the North Shore of Staten Island, New York, in honor of the Staten Island Pizza Rats—the occasional name, for marketing purposes, of the local Major League Baseball farm team. Pizza Rat Pilsner was a hoppier iteration of the lager style—an indication of pilsner's continued evolution. It would appear that what Victory Brewing did in the 1990s with its Prima Pils is happening more and more as smaller producers try their hands at a style most closely associated with bigger operations.

It appears too that pilsner is coming full circle, and might in fact lap itself as the history of the style continues to unfold in our bars and restaurants, supermarkets and specialty shops, ballfields and other arenas, anywhere alcohol is sold. Certainly, the style born in Pilsen in 1842 owed its popularity to the migratory rush of enterprising, hardworking Germans and Czechs to America and to the scientific and technological earthquakes of the nineteenth and twentieth centuries. But it also owed its popularity to tinkerers, like the smaller-scale brewers of today and, going back nearly 180 years now, to the acerbically dour Josef Groll, a brewer against the currents of centuries of practice, who drew beer into the future.

ACKNOWLEDGMENTS

One of the fabulous side effects of craft beer's rise has been an increase in beer writing. This swelling corpus has included not only new insights and story lines but also references to much older works that might otherwise have escaped notice. I am grateful in particular to two writers for works that I returned to repeatedly while writing this book—and that led me to older works that proved invaluable to my research: Evan Rail's online articles on the history of Pilsner Urquell, which serve for many English speakers as the best introduction to the thinking and the mechanics of that brewery's launch in the late 1830s and early 1840s, and Maureen Ogle's *Ambitious Brew*, which I think remains one of the best books on American food and drink of the past half century at least. (Evan also provided some expert advice for navigating Czechia.) Other writers whom I referenced are noted in the bibliography and the endnotes, and I am grateful to have been able to stand on their scholarly shoulders.

For additional research help, I would like to thank the American Breweriana Association and, in particular, its growing online database of *Western Brewer* journals; Tracy Lauer at Anheuser-Busch; Daniel Scholzen and Erik Brooks at Miller Coors; Thomas Hunt at Heineken; Christina Nettek at the Austrian Patent Office; Martin Wittal and others at the Spaten brewery; Jana Domanicka at the Pilsner Urquell brewery, who shared with me a detailed in-house history of the brewery; and Alfred McCoy, whose memoir of his family's time in the brewing industry proved scrupulously insightful. I also could not have imagined completing this book without the aid of the research staff at the Cambridge Public Library in my hometown. There are others too numerous to name here who have helped me along the way in learning about the history of beer and the ever-evolving brewing industry. Many are cited in the bibliography and the endnotes, and their aid was greatly appreciated. They know who they are.

I would also like to give yet another shout-out to my longtime editor Yuval Taylor, who demanded key edits of this book, the entire team at Chicago Review Press, including senior editor Kara Rota and developmental editor Devon Freeny, and copyeditor Miki Alexandra Caputo. I owe a debt of gratitude, too, to my agent Adam Chromy.

Finally, I'd like to thank my family. My father-in-law, John Rudy, provided his usual meticulous proofreading, and this book is dedicated to my brothers Angelo (A.J.) Acitelli and Mark Acitelli for further research help and other things. I'd also like to thank my wife, Elizabeth, and our wee ones, Josephine and Mathieu. They were along for the ride on much of this research, literally and figuratively. If there's one meta-theme in my book beyond how a seemingly obscure style came to dominate the world beer market, I hope it's one about the contribution of talented, ambitious immigrants and their descendants to the fabric of American life. May my children take that to heart.

TJA
Cambridge, Massachusetts
September 23, 2019

NOTES

Introduction: At the Right Place and Time

given generously to the museum effort; *"I am still working"* John Lenger, "Busch-Reisinger Marks a Century," *Harvard Gazette*, November 6, 2003.

Nearly one million Germans "The Germans in America," European Reading Room, Library of Congress, April 23, 2014, https://www.loc.gov/rr/european/imde/germchro.html.

an eightfold increase Ogle, *Ambitious Brew*, 40. Ogle's *Ambitious Brew* is the most thorough accounting of German American brewing in nineteenth-century America.

"Breweries have multiplied" Daniel Dorchester, *The Liquor Problem in All Ages* (New York: Philips & Hunt, 1884), 452.

"in immense quantities" D. W. Mitchell, *Ten Years in the United States* (London: Smith, Elder & Co., 1862), 87.

describe pilsner as "naked" Miles Liebtag, "Three Styles You Need to Drink Fresh," *October*, May 30, 2017, https://oct.co/essays/three-styles-you-need-drink-fresh.

"A dozen years ago" Mitchell, *Ten Years*, 87.

"our next emancipation"; *"Specious pleadings"* Dorchester, *Liquor Problem*, 4, 452.

"A German festival is always"; *"new and pleasant phase"* Ogle, *Ambitious Brew*, 33.

"Imitation pilsners today account" Pete Brown, "Pilsner," *Oxford Companion to Beer*, ed. Oliver, 651.

Harvard delayed the opening; *"lack of coal"* Lenger, "Busch-Reisinger."

"It was a time of endings" Blum, *In the Beginning*, x.

they reached for Trump, for instance, topped a November 2015 poll asking Republican voters which candidate in their party's primary they would like to have a beer with. Seth Stevenson, "A Cold One with Donald," *Slate*, February 11, 2016.

"Today, for most beer drinkers" Brown, "Pilsner," 651.

most naked of beers Garrett Oliver's *The Brewmaster's Table* might have been the first to relate in print how fellow brewers describe pilsner as "naked."

1. A Divine Plan

only surviving full architectural Jeremy Norman, "The Only Surviving Major Architectural Drawing from the Fall of the Roman Empire to Circa 1250," History of Information, accessed July 9, 2019, http://www.historyofinformation.com/detail.php?entryid=246.

an unknown monk Warren Sanderson, "The Plan of St. Gall Reconsidered," *Speculum* 60, no. 3 (July 1985): 615–632.

"a very detailed sketch" Norman, "Only Surviving."

It appears the monks never got Martyn Cornell, "Myth 6: As Early as the Ninth Century, the Abbey of St. Gall in Switzerland Had Three Breweries in Full Operation," Zythophile, accessed June 10, 2019, http://zythophile.co.uk/false-ale-quotes/myth-6-as-early-as -the-ninth-century-the-abbey-of-st-gall-in-switzerland-had-three-breweries-in-full -operation/.

One of the breweries planned for St. Gall Horst Dornbusch, "St. Gallen," *Craft Beer & Brewing*, accessed June 12, 2019, https://beerandbrewing.com/dictionary/zF6EbAU8Vx/.

The word ale to describe Nick R. Jones, "Ale," *Oxford Companion to Beer*, ed. Oliver, 27.

Lord Sidmouth, a British prime minister George Canning, *George Canning and His Friends*, vol. 2 (London: J. Murray, 1909), 66.

wasn't fully understood yet It's a common misconception that yeast's role in fermentation was not understood until the nineteenth century. Brewers at least as early as the Middle Ages knew that yeast played a role; they just did not understand it fully nor grasp how to reliably propagate yeast from batch to batch. Per Unger, *Beer in the Middle Ages*, 152–153. Unger's survey of brewing in Europe premodernity debunks a lot of myths.

nearly one in five commercial brewers; All thirty-two of Antwerp's Unger, *Beer in the Middle Ages*, 182.

"It is better to think of church" Goodreads, accessed June 12, 2019, https://www.good reads.com/quotes/258494-it-is-better-to-think-of-church-in-the-ale-house.

"the king of hops" "Rick Steves' Luther and the Reformation," documentary video special, accessed June 12, 2019, https://www.ricksteves.com/tv-programmers/specials/luther, 55:37.

2. Lager and Its Rivals

sought to put a stop Sepp Wejwar, "The Wittelsbach Family," *Oxford Companion to Beer*, ed. Oliver, 847–848; Horst Dornbusch and Karl Ullrich-Heyse, "Reinheitsgebot," *Oxford Companion to Beer*, ed. Oliver, 692–693.

could help him Unger, *Beer in the Middle Ages*, 109.

all beers made in Bavaria Unger, *Beer in the Middle Ages*, 109. Wilhelm IV's own father, Albrecht IV, had promoted a similar decree originally intended only for brewing in the capital of Munich, suggesting that the son's action, which cemented its reach in all of Bavaria, was less revolutionary than it has come to be seen.

born of a hybrid yeast strain University of Wisconsin-Madison, "Yeast's Epic Journey 500 Years Ago Gave Rise to Lager Beer," *ScienceDaily*, August 22, 2011, https://www.sciencedaily .com/releases/2011/08/110822151019.htm.

became a lager or an ale by accident Horst Dornbusch, Michael Zepf, and Garrett Oliver, "Lager," *Oxford Companion to Beer*, ed. Oliver, 533.

slamming the brakes on any innovation; shoehorned brewers in Bavaria Unger, *Beer in the Middle Ages*, 158; Horst Dornbusch, "Bavaria," *Oxford Companion to Beer*, ed. Oliver, 105.

"For many years" Garrett Oliver, "Dunkel," *Oxford Companion to Beer*, 311.

world's great coin collectors Jaynie Andersen, "A Further Inventory of Gabriel Vendramin's Collection," *Burlington Magazine* 121, no. 919 (October 1979): 640f.

to ban brewing altogether; enhanced the reputation Unger, *Beer in the Middle Ages*, 109; Dornbusch, "Bavaria," 105.

"1 Hogshead best porter" "Enclosure: Invoice to Robert Cary & Company, September 20, 1759," Founders Online, https://founders.archives.gov/documents/Washington /02-06-02-0189-0002.

The author took style descriptions in this chapter and for the book generally from *The Oxford Companion to Beer*, edited by Garrett Oliver, and Michael Jackson's *New World Guide to Beer* as well as from his own experiences. Because, unlike with wines and most spirits, the government does not set regulatory parameters for beer styles, those styles can vary and are often subject to vociferous debate among beer aficionados.

3. Thieves Abroad

The young Austrian visitor Hornsey, *History of Beer*, 625–626.

Dreher was twenty-three years old Pete Brown, "Dreher, Anton," *Oxford Companion to Beer*, ed. Oliver, 299.

"Our art of stealing" Hornsey, *History of Beer*, 625.

Much of that growth Ian Hornsey, "Burton-on-Trent," *Oxford Companion to Beer*, ed. Oliver, 194.

"The Abbot of Burton"; An inventory of rental properties; "At Lichfield, the ale" Ibid., 193–194.

It was probably initially the water Pete Brown, "Burton-on-Trent: The World's Most Important Beer Town," *All About Beer*, March 1, 2007.

were using a wood-barrel Matthew Brynoldson, "Burton Union System," *Oxford Companion to Beer*, ed. Oliver, 195–196.

anyone had ever seen Terry Foster, "Pale Ale," *Oxford Companion to Beer*, ed. Oliver, 638–639. As Foster writes, it was not necessarily that people declared pale ales the clearest beers they had ever seen—it was that the term "originated as a catch-all term for any top-fermented beer that was not dark."

giant leap forward in 1818 Nick Kaye, "Wheeler, Daniel," *Oxford Companion to Beer*, ed. Oliver, 840–841.

the rudimentary filtration system Martin Wheeler, "The Story of Brewing in Burton-on-Trent," *All About Beer*, May 1, 2012.

shipping its stout Author's tour of the Guinness Brewery in Dublin, 2015.

Gabriel Sedlmayr was barely past Ian Hornsey, "Sedlmayr, Gabriel the Younger," *Oxford Companion to Beer*, ed. Oliver, 724–725.

It already had had quite a history Author's tour of the Spaten brewery in Munich, November 2018.

4. Over the Horizon

about the impending arrival Martin W. Sandler, *Atlantic Ocean: The Illustrated History of the Ocean That Changed the World* (New York: Sterling Publishing Company, 2008), 344; Blum, *In the Beginning*, 31.

a collapsed flue caused the explosion Rebecca Onion, "Bloody Accounts of Steamboat Disasters, Sold to Tourists on the 19th-Century Mississippi," *Slate*, March 20, 2015.

THE BEGINNING; *"thus solving the problem"* "Science News a Century Ago," *Nature* 141, no. 759 (1938).

The maiden voyage for that venture; called the Unicorn Bradford Hudson, "Cunard in Boston," *Boston Hospitality Review*, February 1, 2015, https://www.bu.edu/bhr/2015/02/01/cunard-in-boston/.

world's first steam-powered railway "Stockton & Darlington Railway," *Encyclopaedia Britannica Online*, accessed June 1, 2019, https://www.britannica.com/topic/Stockton-and-Darlington-Railway.

"made coaches obsolete" Blum, *In the Beginning*, 10.

"In Bavaria, small-time brewers" Purinton, "Empire," 68.

obtained a congressional subsidy; there were thirteen miles Blum, *In the Beginning*, 33.

announced separate discoveries; mass production of photography Ibid., 37–38.

introduced the penny post; launched a revolution Ibid., 34–37.

became the first surgeon "William Thomas Green Morton," *Encyclopaedia Britannica Online*, accessed June 1, 2019, https://www.britannica.com/biography/William-Thomas-Green-Morton.

fastest sewing machine "Isaac Singer," Biography, accessed June 1, 2019, https://www.biography.com/inventor/isaac-singer.

was starting to keep "Darwin's Beagle Field Notebooks (1831–1836)," Darwin Online, accessed June 1, 2019, http://darwin-online.org.uk/EditorialIntroductions/Chancellor_fieldNotebooks.html. Darwin first started taking notes during the HMS *Beagle* trip in 1831.

tripled in population by 1860 "A Population History of London," Proceedings of the Old Bailey, accessed June 1, 2019, https://www.oldbaileyonline.org/static/Population-history-of-london.jsp#a1815-1860.

sixty thousand to roughly eight times that "Total and Foreign-Born Population," New York City Department of City Planning, accessed June 1, 2019, https://www1.nyc.gov/assets/planning/download/pdf/data-maps/nyc-population/historical-population/1790-2000_nyc_total_foreign_birth.pdf.

enslaved African Americans were worth Benjamin T. Arrington, "Industry and Economy During the Civil War," National Park Service, accessed June 1, 2019, https://www.nps.gov/articles/industry-and-economy-during-the-civil-war.htm.

"To improve the means" Michel Chevalier and Thomas Bradford, *Society, Manners, and Politics: In the United States, Being a Series of Letters on North America* (Boston: Weeks, Jordan and Company, 1839; repr. Carlisle, MA: Applewood Books, 2007), 210.

Sedlmayr's contribution; Dreher's contribution; seen together as a high-water mark Conrad Seidl and Horst Dornbusch, "Märzenbier," *Oxford Companion to Beer*, ed. Oliver, 573–574; Jackson, *New World Guide*, 47.

5. "We Must Have Good and Cheap Beer"

Chapter 7 of Blum's *In the Beginning* (235–268) provides an excellent survey of the Austrian Empire politically, socially, and economically around the time of the birth of pilsner.

perhaps as many as four in five Rail, "Founding, Part III." Rail's research on the origins both of pilsner and of Pilsner Urquell was essential to writing this book, and the author expresses his gratitude.

made Czech-language attractions Ibid.

"had little interest" Blum, *In the Beginning*, 258.

fell under a kind of semifeudalism Rudolf Schlesinger, *Federalism in Central and Eastern Europe* (Routledge Trench, Trubner & Co., 1945), 9–10.

blocked attempts to lay down railroad; not until 1839 Blum, *In the Beginning*, 25.

Bohemia had several breweries; more than one hundred Rail, "Founding, Part I."

"Bavarian beer"; leaders was Václav Mirwald Ibid.

one of the 289 burghers Rail, "Corrections, Comments, Clarifications and Addenda to the Czech Entries of the *Oxford Companion to Beer*," Beer Culture (blog), December 13, 2011, http://www.beerculture.org/2011/12/13/corrections-clarifications-and-addenda-to-the-czech-entries-to-the-oxford-companion-to-beer/.

"We must have good" Rail, "Founding, Part I."

was not totally unfamiliar; samec; warranted a mention; out of Rakovník Rail, "Pre-lager Lager Brewing in the Czech Lands," *Beer Culture* (blog), November 4, 2008, http://www.beerculture.org/2008/11/04/pre-lager-lager-brewing-in-the-czech-lands/.

"Everywhere else they were adapting" Rail, "Founding, Part I." The author cleaned up the end of the quotation, which originally translated as "caused that there were foreign beers to be imported into Pilsen."

as Václav Mirwald saw it Ibid.

thirty-six barrels of beer; "as detrimental to the health" "Plzeňský Prazdroj, a Story That Continues to Inspire," 6. This is an in-house history of Pilsner Urquell, translated into English, that the brewery shared with the author in April 2019.

"the formerly thriving" Rail, "Founding, Part I." Rail quoted from "Novy Poupe," an 1880 Czech brewing handbook that was based on František Ondřej Poupě's "watershed brewing manual from 1794."

"the tradition of our ancestors" Rail, "Founding, Part II."

theirs was a plan to brew Rail, "Founding, Part II."

6. "The Rudest Man in Bavaria" and His Enablers

The monk hid the vial Rail, "Founding, Part III."

Martin Stelzer was an architect Ibid. To describe Stelzer and others involved in the launch of what became Pilsner Urquell, the author also drew from "Plzeňský Prazdroj."

well known for his Romanesque Revival "A Place for Jewish Women and Memory in Plzeň," Jewish Heritage Europe, July 25, 2018, https://jewish-heritage-europe.eu/2018/07/25/on-the-road-in-cz-the-place-of-women-and-memory-in-plzen/.

define a lot of major buildings "Romanesque Architecture in the Czech Republic," HiSoUR.com, accessed June 20, 2019, https://www.hisour.com/romanesque-architecture-in-the-czech-republic-31651/.

He had to travel Roger Protz, "Pilsner Urquell," *Oxford Companion to Beer*, ed. Oliver, 653; "Plzeňský Prazdroj," 8.

largest in Munich This was true by 1867, per "Spaten Brewery History," Munich Beer Gardens, accessed May 29, 2019, https://www.munichbeergardens.com/Spaten_Brewery_history.

first easy-to-read saccharometer Gerard L'Estrange Turner and Margaret Weston, *Nineteenth-Century Scientific Instruments* (Berkeley: University of California Press, 1984), 92–93.

Sedlmayr had bought a hydrometer "Meeting Held at the Midland Hotel, Manchester, on Friday, December 13th, 1907," *Journal of the Institute of Brewing* 14, no. 6 (1908): 45.

"The introduction of the saccharometer" Purinton, "Empire," 57.

Dreher's operation was fast becoming Brown, "Dreher, Anton," 299.

was pivoting away from buildings Rail, "Founding, Part III."

The most famous property Filaus; a grand affair Jan Purkert, "Town Theatre, Pilsen, Czech Republic," Theatre Database, accessed May 9, 2019, https://www.theatre-architecture.eu/en/db/?theatreId=966.

None other than Austrian emperor Ibid.

His work on the Burghers' Brewery "Plzeňský Prazdroj," 8–9.

was popular with pedestrians and diners Ibid., 8.

The burghers intended their new Rail, "Founding, Part III." The current Pilsner Urquell brewery on the site of the original Burghers' Brewery does not bear much of a resemblance to the 1842 original. It's much larger, for one thing.

Stelzer himself would go on Rail, "Founding, Part III." Most of the other buildings that Stelzer would design involved housing, not breweries—but his success with the Burghers' Brewery at such a relative young age almost certainly meant that he was called on to design others in the empire.

first modern production facility; *"The spacious building"* "Plzeňský Prazdroj," 10.

had a reputation for being cantankerous Ibid.

"the rudest man"; *"a simple man"* Pete Brown, "Groll, Josef," *Oxford Companion to Beer*, ed. Oliver, 408.

on October 5 of that year "Plzeňský Prazdroj," 10.

at least three pubs and inns Ibid.

Much has been written about what made Groll's 1842 creation so unique in brewing history. The best source is probably Rail's "On the Founding of Pilsner Urquell, Part III," which details among other things the origin of the yeast and the hops. Many accounts have gotten the origin of the original hops wrong, saying that they came from the acclaimed Saaz (or Žatec) hops-growing region. They very well may have been Saaz hops, but it's unlikely they were from Saaz.

"Bavarian skill had met" Brown, "Pilsner," 652.

just over three thousand barrels "Plzeňský Prazdroj," 20.

in two different forms Rail, "Founding, Part III."

was a sizable amount for a brewery Ibid.

The volume would grow considerably Purinton, "Empire," 60.

before the end of its birth year Ibid.

Vienna by 1856 Rail, "Founding, Part III."

"In the effort to put an end" Purinton, "Empire," 60.

He had wanted to stay on "Plzeňský Prazdroj," 20.

for a head brewer until 1900 Rail, "Founding, Part I."

could not deliver the savings "Plzeňský Prazdroj," 20. Groll's successor—another Bavarian named Sebastian Baumgartner—apparently secured the job in part because he "pledged to achieve substantial savings." Per Ibid.

Groll eventually inherited Brown, "Groll, Josef," 409.

7. New World, Old Beer

"all my crop" "To George Washington from Samuel Washington, 7 July 1797," Founders Online, accessed June 9, 2019, https://founders.archives.gov/documents/Washington /06-01-02-0200.

"I perceive by your letter" "From George Washington to Samuel Washington, 12 July 1797," Founders Online, accessed June 9, 2019, https://founders.archives.gov/documents/Washington/06 -01-02-0209.

Enter James Anderson "George Washington's distillery," Mount Vernon official website, accessed June 9, 2019, https://www.mountvernon.org/the-estate-gardens/distillery/. Dennis J. Pogue's *Founding Spirits: George Washington and the Beginnings of the American Whiskey Industry* (Whitestable, UK: Harbour Books, 2011) is an excellent history of not only Washington's distillery but also the early republic's relationship to distilling and spirits.

was either the biggest; *eleven thousand gallons*; *$120,000* "Ten Facts About the Distillery," Mount Vernon official website, accessed June 9, 2019, https://www.mountvernon .org/the-estate-gardens/distillery/ten-facts-about-the-distillery/.

some thirty-six hundred distilleries Ibid.

likely about one-quarter "Celebrating Our History: Jefferson Bourbon," *Louisville Courier-Journal*, November 14, 2014, https://www.courier-journal.com/story/news/history/river-city-retro/2014/11/14/celebrating-history-jefferson-bourbon/19022425/. The exact number of distilleries in early America is impossible to calculate because of illicit stills and lax regulation.

"Distilling whiskey was good business" Gordon S. Wood, *The Radicalism of the American Revolution* (New York: Vintage, 1993), 306.

Americans of all socioeconomic classes; nearly half the city's physicians Gordon S. Wood, *Empire of Liberty: A History of the Early Republic, 1789–1815* (New York: Oxford University Press, 2009), 339.

"Whiskey accompanied every communal" Ibid., 349.

nearly five gallons of spirits Ibid., 339.

"I am sure the American" Frederick Marryat, "A Diary in America, with Remarks on Its Institutions, Part 2, Volume 1 (1839), Excerpt," via America in Class from the National Humanities Center, accessed June 10, 2019, http://americainclass.org/seminars11-12/prohibition/Marryat.pdf.

licensed to a Samuel Cole; "beer, malt, or other beverages" Schlüter, *Brewing Industry*, 25.

"had gained a remarkable reputation" Ibid., 38.

dropped to below one thousand Ibid.

They began a triangular trade Baron, *Brewed in America*, 56; Schlüter, *Brewing Industry*, 39–41. The triangular trade in molasses, rum, and enslaved laborers actually started picking up at least a couple of decades before the American Revolution. The trend would hit its stride, so to speak, around the time of the conflict.

started once again to climb Schlüter, *Brewing Industry*, 42.

just under 130; in Pennsylvania and New York Ibid., 45–46.

with the 3,600 distilleries "Ten Facts," Mount Vernon official website.

estimated 14,000 Michael Kinstlick, "The U.S. Craft Distilling Market: 2011 and Beyond," accessed June 20, 2019, https://coppersea.com/wp-content/uploads/2012/04/Craft_Distilling_2011_White_Paper_Final.pdf.

dwarfed beer drinking Schlüter, *Brewing Industry*, 42.

8. Of Revolutions and Counterrevolutions

"Sicilians!" Rosemary H. T. O'Kane, ed., *Revolution: Critical Concepts in Political Science*, vol. 1 (London: Routledge, 2000), 214.

became the common source Blum, *In the Beginning*, xv–xvi.

For this chapter, the author drew a lot from the second part of Blum's *In the Beginning* (155–334), which covers the revolutionary and counterrevolutionary upheaval.

poor harvests and an economic downturn; famine spread Eric Vanhaute, Richard Paping, and Cormac Ó Gráda, "The European Subsistence Crisis of 1845–1850: A Comparative Perspective," IEHC 2006 Helsinki Session 123, accessed June 1, 2019, http://www.helsinki.fi/iehc2006/papers3/Vanhaute.pdf.

the revolutions were not unexpected Blum, *In the Beginning*, xv.

Philippe's hasty exit reached Vienna Ibid., 261.

allowed his realm's; the end of having to pay tribute Ibid., 263–265.

also cowered in the wake Ibid., 272–273, 291–292. There were also revolutions in smaller German states such as Hannover and Baden, per Blum, *In the Beginning*, chapter 8.

first large ethnic group to assimilate "The Silent Minority," *Economist*, February 5, 2015, https://www.economist.com/united-states/2015/02/05/the-silent-minority.

9. Spread

"herewith we give notice" Ogle, *Ambitious Brew*, 13.

Milwaukee was one of the fastest-growing Ibid., 10–11.

doubled the city's population "Wisconsin," US Census Bureau, accessed July 9, 2019, https://www2.census.gov/library/publications/decennial/1940/population-volume -1/33973538v1ch10.pdf, 1162.

"The public houses"; arrived sometimes by the dozens Ogle, *Ambitious Brew*, 10–11.

"as if under lions and dragons" Ibid., 9. For more on how Germans viewed their new homeland, see Ogle, *Ambitious Brew*, 8–10; James McPherson, *Battle Cry of Freedom: The Civil War Era* (New York: Oxford University Press, 1988), 7.

the city was known as hospitable; might also have heard Norwegian Ogle, *Ambitious Brew*, 10–11.

was crude and man powered For details on the Bests' start-up phase, see Ogle, *Ambitious Brew*, 4–13, and James Smith Buck, *Pioneer History of Milwaukee, from the First American Settlement in 1833* (Milwaukee: Swain & Tate, 1890), 344–345.

was not heavily involved in the initial Ogle, *Ambitious Brew*, 35.

"the product and sales" Buck, *Pioneer History*, 344.

quickly fell into debt Ogle, *Ambitious Brew*, 35. For more on Miller's takeover of the Plank Road Brewery and Best's mismanagement and misfortune, see "Miller Brewing Company," Encyclopedia.com, accessed July 23, 2019, https://www.encyclopedia.com /books/politics-and-business-magazines/miller-brewing-company.

describe Best's beer Milwaukee Daily Sentinel, January 28, 1861.

was a well-documented race Ogle, *Ambitious Brew*, 73–79, 83–85; Baron, *Brewed in America*, 175–183.

"The really important" Baron, *Brewed in America*, 186.

one ale producer left Ibid., 187.

Francesco Peroni set about "Timeline," Peroni Italia official website, accessed July 3, 2019, http://www.peroniitaly.com/about/timeline; "Peroni Beer Museum," European Route of Industrial Heritage, accessed July 3, 2019, https://www.erih.net/i-want-to-go-there /site/show/Sites/peroni-beer-museum/. For more on Peroni's founding, see Keith Villa, "Peroni," *Oxford Companion to Beer*, ed. Oliver, 647.

For more on the rise of the Italian brewing industry in the nineteenth century, see Gourvish and Wilson, *Dynamics*, chapter 2, "The Italian Brewing Industry, c. 1815–1990."

It went back to ancient Rome; Giovanni Baldassarre Ketter Lorenzo Dabove, "Italy," *Oxford Companion to Beer*, ed. Oliver, 498–500.

family of Anton Dreher Sepp Wejwar, "Austria," *Oxford Companion to Beer*, ed. Oliver, 74; "Dreher-Brewery" [in Italian], Trieste di ieri e di oggi, accessed and translated July 20, 2019, http://www.trieste-di-ieri-e-di-oggi.it/category/dreher-birreria/.

looked and tasted very similar A definitive portrait of Peroni's appearance and taste in the mid-nineteenth century appears impossible, but the brewery itself describes the earliest iteration as "a distinctive pale, medium-strength beer" (per "Timeline," Peroni Italia official website), and within decades Peroni would be routinely shown as golden and effervescent.

add a second brewery Villa, "Peroni."

10. Anti-immigrant Ferment

doctor with round spectacles "Mayor Levi Boone Biography," Chicago Public Library, accessed July 1, 2019, https://www.chipublib.org/mayor-levi-day-boone-biography/.

"I cannot be blind" Ron Grossman, "Chicago's Lager Beer Riot Proved Immigrants' Power," *Chicago Tribune*, September 25, 2015.

"Who does not know" Ibid.

as many as two million Irish "European Immigration to the U.S., 1851–1860," PBS.org, accessed July 1, https://www.pbs.org/destinationamerica/usim_wn_noflash.html.

over two hundred thousand "The E Pluribus Unum Project," Assumption College, accessed July 1, 2019, http://www1.assumption.edu/ahc/irish/overview.html.

most Catholics from southern statelets McPherson, *Battle Cry*, 131. Details on nativism and hostility to immigrant growth taken from McPherson, *Battle Cry*, 130–145, and Ogle, *Ambitious Brew*, 13–21.

nearly half the city's Grossman, "Chicago's Lager."

dropped from an astounding seven gallons Okrent, *Last Call*, 7.

So it came as little surprise Grossman, "Chicago's Lager." Details of the riot and its immediate aftermath are in the Grossman piece.

"They filled the sidewalks" Ibid.

"One German was taken"; "had his nose" Ibid.

Similar violence would grip; killing one Ogle, *Ambitious Brew*, 26–28.

For overview of temperance movement and its origins, see Okrent, *Last Call*.

Millions of Americans turned McPherson, *Battle Cry*, 35; Ogle, *Ambitious Brew*, 24–25.

"Campaigners railed against every" Ibid., 24.

"Intemperance in our land" Anonymous, *The Great Awakening on Temperance and the Great Controversy, Romanism, Protestantism, and Judaism* (St. Louis: Anchor Publishing Company, 1878), 37.

"I claim, sir, that slavery" "Slavery in the Territories," Jefferson Davis speech in the US Senate on February 13 and 14, 1850, Furman University Department of History official website, accessed July 3, 2019, http://history.furman.edu/benson/hst121/davis13feb1850excerpts.html. Details on how the nation began to focus on slavery to the exclusion of other issues, see McPherson, *Battle Cry*, 6–202.

quietly purchased part of a German-language David S. Reynolds, review of *Lincoln and the Power of the Press* by Harold Holzer, *New York Times*, October 31, 2014.

Abraham Lincoln never lost See Frank Baron, *Abraham Lincoln and the German Immigrants: Turners and Forty-Eighters*, Yearbook of German American Studies, supplemental issue, vol. 4 (Lawrence, KS: Society of German-American Studies, 2012).

"It isn't a war" Don H. Doyle, "The Civil War Was Won by Immigrant Soldiers," *Time*, June 29, 2015.

met with resounding opposition; "now mellow in old age" Grossman, "Chicago's Lager."

11. Science Meets Brewing

in operation since 1592 Gourvish and Wilson, *Dynamics*, 21.

he sat down and wrote a letter Smit, *Heineken Story*, 2–3. For background on the Heinekens, see Smit's *Heineken Story*.

he saw the potential in growing Gourvish and Wilson, *Dynamics*, 21.

dream of exporting English-style Ibid.

De Hooiberg also made a porter "Heineken 1864–1900," *Van Der Meer* (blog), accessed January 5, 2020, http://famvandermeer.com/green-room/heineken-1864-1900.

Heineken had a deal "Gerard Heineken, Man of the World," Heineken Collection Foundation, accessed June 21, 2019, https://heinekencollection.com/en/stories/gerard-heineken-man-world.

quickly disabused himself of exporting; refocused on the Dutch market Gourvish and Wilson, *Dynamics*, 21.

traveled to Bavaria Ibid. For more on the Heineken-Feltmann relationship, see Gourvish and Wilson, *Dynamics*, 21–22. It is unclear if Heineken met Feltmann in Bavaria or in another part of what became Germany, but Feltmann was undoubtedly a devotee of Bavarian brewing methods, per Gourvish and Wilson, *Dynamics*, 21.

started producing lighter-colored lagers; was particularly a fan of Dreher's Ibid.

Heineken saw a similar track Ibid., 21–22.

allowed the company to start "Heineken 1864–1900," *Van Der Meer*.

Heineken's operation represented the first time Gourvish and Wilson, *Dynamics*, 23–25; Smit, *Heineken Story*, 4–5.

edged out not only Germanic Gourvish and Wilson, *Dynamics*, 23–30.

"It was not only the conversion" Ibid., 23.

On April 23, 1859 Author's e-mail exchange with the Austrian Patent Office, August 2019. The office generously provided a scanned copy of the trademark document, which showed the date as well as the owner of the brand: "Brauberechtigte Bürgerschaft in Pilsen," or Civic Brewery in Pilsen.

"This convergence of science" K. Florian Kemp, "Pilsner," *All About Beer*, September 1, 2010, http://allaboutbeer.com/article/pilsner-4/.

12. "Beer of Revenge"

Louis Pasteur meticulously noted; "the continual rising" Debré, *Louis Pasteur*, 104–105.

a revolutionary conclusion Ibid., 105.

"For there can be no hesitation" Ibid., 104.

The author took biographical information throughout from Patrice Debré's authoritative *Louis Pasteur* and from the website of the Institut Pasteur in Paris, accessed June 3, 2019, https://www.pasteur.fr/en.

"Thanks to Pasteur" Debré, *Louis Pasteur*, 51.

Take the friend of Pasteur's; "At most, people knew" Ibid., 250.

The French beer of Pasteur's time Ibid., 227. For more on the history of beer in France, see Phil Markowski's entry "France" in *Oxford Companion to Beer*, ed. Oliver, 373–375.

grew tenfold over sixty years Debré, *Louis Pasteur*, 227.

"Every good bourgeois" Ibid., 226.

For how the French saw wine and the quality of that wine, see Debré, *Louis Pasteur*, 226–227.

"it was still widely thought that winemaking" Ibid., 227.

he saw the unpredictability Ibid., 227–228.

wrote to Pasteur in the summer; "The Emperor is firmly" Ibid., 219.

threw himself into the task Ibid., 228–234.

By early 1864 C. N. Trueman, "Louis Pasteur," History Learning Site, March 16, 2015, https://www.historylearningsite.co.uk/a-history-of-medicine/louis-pasteur/.

"Are you continuing your studies" Debré, *Louis Pasteur*, 222.

took enthusiastically to pasteurization; "Pasteur is as popular" Ibid., 238.

which drew to Paris entrants "Expo 1867 Paris," Bureau International des Expositions, accessed June 3, 2019, https://www.bie-paris.org/site/en/1867-paris.

had little long-term effect; "The practice of heating" Debré, *Louis Pasteur*, 238.

proved much more popular Baron, *Brewed in America*, 238–239; Debré, *Louis Pasteur*, 253–254.

"Within a few short" Plavchan, *History of Anheuser-Busch*, 68.

"I was inspired to do this research" Debré, *Louis Pasteur*, 249.

"beer of revenge" Ibid.

Pasteur showed the usefulness Ibid., 250–256.

became a kind of bible Fritz Maytag, one of the pioneers of American craft beer as the financial rescuer of San Francisco's Anchor Brewing Company, once named Pasteur as the most influential figure in beer from the late nineteenth century to the twenty-first century. Per the 2011 Michael Jackson documentary *Beer Hunter*, directed by J. R. Richards.

13. The Eternal Optimist

mustered out of the United States Army It is likely Busch served in Company E of the third regiment of the US Reserve Corps, which was a largely German American outfit that Missouri power broker Francis Blair Jr. set up to aid the Union cause. It's likely, then, that the young Busch joined out of a combination of peer pressure and loyalty to his new homeland. Per "Adolphus Busch (1839–1913)," Immigrant Entrepreneurship, accessed June 3, 2019, https://www.immigrantentrepreneurship.org/entry.php?rec=152; "Adolphus Busch (1839–1913)," State Historical Society of Missouri, accessed June 3, 2019, https://historicmissourians.shsmo.org/historicmissourians/name/b/busch/. Also, enlistments in the North were generally only months long early in the war. Per "American Civil War," *Encyclopaedia Britannica Online*, accessed February 12, 2020, https://www.britannica.com/event/American-Civil-War.

Busch's biographical information came from various sources, including Ogle, *Ambitious Brew*, 41–159 and Knoedelseder, *Bitter Brew*, 15–23. The author is also grateful to Tracy Lauer, archives and chief storytelling officer at Anheuser-Busch, for her aid in fact-checking and other information.

Missouri city was booming then "Population of 100 Largest Urban Places: 1850," US Census Bureau, June 15, 1998, https://www.census.gov/population/www/documentation/twps0027/tab08.txt; Ogle, *Ambitious Brew*, 40–42.

"We found it almost necessary" James Neal Primm, *Lion of the Valley: St. Louis, Missouri, 1764–1980* (Missouri Historical Society Press, 1998), 196.

thirty to forty pre–Civil War breweries "St. Louis Brewing History," St. Louis Brewers Heritage Foundation official website, accessed June 3, 2019, https://stlbeer.org/history. The author also consulted Henry Herbst et al, *St. Louis Brews: The History of Brewing in the Gateway City*, 2nd ed. (St. Louis: Reedy Press, 2015).

"well nigh universally adopted" Ogle, *Ambitious Brew*, 40.

the year when a German immigrant Chris Naffziger, "Unveiling the Real Johann Adam Lemp," *St. Louis Magazine*, August 2, 2017; Chris Naffziger, "Adam Lemp's Riverfront Brewery Was the Birthplace of Lager Beer in St. Louis—and Perhaps America," *St. Louis Magazine*, August 9, 2017.

"This light, clear, pleasant-tasting" Primm, *Lion of the Valley*, 195.

"had captured the lion's share" Ibid., 196.

Two dozen St. Louis breweries; "when the lager beer gave out" Ibid.

One of the St. Louis breweries Ogle, *Ambitious Brew*, 42–43; Knoedelseder, *Bitter Brew*, 16.

gone for the Union or the Confederacy; "The war in Missouri" Walter Stahr, *Stanton: Lincoln's Secretary of War* (New York: Simon & Schuster, 2017), 188.

"Everybody—almost—drinks"; particular favorite of these soldiers Ogle, *Ambitious Brew*, 44.

Hundreds of breweries in Missouri; "a valuable substitute" Ibid.

"beer, lager beer, ale" Charles Frederick Estee, *The Excise Tax Law, Approved July 1, 1862; and All the Amendments* (New York: Fitch Estee, 1863), 35.

at other so-called luxury items McPherson, *Battle Cry*, 447–448.

required brewers to purchase; cleared $369 million Ogle, *Ambitious Brew*, 44.

that was unusual for American business Baron, *Brewed in America*, 214–215.

pegged it at thirty-seven Mittelman, *Brewing Battles*, 28.

marked a watershed Baron, *Brewed in America*, 214–215.

charting new territory in lobbying Ibid., 218.

constitued nearly the entire Schlüter, *Brewing Industry*, 77.

helped persuade Congress Baron, *Brewed in America*, 215–216.

"the brewers learned" Ogle, *Ambitious Brew*, 45.

provided his son-in-law Ibid. 45–46. Busch also purchased a share of the brewery in 1865, per Ogle.

would grow exponentially For more on the growth of Anheuser-Busch under Busch's early management, see Plavchan, *History of Anheuser-Busch*, 26–46. Production figures vary, depending on the source, but all agree that Anheuser-Busch's production volume increased along with its distribution. By the end of the century, it would be one of the world's largest breweries.

with a majority of the company's shares Knoedelseder, *Bitter Brew*, 16.

"I am an eternal optimist" Ogle, *Ambitious Brew*, 47.

14. International Splash

There were fifty-three thousand "Site Plan of the Vienna World Exhibition, 1873," Technische Museum Wien official website, accessed June 2, 2019, https://www.technischesmuseum.at/object/situationsplan-der-wiener-weltausstellung-1873. Details on world's fairs were also taken from the Smithsonian Libraries' online collection of information about the expos, accessed June 2, 2019, https://library.si.edu/digital-library/collection/worlds-fairs and from Robert W. Rydell, *All the World's a Fair: Visions of Empire at American International Expositions, 1876–1916* (Chicago: University of Chicago Press, 1987).

the latest in beer Rydell, *All the World's*, 20.

a medal the brewery displays Author's Spaten visit, November 2018.

"Of course all the great" *Reports on the Vienna Universal Exhibition of 1873*, part 4 (London: George E. Eyre and William Spottiswoode, 1874), via the Library of Princeton University, 159. Henry Vizetelly was the writer quoted.

"a pyramid of beer casks" Ibid.

"was constructed in the form" Ibid.

"The restaurants and beer halls" W. P. Blake and Henry Pettit, *Reports on the Vienna Universal Exhibition, 1873, Made to the US Centennial Commission* (Philadelphia: Mclaughlin Brothers, 1873), https://archive.org/stream/reportsonviennau00blak/reportsonviennau00blak_djvu.txt.

was a mixed bag Ibid., 159–178.

"The Austrian beers" Ibid., 160.

"Most of the Austrian beers" Ibid., 163.

"medal for progress"; "by far the largest quantity" Ibid.

"drink of fashionable London" Pete Brown, "India Pale Ale," *Oxford Companion to Beer*, ed. Oliver, 484.

attracted visitors from Missouri; unclear if Busch himself Ogle, *Ambitious Brew*, 74. Lademan's father-in-law was brewer Joseph Uhrig per ibid., 48.

one Lademan learned about Ibid., 74.

15. Beyond Ice

reached agreements with the Dreher Linde AG, *125 Years of Linde: A Chronicle*, 9, accessed June 9, 2019, https://www.the-linde-group.com/en/images/chronicle_e%5B1%5D14 _9855_tcm14-233340.pdf

while competing in a university contest Ibid.

not a new idea Horst Dornbusch, "Linde, Carl von," *Oxford Companion to Beer*, ed. Oliver, 549.

"The thought immediately struck" Linde AG, *125 Years of Linde*, 9.

published his initial research Ibid.

reached out to Linde Thomas Flynn, *Cryogenic Engineering*, 2nd ed. (New York: Marcel Decker, 2004), 367.

"improved ice and refrigeration" Linde AG, *125 Years of Linde*, 9. He would also call his invention "ammonia cold machine," per Dornbusch, "Linde, Carl von," 550.

which hinged on Dornbusch, "Linde, Carl von," 550; Linde AG, *125 Years of Linde*, 9.

installed there in January 1874; "This design was not a suitable" Ibid.

Build it he and his partners; Linde tested it Ibid., 9, 11.

bought the first commercial machine Ibid., 10.

ran more than thirty years Hans-Liudger Dienel, *Linde: History of a Technology Corporation, 1879-2004* (New York: Palgrave Macmillan, 2004), 261.

went full-time Linde AG, *125 Years of Linde*, 88.

the kaiser knighted him Dornbusch, "Linde, Carl von," 550.

"It was Linde's closer relationship" Dienel, *Linde*, 33.

"My cellars and fermenting" Jonathan Rees, *Refrigeration Nation: A History of Ice, Appliances, and Enterprise in America* (Baltimore: Johns Hopkins University Press, 2013), 45.

reaching dusty, hot Texas Ogle, *Ambitious Brew*, 64.

250 railroad cars Knoedelseder, *Bitter Brew*, 17. More on Busch's shipping and refrigeration can be found in Ogle, *Ambitious Brew*, 62–64; and Plavchan, *History of Anheuser-Busch*, 55–56.

the form of Frederick Pabst Author took biographical information on Pabst—including the shipwreck and employment and partnership with the Bests—from Ogle, *Ambitious Brew*, 49–57; and Cochran, *Pabst Brewing*, 46–49.

They adopted pilsner Based on their embraces of pilsner brands, including Budweiser, as flagships for their respective companies. Also, as an example of how big their companies had become, Anheuser-Busch had 250 employees by the mid-1870s, per Ogle, *Ambitious Brew*, 64.

"commanded any room" Ogle, *Ambitious Brew*, 50.

16. Farther and Wider

an entire barge loaded "The Market for Bottled Ales," *Western Brewer* 12 (1877): 518.

transferred its bottling Plavchan, *History of Anheuser-Busch*, 72; Baron, *Brewed in America*, 244–245

Its leader saw the potential Baron, *Brewed in America*, 245; Plavchan, *History of Anheuser-Busch*, 72.

Bottled beer was not new Horst Dornbusch and Garrett Oliver, "Bottles," *Oxford Companion to Beer*, ed. Oliver, 150–151. For more on the challenges in bottling beer, particularly beer such as pilsner with lots of carbonation, see Plavchan, *History of Anheuser-Busch*, 71, and Baron, *Brewed in America*, 242.

done by hand; any bottles it sold; usually six dozen quart bottles Plavchan, *History of Anheuser-Busch*, 73–74.

largest bottling plant in the United States; one hundred thousand bottles This is based on production figures during the mid-1870s (per Plavchan, *History of Anheuser-Busch*, 76–77) compared with other breweries and bottle-using industries. The one hundred thousand bottles a day comes from Plavchan, *History of Anheuser-Busch*, 52.

Henry Barrett had developed David Hughes, *A Bottle of Guinness, Please: The Colorful History of Guinness* (Workingham, UK: Phimboy, 2006), chapter 10. The author also drew from this chapter for information on bottle seals in general.

Anheuser-Busch's explosive growth; "embarked upon a building program" Plavchan, *History of Anheuser-Busch*, 50–51.

Steam powered much of Ibid.; "The Chemistry of the Mash-Tun," *Western Brewer* 3 (March 15, 1878): 158.

were an inspiration for Henry Ford's Author's e-mail exchange with The Henry Ford, March 2019. William Klann, head of Ford Motor Company's engine department at the time Henry Ford implemented the assembly line, had worked servicing brewery conveyors before going to work for Ford.

"a model to other businessmen"; a special Western Union telegraph Plavchan, *History of Anheuser-Busch*, 52.

Millions of its citizens Howe, *What Hath God Wrought* (Oxford: Oxford University Press, 2009), 525–539.

grew from about one-fourth "Population Distribution," US Census Bureau, Census Atlas, accessed June 30, 2019, https://www.census.gov/population/www/cen2000/censusatlas /pdf/2_Population-Distribution.pdf; "Population: 1790–1990," US Census Bureau, accessed June 30, 2019, https://www.census.gov/population/censusdata/table-4.pdf, 9.

automated production; belching out goods Howe, *What Hath God Wrought*, 525–539. Also, Ogle's *Ambitious Brew*, 52–55, has a good overview of America's rapid pivot from farm to factory and brewing's place in that.

McCormick Harvesting Machine Company; Campbell produced Howe, *What Hath God Wrought*, 525–539; Ogle, *Ambitious Brew*, 52–55.

more than fifteen million "Campbell Soup Corporate History," Marketplace, December 18, 2007, https://www.marketplace.org/2007/12/18/campbell-soup-corporate-history/. The figure was more than sixteen million by 1904, suggesting the fifteen million threshold before that at the turn of the century.

nearly twenty-seven hundred in 1876 "National Beer Sales & Production Data," Brewers Association official website, accessed June 30, 2019, https://www.brewersassociation .org/statistics-and-data/national-beer-stats/.

"much of the local beer" Ogle, *Ambitious Brew*, 84.

not keeping up with the latest; "We use bicarbonate"; "depends not so much" Ibid. 84–85.

"I wish it understood" Ibid., 70.

not many brewers of ale left Baron, *Brewed in America*, 189, 228.

"by far the greater" "The Million's Beverage," *New York Times*, May 20, 1877.

fewer than four thousand barrels; fewer than one thousand Ogle, *Ambitious Brew*, 68.

turned out so much more Ibid.

never enjoyed the consistent reach Author's tour of the Guinness Brewery in Dublin, 2015.

17. How It Sparkles

not a beer man; imported wine; business side of the restaurant trade Ogle, *Ambitious Brew*, 76–77; Knoedelseder, *Bitter Brew*, 16–17.

how Conrad came to know Adolphus Knoedelseder, *Bitter Brew*, 16.

St. Louis Lager, a conscious imitation; Developed by Busch's Ogle, *Ambitious Brew*, 84.

St. Louis Lager used rice Ibid. The author drew from Ogle, *Ambitious Brew*, 70–75, and from Chris Holliland, "Rice," *Oxford Companion to Beer*, ed. Oliver, 695–696, as well as Charles W. Bamforth, "Corn," *Oxford Companion to Beer*, ed. Oliver, 267–268, for information on the rise of adjuncts in American brewing.

"A glass of sparkling" Ogle, *Ambitious Brew*, 74.

were blessed with copious volumes; six-row rarely appeared Colin J. West, "Barley," *Oxford Companion to Beer*, ed. Oliver, 86.

For much of the nineteenth century Ogle, *Ambitious Brew*, 75; Greg Kitsock, "Craft Beer: Corn Gets a New Look from Brewers, and Not as a Mere Filler," *Washington Post*, August 5, 2014.

neither had a lot of protein; less oily than corn Ogle, *Ambitious Brew*, 75.

his own European travels Plavchan, *History of Anheuser-Busch*, 69.

also steeped in Bavarian lagering The role of Erwin Spraul (spelling per Plavchan drawing from Anheuser-Busch board of director minutes from August 1875, page 39, though he appears as Irwin Sproul elsewhere) in the creation of both St. Louis Lager and Budweiser strongly suggests he knew the latest revolutionary brewing techniques out of Bavaria.

the idea for the new beer Ogle, *Ambitious Brew*, 76–77; Baron, *Brewed in America*, 245.

legend has it Bill Lockhart et al., "Carl Conrad & Co.—the Original American Budweiser," Society for Historical Archaeology official website, https://sha.org/bottle/pdffiles/CarlConradCo.pdf, 133.

"the best he ever tasted" Ibid. For more on how Conrad and Busch discovered what became Budweiser, see Ogle, *Ambitious Brew*, 76. Conrad's subsequent—though short lived—success in marketing and selling Bud suggests that he really did want in on St. Louis's booming beer business. See Lockhart et al., "Carl Conrad," 134.

The recipe he hired; "special characteristic"; "Taking [the grain]" Ogle, *Ambitious Brew*, 77.

nor Busch had ever visited Ibid., 76.

proved ravishingly popular Ibid., 77–85; Plavchan, *History of Anheuser-Busch*, 27, 53, 64.

"sparkles"; "It has a very pretty" Ogle, *Ambitious Brew*, 77.

would sell a quarter of a million Ibid., 80.

would produce six thousand barrels Ibid.

"Can't you give us" Ibid., 78.

urgently wrote his brewmaster; "There is no doubt" Ibid.

hiring brewers knowledgeable; was on its way to becoming Cochran, *Pabst Brewing*, 216–217.

its own pilsner interpretations Ibid.

"We have done & are doing" Ogle, *Ambitious Brew*, 113.

The company missed its master's; "We will lead Busch" Ibid.

a list from 1895 Downard, *Dictionary*, 240.

more than double from 1870 Robin A. LaVallee and B.A. Hsiao-ye Yi, "Surveillance Report #92, Apparent Per Capita Alcohol Consumption: National, State, and Regional Trends, 1977–2009," National Institute on Alcohol Abuse and Alcoholism, August 2011, 12.

18. "All the Old Styles Were All but Gone"

Emil Christian Hansen Biographical information on Hansen taken from Arthur R. Ling, "Prof. Emil Christian Hansen," *Nature* 81 (September 9, 1909): 310; Louise Crane, "Legends of Brewing: Emil Christian Hansen," Beer 52 official website, December 6, 2017, https://www.beer52.com/ferment/article/159/EmilChristianHansen; "Hansen, Emil Christian," Encyclopedia.com, accessed August 2, 2019, https://www.encyclopedia .com/science/dictionaries-thesauruses-pictures-and-press-releases/hansen-emil -christian.

Panum was best known J. L. Little, "Peter Ludwig Panum 1820–1885: A Pioneer in the Epidemiology of Measles," *Canadian Public Health* 22, no. 10 (October 1931): 509–516.

brewers still struggled Cochran, *Pabst Brewing*, 110–114.

refused to send out a batch Ogle, *Ambitious Brew*, 78–79.

Jacobsen had been running Biography information on Jacobsen taken from "Who We Are," Carlsberg Group, accessed August 2, 2019, https://www.carlsberggroup.com /who-we-are/about-the-carlsberg-group/our-rich-heritage/; Anders Brinch Kissmeyer, "Carlsberg Group," *Oxford Companion to Beer*, ed. Oliver, 223–225.

with a hatbox full Michael Jackson, "Can Big Be Beautiful?" Beer Hunter, January 23, 2002, http://www.beerhunter.com/documents/19133-001656.html.

a darker Bavarian-style dunkel Kissmeyer, "Carlsberg Group," 225.

November 1847; "an instant success" Roger Protz, "Arts That Others Don't Reach . . ." *Guardian* (UK), February 11, 2001.

ale had reigned in Denmark; known in particular for using honey; "swept quickly through Denmark" Jens Eiken, "Denmark," *Oxford Companion to Beer*, ed. Oliver, 284–285.

Carlsberg was exporting its lager Kissmeyer, "Carlsberg Group."

Jacobsen's commitment to the science; sought to codify; "J.C. believed that the art" Ibid.

generous in his approach; would share with the rest Ibid.; Crane, "Legends of Brewing."

For information on Hansen's groundbreaking yeast work, the author mined Anders Brinch Kissmeyer's "Carlsberg Group" entry in *Oxford Companion to Beer*, ed. Oliver; and Crane's "Legends of Brewing."

"In 1883, the work was" Anders Brinch Kissmeyer, "Hansen, Emil Christian," *Oxford Companion to Beer*, ed. Oliver, 420–421.

shared the discovery Crane, "Legends of Brewing."

included with Tuborg; started in 1875; marketed as a pilsner Anders Brinch Kissmeyer, "Tuborg Brewery," *Oxford Companion to Beer*, ed. Oliver, 800–801.

would become Denmark's bestselling Ibid.

"pure culture of the best" Kissmeyer, "Hansen, Emil Christian."

in November 1883 Chandra J. Panchal, ed., *Yeast Strain Selection*, (Boca Raton: CRC Press, 1990), 67. More on the spread of Carlsberg's yeast to other breweries can also be found here.

every brewery in Denmark Crane, "Legends of Brewing." This is based on a claim by Hansen for which the author could not find any challenge.

19. The Right Kind of Lager

Ballantine was born The author took Ballantine's biographic information from Baron, *Brewed in America*, 188, and from Jay R. Brooks, "Ballantine, Peter," *Oxford Companion to Beer*, ed. Oliver, 80–81. There is some uncertainty over the facts of Ballantine's life and brewery he steered. See *A Good Beer Blog*'s entry-by-entry critique of the *Oxford*

Companion to Beer, accessed June 28, 2019, https://abetterbeerblog427.com/oxford
-companion-to-beer-commentary/articles-b/.

was ale country Schlüter, *Brewing Industry*, 51.

beers made from wheat; *a vestige of the Dutch* Craig Gravina, "Albany, New York: America's
Forgotten Beer City," *Beer Advocate Magazine*, November 2017.

about seventeen thousand residents World Population Review, based on US Census data,
accessed June 3, 2019, http://worldpopulationreview.com/us-cities/newark-population/.

nation's fourth-largest brewer; *nation's largest*; *number-two* Downard, *Dictionary*, 240. The
third largest was Philadelphia-based Bergner & Engel, which was well known for a
lighter-colored and lighter-tasting lager known as Tannhauser Export, per Sandy
Hingston, "10 Things You Might Not Know About Beer in Philly," *Philadelphia
Magazine*, June 1, 2016.

mercenaries and executives from the East India Company William Dalrymple, "Lessons
on Capitalism from the East India Company," *Financial Times*, August 30, 2019.

myths have shrouded IPA India pale ale is probably the most debated style in American
craft beer in terms of its origins and its characteristics. Pete Brown's "India Pale
Ale" entry in the *Oxford Companion to Beer,* ed. Oliver, 482–486, and Jeff Alworth's
coverage in his *Beer Bible*, 106–107, are great starting points for understanding the
debate. Readers can go deeper with Mitch Steele's book *IPA*.

much more organically; *made the trek just fine* Martyn Cornell, "Four IPA Myths That
Need to Be Stamped out for #IPADay," Zythophile, August 4, 2011, http://zythophile
.co.uk/2011/08/04/four-ipa-myths-that-need-to-be-stamped-out-for-ipaday/.

"The Messers. Ballantine manufacture" Alan McLeod, "Articles—B," *A Good Beer Blog*,
accessed June 12, 2019, https://abetterbeerblog427.com/oxford-companion-to-beer
-commentary/articles-b/.

was number five Downard, *Dictionary*, 240.

purchased a lager-brewing Newark rival McLeod, "Articles—B." The rival was the Schalk
Bros. Lager Beer Brewing Co.

dwarfed those Ogle, *Ambitious Brew*, 55.

gradually peter out Dick Cantwell, "Ballantine IPA," *Oxford Companion to Beer*, ed. Oliver,
80.

it was a rout Baron, *Brewed in America*, 186–187.

ale held on Ibid., 187–190.

been one of the largest; *sales declined*; *all but gone* Samuel Wagner, "The Rise and
Fall of M. Vassar and Co.," Welcome to the Hudson Valley: A Guidebook of
Topics in Local Environmental History, June 3, 2013, https://pages.vassar.edu
/hudsonvalleyguidebook/2013/06/03/the-rise-and-fall-of-m-vassar-and-co/.

Manhattan's Park Avenue; *several lagering caves* Ogle, *Ambitious Brew*, 56; Baron, *Brewed
in America*, 230.

"genuine old"; *"the rich"*; *"a general growl"* Ogle, *Ambitious Brew*, 85.

brewers reinvigorated the local style; *made it brighter and lighter*; *"pilsner was thus stopped"*
Karl-Ullrich Heyse, "Kölsch," *Oxford Companion to Beer*, ed. Oliver, 519.

would not extend much beyond Tom Acitelli, "Kölsch: Where Ale Meets Lager," Food
Republic, June 11, 2015, https://www.foodrepublic.com/2015/06/11/kolsch-where
-ale-meets-lager/.

conscious pilsner imitation Conrad Seidl, "Helles," *Oxford Companion to Beer*, ed. Oliver, 430.

which remained the everyday tipple Oliver, *Oxford Companion to Beer*, 310.

introduced a style Ibid., 430; K. Florian Kemp, "Munich Helles," *All About Beer*, July 1,
2011, http://allaboutbeer.com/article/munich-helles-5/.

was a conscious imitation Munich Beer Gardens, accessed September 3, 2019, https://www
.munichbeergardens.com/Spaten_Brewery_history; Eric Toft, "Münchner Helles,"
New Brewer 29, no. 1 (January/February 2012).

A Munich competitor called; "recognized as the most" Oliver, *Oxford Companion to Beer*, 430.

about one-quarter of the region's Ibid.

"declared that they had" Ibid.

more than thirty-six million; nearly twenty-four gallons Schlüter, *Brewing Industry*, 83.

agreed to disagree Oliver, *Oxford Companion to Beer*, 430.

not the first plague; caused major hiccups John Wilson, "Phylloxera: The Parasite That
Changed Wine Forever," *Irish Times*, January 3, 2015. For more on phylloxera's effects
and the fight against it, see Christy Campbell, *Phylloxera: How Wine Was Saved for
the World* (New York: Harper Perennial, 2010).

It all started; Starting in France's Kelli White, "The Devastator: Phylloxera Vastatrix &
the Remaking of the World of Wine," GuildSomm, December 30, 2017, https://www
.guildsomm.com/public_content/features/articles/b/kelli-white/posts/phylloxera
-vastatrix.

"The phylloxera, a true gourmet" Edward Linley Sambourne, cartoon, *Punch*, September 6, 1890, via Wikimedia Commons, accessed March 2, 2020, https://commons.wiki
media.org/wiki/File:Phylloxera_cartoon.png.

rootstocks were carefully yet quickly Nellie Ming Lee, "Vines That Survived Europe's Phylloxera Epidemic in the 1800s, and the Wines Made from Them," *South China Post*,
November 2, 2018.

Unscrupulous practices, too, ran amok; led to France's groundbreaking Acitelli, *American
Wine*, 8.

did particularly well in the wake Jared Ranahan, "How Phylloxera Jumpstarted the Modern
Whiskey Industry," *Bourbon Review*, July 12, 2019.

used those emptied sherry casks "Phylloxera: The Bug That Saved the Whisky Industry,"
Whiskystories (blog), November 18, 2015, https://whiskystories.com/2015/11/18
/phylloxera-saved-whisky/.

"By the 1870s" Baron, *Brewed in America*, 228.

United States would surpass; a matter of time Schlüter, *Brewing Industry*, 82.

20. Toward a Better Pilsner

1893, broke cold Reid Badger, *The Great American Fair: The World's Columbian Exposition and American Culture* (Chicago: Nelson Hall, 1979), xi–xiii. The author also
used details about the expo found in chapter 2 of Rydell's *All the World's*, 38–71.

"Millions of people" Joseph Gustaitis, *Chicago's Greatest Year, 1893: The White City and
the Birth of a Modern Metropolis* (Carbondale: Southern Illinois University Press,
2013), 15.

"a coming out" Ibid.

Paris in 1889; Chicago's would cover Ibid., 18.

"the most stalwart"; which spurred Ibid.

"Never before" David Lowe, *Lost Chicago* (Chicago: University of Chicago Press, 2010), 153.

130,000; starting with a group Gustaitis, *Chicago's Greatest Year*, 19; Badger, *Great American Fair*, xi–xii.

"aflame with flags"; "like that of distant"; "stupendous results" Badger, *Great American
Fair*, xii.

pressed a golden Ibid., xii–xiii.

ran to 104 pages; it listed 968; "This was an exposition" Gustaitis, *Chicago's Greatest Year*, 20.

twenty-four brewers and their beers "Classification of the World's Columbian Exposition, Chicago, USA, 1893," Digital Research Library of Illinois History, accessed February 26, 2020, http://livinghistoryofillinois.com/pdf_files/Classification%20of%20the%20 Worlds%20Columbian%20Exposition,%20Chicago,%20USA,%201893.pdf.

"Adolphus Busch as well" Plavchan, *History of Anheuser-Busch*, 101.

"In an era before" Nick Andersen, "When You Couldn't Bring Technology to People, Ambitious Cities Brought People to World's Fairs," *Boston Globe*, September 1, 2018.

none more so than Busch and Pabst Ogle, *Ambitious Brew*, 125–131.

Ogle provides an excellent summary and analysis of the Busch-Pabst rivalry before, during, and after the World's Columbian Expo. The author drew on this account.

For details on Busch's wealth and lifestyle, see Knoedelseder, *Bitter Brew*, 18–20, and Ogle, *Ambitious Brew*, 122–124. For details on Pabst's wealth and lifestyle, see Ogle, *Ambitious Brew*, 122.

particularly gratifying for Busch Ogle, *Ambitious Brew*, 123.

obtained from a financially struggling Carl Plavchan, *History of Anheuser-Busch*, 72–73.

"puny"; "correct to the minutest" Ogle, *Ambitious Brew*, 125.

"Nothing has been omitted" Ibid., 126.

would overshadow everything The author drew from Ogle, *Ambitious Brew*, 127–133, and Plavchan, *History of Anheuser-Busch*, 101–103, regarding the awards competition, controversy, and aftermath.

ANHEUSER BUSCH WINS The ad can be found on page 8 of the October 29, 1893 edition of the *St. Paul Daily Globe*, Library of Congress' digital archives, https://chroniclingamerica .loc.gov/lccn/sn90059522/1893-10-29/ed-1/seq-8/.

"The stuff published" Ogle, *Ambitious Brew*, 130.

PABST MILWAUKEE BEER WINS; *in blue ribbon* Ibid., 131.

no formalized appeal Herbert W. Hess, "History and Present Status of the 'Truth-in-Advertising' Movement as Carried on by the Vigilance Committee of the Associated Advertising Clubs of the World," *American Academy of Political and Social Science* 101, no. 1 (May 1922): 211–220.

"You have no idea" Ogle, *Ambitious Brew*, 132.

had a major hand "Adolphus Busch (1839–1913)," State Historical Society of Missouri, Historic Missourians, accessed June 30, 2019, https://historicmissourians.shsmo.org /historicmissourians/name/b/busch/.

21. The Inevitable Beer

was doing pretty well for himself Ohlsson's background and his rise in South African brewing comes from Purinton, "Empire," 127–137.

a remarkable 64 percent; *Large piles of empty beer*; *Of the 167 companies* Purinton, "Empire," 132.

a kind of forced Anglicization Ibid., 125.

"In the 1830s" Ibid., 126.

"They used an English"; *dispatched one of his* Ibid., 128.

Cape Town gained a reputation Ibid. 128–129. The author also consulted Lucy Corne's *African Brew: Exploring the Craft of South African Beer* (New York: Random House Struik, 2014) for more context on South African brewing history.

acquired other breweries; *He even exported* Purinton, "Empire," 128–129.

the ground under Ohlsson; *but the techniques and the equipment* Ibid., 131–135.

the treasurer-general of Cape Town inquired Ibid., 134–135.

had been good for business Ibid., 135.

That was certainly what spurred Ibid., 137–140; "South African Breweries Ltd," International Directory of Company Histories, Encyclopedia.com, accessed September 9, 2019, https://www.encyclopedia.com/books/politics-and-business-magazines/south-african -breweries-ltd.

"large and beer-loving" Purinton, "Empire," 139.

poured into southern Africa Ibid., 139–140.

through buying up; was laying the foundations Ibid., 140–142.

"there was no comparison"; "had been called" Ibid., 141.

formed a joint stock company Bryan Denton, "A Beer Festival in China Has German Roots, but No Lederhosen," *New York Times*, October 30, 2017; Bev Robertson, "China," *Oxford Companion to Beer*, ed. Oliver, 245.

"They wanted the relief" Robert Bickers, "Tsingtao Beer: A Complex Brew," *China Beat* (blog), June 3, 2009, http://thechinabeat.blogspot.com/2009/06/tsingtao-beer-complex -brew.html.

followed a similar approach Pete Brown, "Foster's," *Oxford Companion to Beer*, ed. Oliver, 370–372.

"supplied in the proper way"; less than what it cost Ibid., 371.

"When consumers ordered" Purinton, "Empire," 14. Purinton in general spells out pilsner's early appeal to brewers and the public. See also Ogle, *Ambitious Brew*, 71–73, for more on the appeal of lighter-tasting, lighter-colored lager.

"the first global" Purinton, "Empire," 144.

"lager brewing required large" Ibid., 67.

It was the "Yesterday" The Beatles hit has been one of the most covered—if not the most covered—song since its 1965 release. Per John Elmes, "The 10 Most Covered Songs," *Independent* (UK), December 5, 2008.

22. The Biggest Threat

a new group formed in Oberlin Baron, *Brewed in America*, 286. For more on the origins of the American temperance movement, see Baron, *Brewed in America*, 191–198.

loved to tell audiences The dialogue that Russell would recount is described in "Howard Hyde Russell," Westerville (OH) Public Library, accessed September 9, 2019, http://www.westervillelibrary.org/antisaloon-russell/.

approximately four million "Immigration," Library of Congress, accessed September 1, 2019, https://www.loc.gov/teachers/classroommaterials/presentationsandactivities /presentations/immigration/italian3.html. These immigrants included all four of the author's grandparents.

the new movement saw success The Anti-Saloon League has been called the first single-issue, nonpartisan interest group in modern US politics, per McCoy, *Beer of Broadway*, 101–102, and "Anti-Saloon League," Encyclopedia.com, Dictionary of American History, accessed September 9, 2019, https://www.encyclopedia.com/history/dictionaries -thesauruses-pictures-and-press-releases/anti-saloon-league.

"regardless of their name" "Howard Hyde Russell," Westerville (OH) Public Library.

In December 1895; "It has not come" "Anti-Saloon League Is Formed," Westerville (OH) Public Library, accessed September 9, 2019, https://www.westervillelibrary.org/antisaloon -history-saloon.

much-needed coordination Plavchan, *History of Anheuser-Busch*, 116.

Brewers hardly noticed Ibid.; Baron, *Brewed in America*, 286–287.

came up with what he called; *"They were designed"* "William Painter," Lemelson-MIT Program, accessed September 9, 2019, https://lemelson.mit.edu/resources/william -painter; Baron, *Brewed in America*, 243.

patented an opener "William Painter," Lemelson-MIT Program.

a vast improvement Baron, *Brewed in America*, 243.

wave of consolidation Ibid., 265–272.

hosted more than forty-one hundred "National Beer Sales," Brewers Association official website.

owned or had sizable stakes Plavchan, *History of Anheuser-Busch*, 106.

trying to thwart Baron, *Brewed in America*, 292–293. Despite brewers' best efforts, the excise tax per barrel doubled to two dollars.

a fact of American civic life Kathryn L. MacKay, "Notable Labor Strikes of the Gilded Age," Weber State University, accessed August 31, 2019, http://faculty.weber.edu/kmackay /notable_labor_strikes_of_the_gil.htm; part 3, 89–280, of Schlüter's *Brewing Industry* gives a fine account of labor-capital relations in the nineteenth-century brewing industry.

"has had the bloodiest" MacKay, "Notable Labor."

tended to make more Baron, *Brewed in America*, 280.

an extra two dollars Schlüter, *Brewing Industry*, 182.

so ineffective and disjointed Plavchan, *History of Anheuser-Busch*, 116; Baron, *Brewed in America*, 286–287. The temperance movement was in particular disjointed, with various groups before 1893 "more interested in fighting among themselves than against the growing power of the liquor industry," per Plavchan, *History of Anheuser-Busch*, 116.

"I drink beer" Baron, *Brewed in America*, 296.

"It pierces the thickest"; *Theodore Roosevelt used* Gary Younge, "Blood, Sweat and Fears," *Guardian* (UK), August 4, 2006.

"a steady stream"; *"the liquor problem"* Plavchan, *History of Anheuser-Busch*, 120.

to publicly condemn; *"Divorce the saloon"* Ibid., 126–127. Drys also advocated temperance as a way to reduce and prevent domestic violence. It does not appear that brewers countered this argument at all.

the modern equivalent Ibid., 127–128.

newly elected governor Ibid., 129.

rejected by a wide margin; *"all intoxicating liquors"* "Florida Prohibition, Amendment 3 (1910)," Ballotpedia, accessed September 10, 2019, https://ballotpedia.org/Florida _Prohibition,_Amendment_3_(1910). The author also drew from Plavchan, *History of Anheuser-Busch*, 128–133, and Baron, *Brewed in America*, 295–307, for details on the slow success of temperance advocates.

"You will hardly suspect" Baron, *Brewed in America*, 296.

He vetoed legislation Ibid., 300.

"I can not & will not" Ibid., 299.

"I notice in the papers" "Prohibition: Early Days," Woodrow Wilson Presidential Library & Museum, November 14, 2018, https://www.woodrowwilson.org/blog/2018/11/14 /prohibition-early-days.

four thousand men and women "The March to National Prohibition," Westerville Public Library, accessed September 10, 2019, https://www.westervillelibrary.org/antisaloon -national-prohibition-march.

brewers were awakening; *leaned on images* Plavchan, *History of Anheuser-Busch*, 127–128; Baron, *Brewed in America*, 301.

"*to take care*" Ibid.

the drys could tug on Baron, *Brewed in America*, 301–302.

"*There is no doubt*" Ibid., 301.

23. War

When in late 1914 Author's visit to Achel, May 2011. The author returned to Barbara Tuchman's *Guns of August* (New York: Presidio Press, 2004) for information on World War I.

"*without letting out the slightest*" Smit, *Heineken Story*, 11.

"*The epitome of the dynastic*" Baron, *Brewed in America*, 288.

his will entrusted Plavchan, *History of Anheuser-Busch*, 130.

well over one million barrels Ibid., 111.

likely made Anheuser-Busch the largest Downard, *Dictionary*, 240.

made him immensely wealthy Baron, *Brewed in America*, 288–289.

"*was said to have been unprecedented*"; *Roosevelt sent gifts; estimated his wealth at some $60 million* "Adolphus Busch Dies in Prussia," *New York Times*, October 11, 1913.

"*Our gardens*"; *private train; 1 Busch Place; fired salutes* Baron, *Brewed in America*, 288–289.

appropriated and repurposed; used as stables Christopher Barnes, "Beer in the Shadow of War," *All About Beer*, May 28, 2018.

the largest brewery in continental Europe; 825,000 barrels "History of a Czech Legend," Pilsner Urquell brewery official website, accessed September 5, 2019, https://www .prazdroj.cz/en/our-story/history.

majority of the brewery's output Peter A. Ensminger, "The History and Brewing Methods of Pilsner Urquell," MoreBeer.com, November 30, 2001, https://www.morebeer.com /articles/Pilsner_Urquell. Export figures for Pilsner Urquell—and for many breweries in Europe in the nineteenth century—are somewhat sketchy, but it is clear that by 1865 the majority of the Burghers' Brewery's output was going well beyond Pilsen and the surrounding Bohemian countryside. See "Plzeňský Prazdroj," 29–41.

in Racine, Wisconsin Evan Rail, "Well, Actually—Why the Pilsner Urquell Story Is Still Coming to America," *Good Beer Hunting* (blog), July 5, 2017, https://www.goodbeerhunting .com/blog/2017/7/3/coming-to-america-pilsner-urquell.

a further trademark on February 8 Author's e-mail exchange with the Austrian Patent Office, September 2019. The office generously provided a scan of the trademark registration.

would not scratch Ensminger, "History and Brewing."

"*The sudden outbreak*" McCoy, *Beer of Broadway*, 95.

could even expand their reach Ibid.

helpfully offered to fill the void; wrote a personal letter Plavchan, *History of Anheuser-Busch*, 135.

"*prove indistinguishable*"; "*The pilsener sales*"; "*propagation apparatus*" McCoy, *Beer of Broadway*, 95.

"*repeated acts of war*" "Public Laws of the Sixty-Fifth Congress of the United States," *The Statutes at Large of the United States of America, from April 1917 to March 1919*, vol. 40 (Washington, DC: Government Printing Office, 1919), 1.

the United States had just over Jim Garamone, "World War I: Building the American Military," Department of Defense News, Defense Media Activity, April 3, 2017.

The United States was in a bind For more on the grain situation during the war, see Tom G. Hall, "Wilson and the Food Crisis: Agricultural Price Control During World War I," *Agricultural History* 47, no. 1 (January 1973): 25–46.

Woodrow Wilson would exercise; *He cut the allowable amount* Baron, *Brewed in America*, 302–303.

"I am informed" Ibid., 305.

Anti-Saloon League knew of an investigation Ibid.

revealed a laundry list; *efforts to combat the temperance* Ibid. For more on anti-German—and anti–German brewer—hysteria during the war, see McCoy, *Beer of Broadway*, 114–115.

"Everything in this country" Plavchan, *History of Anheuser-Busch*, 144.

"We have German enemies" Smit, *Heineken Story*, 42.

financial support behind the US; *scions of many* Baron, *Brewed in America*, 304–305.

"By equating the brewers' defense" McCoy, *Beer of Broadway*, 115.

"For German Americans as a whole" Ibid., 144.

"of enemy character"; *Lilly Busch had been vacationing*; *fair game in Palmer's eyes* Ibid., 115; Ogle, *Ambitious Brew*, 175.

relying on the taxes on beer Joseph Bishop-Henchman, "How Taxes Enabled Alcohol Prohibition and Also Led to Its Repeal," Tax Foundation, October 5, 2011, https://taxfoundation.org/how-taxes-enabled-alcohol-prohibition-and-also-led-its-repeal/.

40 percent of all Baron, *Brewed in America*, 293.

three-fourths of its revenue Michael Lerner, "Unintended Consequences," PBS.org, accessed September 10, 2019, http://www.pbs.org/kenburns/prohibition/unintended-consequences/.

though originally just intended Erik M. Jensen, "The Taxing Power, the Sixteenth Amendment, and the Meaning of 'Incomes,'" Tax History Project, October 4, 2002, http://www.taxhistory.org/thp/readings.nsf/cf7c9c870b600b9585256df80075b9dd/736db4705b4ee21d85256f2b00548fa3.

For a solid study of how the Eighteenth Amendment played out in state legislatures, see R. M. Boeckel, "The States and the Prohibition Amendment," Editorial Research Reports, February 25, 1931, via CQ Press, http://library.cqpress.com/cqresearcher/cqresrre1931022500.

24. "A Good Time for Beer"

"We are fighting Germany"; *King George V pledged* Tom Acitelli, "How World War I Affected Beer," *All About Beer*, June 30, 2014, http://allaboutbeer.com/world-war-i-beer/.

In Canada Gerald Hallowell, "Prohibition in Canada," *Canadian Encyclopedia Online*, March 4, 2015, https://www.thecanadianencyclopedia.ca/en/article/prohibition.

tried some forms of partial or total "Prohibition," *Encyclopaedia Britannica Online*, accessed August 30, 2019, https://www.britannica.com/topic/prohibition-alcohol-interdict.

"Essentially our business" Plavchan, *History of Anheuser-Busch*, 156.

moved into the manufacture; *even talk of converting* Ibid., 154–195; Baron, *Brewed in America*, 312–314.

packaging the flesh Ibid., 314.

Brewers drew particular hope; *"The leading New York brewers"*; *Closings and consolidations became common* Baron, *Brewed in America*, 315.

"Brewing on a national scale" Ibid., 313.

Pabst by 1910; *pivoting to the production* Cochran, *Pabst Brewing*, 247.

"My position may surprise you" Rockefeller's letter was so widely disseminated it was even read into the congressional record. *Congressional Record: Proceedings and Debates*, vol. 75, part 11 (Washington: Government Printing Office, 1932), 12144.

prominent business leaders Baron, *Brewed in America*, 318–319.

called for returning regulatory authority "Dr. Butler Offers Plank for Repeal," *New York Times*, June 6, 1932.

Nothing illustrated that more Terry Golway, *Frank & Al: FDR, Al Smith and the Unlikely Alliance That Created the Modern Democratic Party* (New York: St. Martin's Press, 2018), 192–210.

lustily supported Prohibition Lerner, "Unintended Consequences."

"the Mother of ignorance" Okrent, *Last Call*, 89.

got more than fifteen million "United States Presidential Election of 1928," *Encyclopaedia Britannica Online*, accessed August 30, 2019, https://www.britannica.com/event/United-States-presidential-election-of-1928.

contributed to a spike Cochran, *Pabst Brewing*, 361.

to 63 percent "History of Federal Income Tax Rates: 1913–2019," Bradford Tax Institute, accessed August 30, 2019, https://bradfordtaxinstitute.com/Free_Resources/Federal-Income-Tax-Rates.aspx.

a couple of banks "Bank Run," History.com, June 10, 2019, https://www.history.com/topics/great-depression/bank-run.

did adopt a call; "allow the States to deal" "Republican Party Platform of 1932," June 14, 1932, American Presidency Project, https://www.presidency.ucsb.edu/documents/republican-party-platform-1932.

called for outright repeal; "immediate modification" "Democratic Party Platform of 1932," June 27, 1932, American Presidency Project, https://www.presidency.ucsb.edu/documents/1932-democratic-party-platform.

Congress passed; up to 3.2 percent alcohol by weight Baron, *Brewed in America*, 320–321.

picked the percentage arbitrarily Dan Nosowitz, "Weak but Powerful: The Legacy of 3.2 Percent Beer Endures," New Food Economy, July 12, 2019, https://newfoodeconomy.org/3-2-beer-alcohol-prohibition-liquor-laws-abv/.

when Utah became Allan Kent Powell, "Prohibition," *Utah History Encyclopedia*, accessed August 29, 2019, https://www.uen.org/utah_history_encyclopedia/p/PROHIBITION.shtml.

Brewers were ready even before Baron, *Brewed in America*, 322.

in a remark to guests; "I think this would be" Ernest K. Lindley, *The Roosevelt Revolution: First Phase* (New York: The Viking Press, 1933), 91. Special thanks to the Franklin Delano Roosevelt Library & Museum in Hyde Park, New York, for helping track down this quotation from one of FDR's dinner guests that night.

25. The Americans' Century

steamed into Hoboken; Smit, *Heineken Story*, 43–44.

a capacity for more than "SS Statendam Passenger Lists," GG Archives, accessed August 30, 2019, https://www.gjenvick.com/Passengers/Ships/Statendam-PassengerLists.html.

"The first legal shipment" Smit, *Heineken Story*, 43–44.

steep tariffs; foreign beer accounted for Ibid., 45.

"It's a risk, I know"; Pabst pilsner readily available Cochran, *Pabst Brewing*, 364–365.

Police estimated; "tooted their German tunes" "Crowds in Cafés, Hotels Give Beer Rousing Welcome," *St. Louis Post-Dispatch*, April 7, 1933.

rolling out its wares; million-dollar advertising Plavchan, *History of Anheuser-Busch*, 218–219; J. Anne Funderburg, *Bootleggers and Beer Barons of the Prohibition Era* (Jefferson, NC: McFarland and Company, 2014), 364–365.

a train carried six; *"Surely it is a happy"* Plavchan, *History of Anheuser-Busch*, 221–222.

also got a special airborne; *Some fifty-five additional* Ibid., 219; "Crowds in Cafés," *St. Louis Post-Dispatch.*

would ship a remarkable forty-five Plavchan, *History of Anheuser-Busch*, 221.

had either not survived Knoedelseder, *Bitter Brew*, 31–32.

would have it no other way Plavchan, *History of Anheuser-Busch*, 131. For more on August A. Busch's management style and lifestyle, see Plavchan, *History of Anheuser-Busch*, 131–223; and Knoedelseder, *Bitter Brew*, 30–31.

He had to be Baron, *Brewed in America*, 287–289, covers the hand-offs between brewery founders and later generations.

took to the radio; *"Happy days"*; *"for all time, divorce"* Plavchan, *History of Anheuser-Busch*, 219–220.

Sales surged so much; *"The reason the supply"* Plavchan, *History of Anheuser-Busch*, 220.

"an article formerly contraband" Thomas Pinney, *A History of Wine in America*, vol. 2, *From Prohibition to the Present* (Berkeley: University of California Press, 2005), 51. For more on the public's post-Prohibition perception of beer and drinking, see Baron, *Brewed in America*, 326–328; and Ogle, *Ambitious Brew*, 208–210.

a dramatic decline Mark H. Morse, "Actually, Prohibition Was a Success," *New York Times*, October 16, 1989.

went from being an industrial flyspeck Baron, *Brewed in America*, 324.

26. Crushing It

On January 24, 1935 For Gottfried Kruger's can rollout, the author drew from Ogle, *Ambitious Brew*, 214–215; Baron, *Brewed in America*, 327; and Horst Dornbusch, "Canning," *Oxford Companion to Beer*, ed. Oliver, 214–216.

nation's fifty largest "American Can Company," Ohio History Central, accessed September 14, 2019, https://ohiohistorycentral.org/w/American_Can_Company.

from heavy-gauged steel Christina Perozzi, "From Church Key to Pop Top, a Look Back at Canned Beer," Eater, July 15, 2015, https://www.eater.com/drinks/2015/7/15/8942369/dirt-cheap-week-canned-beer.

about four ounces "Beer Can History," Brewery Collectibles Club of America, accessed September 9, 2019, https://www.bcca.com/beer-can-history/.

as boilerplate as they came; *"in wooden shoes and leather"*; *grown into a major investor* William Starr Myers, ed., *Prominent Families of New Jersey*, vol. 1 (Baltimore: Genealogical Publishing Company, 2000), 360–362.

had led the way; *Pabst researchers found salvation* Cochran, *Pabst Brewing*, 380–381.

"the brewing industry" Ibid., 381.

Perlstein did. Three times. Ibid.

came in—albeit cautiously; *Nearly all the respondents* Ogle, *Ambitious Brew*, 214–215.

"The results surprised" Ibid., 214.

striking a deal "Krueger Ale: 1951," RustyCans.com, April 2006, http://www.rustycans.com/COM/month0406.html.

more than 80 percent; *lost sales in Richmond* Ogle, *Ambitious Brew*, 215.

since that first decade Dornbusch, "Canning," 215.

found its lining Ibid., 214.

worked so well "Union Carbide to Make Vinylite at New Bound Brook Unit," *New York Times*, December 13, 1940.

explosive cans had also hindered Dornbusch, "Canning."

an early brochure "Krueger Pop-Up Brochure," Breweriana.com, accessed December 21, 2019, http://breweriana.com/miscellaneous/krueger-pop-up-brochure-8738/.

The returnable bottle system For a fine rundown of the history of bottling and bottling reuse and return, see Jane Busch, "Second Time Around: A Look at Bottle Reuse," *Historical Archaeology* 21, no. 1 (1987): 67–80.

"That period of the year"; "the Massachusetts Bottlers'" Ibid., 71.

ice reigned a little longer; especially big hit in 1927 Nancy Mitchell "A Brief but Fascinating History of the Refrigerator," Apartment Therapy, accessed September 10, 2019, https://www.apartmenttherapy.com/history-of-the-refrigerator-248166.

Indeed, there were fatalities Ibid.

"miracle compound" Mary Bellis, "The History of Freon," ThoughtCo, March 4, 2019, https://www.thoughtco.com/history-of-freon-4072212.

ended up leading; owned a refrigerator Mitchell, "Brief but Fascinating History."

"The refrigerator came to be" Matt Novak, "The Great Depression and the Rise of the Refrigerator," *Pacific Standard*, June 14, 2017, https://psmag.com/environment/the-rise-of-the-refrigerator-47924.

had rolled out canned; included Pabst Export Lager Dornbusch, "Canning," 215.

first canned beer outside; its production quintuple Ibid.

three in four beers sold Baron, *Brewed in America*, 326.

27. Share of Throat

Munching was a tall; to seize a life-changing moment Smit, *Heineken Story*, 39–41, 44–45.

one last sales pitch; would spend the next several Ibid., 44.

would look aghast; wanted the other diners Ibid., 39–40.

"Snob appeal" Ibid., 40.

one of his coups was a float Ibid., 46.

twelve hundred acres; forty-four million Alan Taylor, "The 1939 New York World's Fair," *Atlantic*, November 1, 2013.

was a replica "1939 World's Fair," Museum of the City of New York, federal art project, accessed September 12, 2019, https://collections.mcny.org/Explore/Highlights/1939-World's-Fair/.

serving more than 264 Smit, *Heineken Story*, 46.

the number of breweries "National Beer Sales," Brewers Association official website.

at least one million barrels; per capita beer consumption Baron, *Brewed in America*, 330–331.

was growing fiercer Ogle, *Ambitious Brew*, 225–229.

no larger than 5.5; "A preview of television" RCA Brochure (1939), TVHistory.tv, accessed September 12, 2019, http://www.tvhistory.tv/1939-RCA-Brochure-1.JPG.

got their biggest public airing Keri Blakinger, "A Look Back at Some of the Coolest Attractions at the 1939 World's Fair," *Daily News*, April 30, 2016.

"Will Television programs" A Preview of Television: Radio's Newest Contribution to Home Entertainment, RCA Brochure (1939), EarlyTelevision.org, accessed September 13, 2019, http://www.earlytelevision.org/pdf/preview_of_tv.pdf.

first US president Andrew Glass, "First White House Speech Airs on TV, October 5, 1947," *Politico*, October 5, 2010, https://www.politico.com/story/2010/10/first-white-house-speech-airs-on-tv-october-5-1947-043100.

"with great happiness"; "Often I think" "President Roosevelt Opens 1939 New York World's Fair," April 30, 1939, C-Span video, https://www.c-span.org/video/?319178-1/president-roosevelt-opens-1939-york-worlds-fair, 02:32.

would shroud that nation's Blakinger, "Look Back."

28. A Different War

including two-thirds History.com editors, "Nazis Take Czechoslovakia," History.com, July 28, 2019, https://www.history.com/this-day-in-history/nazis-take-czechoslovakia.

disrupted the flow; "less robust domestic varieties" McCoy, *Beer of Broadway*, 233.

cut their barley usage; "To make up for" Baron, *Brewed in America*, 335.

figures did not slip "Beer and WWII," EuropeanBeerGuide.net, accessed September 13, 2019, https://www.europeanbeerguide.net/warbeer.htm.

to a record eighty million Baron, *Brewed in America*, 335.

discovered greater demand McCoy, *Beer of Broadway*, 235. For more on how the US brewing industry weathered and even thrived during World War II, see Baron, *Brewed in America*, 331–335.

filled Madison Square Garden Diane Bernard, "The Night Thousands of Nazis Packed Madison Square Garden for a Rally—and Violence Erupted," *Washington Post*, December 10, 2018.

"The Germans leave mankind"; "Sooner or later" McCoy, *Beer of Broadway*, 234–235.

"We must, perhaps" Baron, *Brewed in America*, 332.

"America's oldest lager" Rudolph J. Schaefer Jr., "The Schaefer Story: History of the F&M Schaefer Brewing Co.," accessed September 13, 2019, https://theschaeferstory .wordpress.com/chapter-iv/.

to ban alcohol sales; "It would be harmful" Baron, *Brewed in America*, 333.

ordered it stopped; "an essential industry" Ibid., 334.

"a greatly improved financial position" Ibid., 335.

"flourished" McCoy, *Beer of Broadway*, 235.

29. Beyond the Brewery

died of a cerebral hemorrhage Knoedelseder, *Bitter Brew*, 49; "Adolphus Busch 3D, Brewery Head, 65," *New York Times*, August 30, 1946.

The brewery had diversified; "caught with all its eggs"; obituary rattled off Ibid.

MEDIUM STATURE Robert Mcg. Thomas Jr., "August A. Busch Jr. Dies at 90," *New York Times*, September 30, 1989.

the former from suicide Tim O'Neil, "The Day August A. Busch Sr. Killed Himself at Grant's Farm," *St. Louis Post-Dispatch*, February 13, 2019.

"possibly the most brilliant" Knoedelseder, *Bitter Brew*, 50.

"master showman" Thomas, "August A. Busch."

Busch was volatile; "My name is Gussie" Knoedelseder, *Bitter Brew*, 49–51.

was largest by production Maureen Ogle, "Historical Tidbits: The 'Rise' of Miller Brewing," MaureenOgle.com, October 7, 2008, https://www.maureenogle.com/maureen -ogle/2008/10/07/historical-tidbits-beer-the-rise-of-miller-brewing.

losing ground domestically Knoedelseder, *Bitter Brew*, 51.

particularly strong Cochran, *Pabst Brewing*, 389–391.

had approached his good friend Kenan Heise, "Harris Perlstein, 93, Ex-Pabst Chairman," *Chicago Tribune*, August 19, 1986.

was emerging as the bestselling Cochran, *Pabst Brewing*, 397–398.

second act of a storied life; "a swarthy skinned" "Fred Miller Is Elected Notre Dame Captain," *Milwaukee Journal*, February 2, 1928.

not even among the top Ogle, "Historical Tidbits"; Downard, *Dictionary*, 119–120.

courtly and reserved; Heineken started working; plodded the streets; "I don't sell beer" Paul Meller, "Alfred Heineken, 78, Dies; Made Dutch Brewer a Giant," *New York*

Times, January 5, 2007. Barbara Smit also has good background on Heineken's early contributions to the family firm in *Heineken Story*, 63–67.

neck-and-neck; that was unacceptable Knoedelseder, *Bitter Brew*, 49.

"Being second isn't worth"; cleaned up the quotation Ibid.

the style had been settled Baron, *Brewed in America*, 337. Baron makes this point about the wider brewing industry—that what happened after the beer was brewed mattered infinitely more and drew most of the money breweries spent post–World War II. Since pilsner was the reigning style, this would have been especially true of it.

to outsell draft; the difference grew Ibid., 326.

would peak in 1946 Tim Purtell, "1946: The Year for Movie-Going," *Entertainment Weekly*, April 29, 1994.

might have consumed Ogle, *Ambitious Brew*, 228.

Raytheon introduced in 1947 Priya Ganapati, "Oct. 25, 1955: Time to Nuke Dinner," *Wired*, October 25, 2010, https://www.wired.com/2010/10/1025home-microwave-ovens/.

selling thirteen million Andrew F. Smith, *Eating History: 30 Turning Points in the Making of American Cuisine* (New York: Columbia University Press, 2009), 172.

a multibillion-dollar one Bill Ganzel, "Frozen Foods Explode (So to Speak)," Wessels Living History Farm, 2007, https://livinghistoryfarm.org/farminginthe50s/life_15.html.

with White Castle Andrew F. Smith, *Encyclopedia of Junk Food and Fast Food* (Westport, CT: Greenwood Press, 2006), 284–285.

really revolutionized things Ibid., 169–177.

"In the days of draught" Baron, *Brewed in America*, 346.

30. Never Break the Chain

originated from a small German Griesedieck, *Falstaff Story*, 9.

the Griesediecks had a connection Ibid., 134–135.

one of the largest producers; 1937 acquisition enormously expanded Ibid., 138.

gave Falstaff a headache; "Falstaff was literally" Griesedieck covers his family's adventures in New Orleans in his book *Falstaff Story*, 163–166.

Other breweries watched Falstaff; were embracing the trend Baron, *Brewed in America*, 340–342.

fewer than 200 "National Beer Sales," Brewers Association official website.

All the major players; "in the years" Baron, *Brewed in America*, 340–342.

future brewers to understand; "I cannot emphasize" Griesedieck, *Falstaff Story*,166.

$34 million Knoedelseder, *Bitter Brew*, 50.

"a crushing capacity" McCoy, *Beer of Broadway*, 262.

"Nothing said more" Ogle, *Ambitious Brew*, 224.

Competitors such as Pabst; jump more than 48 percent Baron, *Brewed in America*, 340–341.

either closed or sold out; top fifteen companies; "It is not uncommon" Ibid., 343.

most severe bombing run; 111 bombs landed; to toast their liberators "Plzeňský Prazdroj," 135.

in 1950 "to promote" "About the National Science Foundation," National Science Foundation official website, accessed September 17, 2019, https://www.nsf.gov/about.

when it came to agriculture Colleges of Agriculture at the Land Grant Universities: A Profile (Washington, DC: National Academy Press, 1995), 11.

"Here I was, a black kid" Cornelia Dean, "When Science Suddenly Mattered, in Space and in Class," *New York Times*, September 25, 2007.

moved to spacious, modern Michell Eloy, "A Short History of Siebel Chicago's Beer School," *Chicago Magazine*, June 21, 2011.

"In effect" Griesedieck, *Falstaff Story*, 164.

"generally sat out" Thomas E. Ricks, *Churchill & Orwell: The Fight for Freedom* (New York: Penguin Books, 2017), 204. Pages 194–197 amply summarize the mid-twentieth century's wave of scientific devotion as being a distinctly America-driven one.

one million case sales Meller, "Alfred Heineken, 78, Dies."

after the surname Downard, *Dictionary*, 45.

"to saturate all regions" Baron, *Brewed in America*, 342.

Black Label powered; *"two hundred or so"* Ibid., 343.

31. The Soft Sell

Approached Gussie; *"Gussie didn't give"* Knoedelseder, *Bitter Brew*, 58.

in all the United States; *"As the farthest west"* Ibid., 59.

had pleaded guilty Tim O'Neill, "A Look Back," *St. Louis Post-Dispatch*, January 5, 2014.

acquired the Cardinals; *"a couple of dribblers"* Knoedelseder, *Bitter Brew*, 60–61. Busch's company also bought the stadium for $800,000 and paid half that to upgrade it, per Knoedelseder, *Bitter Brew*, 60–61.

"This is one of the finest"; *to name it Budweiser Stadium* Ibid., 60. It was also not unusual for baseball stadiums to be named after owners.

"a giant outdoor tavern"; *helped force the Griesedieck* Ibid., 59.

Brewer Jacob Ruppert Kevin Reichard, "The Glory Days of Baseball and Beer Marketing," *Ballpark Digest*, February 2, 2017, https://ballparkdigest.com/2017/02/02/the-glory -days-of-baseball-and-beer-marketing/.

first brewery to straight-up; *were double those* Knoedelseder, *Bitter Brew*, 59.

was earning $0.73; *was pulling in $1.80* McCoy, *Beer of Broadway*, 262.

Enter Ed Graham McCoy, *Beer of Broadway*, 267–273, is the best account of the rise and fall of the Bert and Harry campaign, including the reaction of fans and the effect on beer sales.

"less N.F.S." Ibid., 252–253.

"pretty horrible" Ibid., 267.

"One of the most effective" "Spiel for Piel," *Time*, May 21, 1956.

"Encouraged by the success" McCoy, *Beer of Broadway*, 269.

"The big mistake"; *"Unfortunately, the beer itself"* Ibid., 271.

croaked Bert and Harry in 1960 Robert Alden, "Curtains for Bert and Harry," *New York Times*, December 1, 1960.

"The question now is" Ibid.

32. The Customer Is Always Right

"I think we have"; *barely extended beyond the Northeast*; *had been trying to develop*; *one million barrels* Tom Acitelli, "How Cream Ale Rose," *All About Beer*, August 17, 2015, http://allaboutbeer.com/the-birth-of-genesee-cream-ale/.

Some considered it the American Jeremy Marshall, "Cream Ale," *Oxford Companion to Beer*, ed. Oliver, 273.

number of likely beer drinkers was shrinking; *sliding to historic lows* Ogle, *Ambitious Brew*, 226.

accounted for nearly one-fourth Dane Huckelbridge, *Bourbon: A History of the American Spirit* (New York, William Morrow, 2014), 227–228.

drove a branch of the Smirnoff Victorino Mathus, *Vodka: How a Colorless, Odorless, Flavorless Spirit Conquered America* (Guilford, CT: Lyons Press, 2014), 27–28.

"One of the most important" Ogle, *Ambitious Brew*, 228.

spurred a tripling Heather Rogers, "A Brief History of Plastic," *Brooklyn Rail*, May 1, 2005, https://brooklynrail.org/2005/05/express/a-brief-history-of-plastic.

"Virtually nothing was made" Ogle, *Ambitious Brew*, 228.

proliferated in kitchens Sarah Archer, "Inventing the Kitchen of Tomorrow," Curbed, May 8, 2019, https://www.curbed.com/2019/5/8/18536810/sarah-archer-the-midcentury -kitchen-excerpt.

doubled to more than twenty-five hundred Elizabeth L. Maurer, "How Highly Processed Foods Liberated 1950s Housewives," National Women's History Museum, May 11, 2007, https://www.womenshistory.org/articles/how-highly-processed-foods-liberated -1950s-housewives.

Industrial output increased 54 percent; beer sales started to stagnate; per capita consumption Ogle, *Ambitious Brew*, 225.

"A careful and impartial student" Purinton, "Empire," 155.

"alcoholic soda pop" Author's interview with Jim Koch.

halved the amount of hops; drop even further Ranjit Dighe, "Why Bland American Beer Is Here to Stay," Conversation, March 13, 2018, https://theconversation.com/why -bland-american-beer-is-here-to-stay-91737.

urged members to brew Ogle, *Ambitious Brew*, 229.

when US corn production took off "Historical Corn Grain Yields for the U.S.," Purdue University Agronomy Department, May 2017, https://www.agry.purdue.edu/ext/corn /news/timeless/yieldtrends.html.

"Indeed, what consumers understood" Purinton, "Empire," 13.

The theory about World War II eating into material became a favorite of the craft beer movement in the late twentieth century, which blamed wartime shortages for the introduction of adjuncts such as corn and rice and therefore for the perceived corruption of American beer. Corn and rice, however, began appearing in American pilsners in the late nineteenth century.

33. A Gnat at an Elephant

"first camp-decor"; "bohemian businessman" J. L. Pimsleur, "Obituary—Frederick Walter Kuh," SF Gate, November 12, 1997, https://www.sfgate.com/news/article/OBITUARY -Frederick-Walter-Kuh-2796413.php.

One of those regulars; to figure out what he wanted Patrick Cain, "Tapping a Fresh Beer Market," *Investor's Business Daily*, February 24, 2010; Robert Sullivan, "Head of Steam," *Stanford Magazine*, September–October 1996.

"Fritz, have you ever" Sullivan, "Head of Steam."

"Have you anything to do" Ibid.

"less than the price" Cain, "Tapping a Fresh."

"We were doing a hundred kegs" Sullivan, "Head of Steam."

as one of the ten largest Baron, *Brewed in America*, 345

"When an industry starts" Roger Fillion, "Bill Coors: 69 Years and Still Brewing," *Rocky Mountain News* (Denver), May 23, 2008.

an already low 188 "Statistics," Brewers Association official website, accessed May 22, 2019, https://www.brewersassociation.org/statistics/number-of-breweries/.

The Narragansett Brewing Company Baron, *Brewed in America*, 345.

"Since 1937" Ibid.

acquired its Dutch archrival; launched its first "Heineken 1864–1900," Van Der Meer.

biggest casualty of the period Ogle, *Ambitious Brew*, 237–238.

trying to merge and acquire Ibid.; "Merger with Pabst Brewing Ruled Out by Barnet," *New York Times*, May 15, 1958.

"the beer that made"; undoubtedly turned off Martyn Cornell, "How Milwaukee's Famous Beer Became Infamous," *Beer Connoisseur*, January 10, 2010.

increasingly built on advertising and marketing; with acquisitions as diverse Ogle, *Ambitious Brew*, 248–249.

"Beer to us" Ibid., 249.

"Schaefer is the one" "The Best Beer Jingles Ever Made," *Rapid City Journal*, September 16, 2016.

"The beer consumer is a very unforgiving" Leslie Wayne, "How a Popular Beer Fell out of Favor," *New York Times*, March 3, 1985.

Its production and sales footprints grew; the first major brewery Ogle, *Ambitious Brew*, 231–232.

nearly thirty million barrels annually Downard, *Dictionary*, 241.

approximately one million-square-foot brewery Acitelli, *Audacity of Hops*, 227.

Adolphus Busch himself likely knew this Roger Protz, "Budweiser Budvar," *Oxford Companion to Beer*, ed. Oliver, 191. Legal and popular disputes have dogged the Budweiser names since at least 1907, largely because of the stunning success of the American-born brand and the fact there is a brewery in Budweis that produces a Budweiser of its own (though that Budweiser is some three decades younger than the American one). The Budweis-made pilsner is generally known as Budweiser Budvar in continental Europe, while the American-born Budweiser is known there simply as Bud. Budvar in the United States goes by the name Czechvar. Per Randy Mosher, "Budweiser," *Oxford Companion to Beer*, ed. Oliver, 189.

"the king of bottled beers" Author's e-mail exchange with Tracy Lauter, May 24, 2019. Anheuser-Busch advertisements and bric-a-brac sometimes rendered the phrase "king of bottled beer."

34. "Yeccch"

"I have tried them"; "Go to hell" Tom Acitelli, "Was American Beer 'Brewed Through a Horse'?," *All About Beer*, April 11, 2017, http://allaboutbeer.com/american-beer -brewed-through-horse-mike-royko/.

"the Gallo Winery sold" "American Wine Comes of Age," *Time*, November 27, 1972.

"Beer is the star" Ann Crittenden, "It's Miller vs. Bud in the War of the Brewers," *New York Times*, August 7, 1977.

"Coors is a light-bodied beer" Grace Lichtenstein, "Sold Only in the West, Coors Beer Is Smuggled to the East," *New York Times*, December 28, 1975.

"a picnic beer smell" Acitelli, "Was American Beer."

35. Lite and Everything After

Weissman was chairman; "I'm no cowboy" Douglas Martin, "George Weissman, Leader at Philip Morris and in the Arts in New York, Dies at 90," *New York Times*, July 27, 2009.

lawyer who had been with Philip Rob Walker, "Let There Be Lite," *New York Times*, December 29, 2002.

Might the waiter Ibid.

pilsner for diabetics; with especially thorough fermentations Ibid.; Michael Jackson, "Diat Pils," Beer Hunter, accessed May 27, 2019, http://www.beerhunter.com/styles/diat _pils.html.

"There's room"; exhibited a keen knack for marketing Walker, "Let There Be Lite."

nearly half the American beer market Ibid.

had poked at the idea Not all of these initial light beers were necessarily lower in calories nor intended to be. They were instead meant as just that—lighter-colored and lighter-tasting than even the paler pilsners on the market. Ogle, *Ambitious Brew*, 229–231.

had a light beer offering McCoy, *Beer of Broadway*, 237.

called Trommers Red Letter Steven P. Schnaars, *Managing Imitation Strategies* (New York: Free Press: 2002), 99.

gummed up the marketing Walker, "Let There Be Lite."

"Not only did no one" Adam Bernstein, "Joseph Owades Dies at 86; the Father of Light Beer," *Washington Post*, December 21, 2005.

Federal government pushback; "special dietary uses"; sued Rheingold for false advertising Schnaars, *Managing Imitation Strategies*, 100–101.

gave Joseph Owades permission Ibid. The debut of Meister Bräu Lite so soon after Gablinger's also makes it likely that Owades shared his recipe with the Chicago brewery without Rheingold's knowledge. Owades died in 2005.

"genuine pilsner type" Ibid., 100–102.

It faced legal pushback; to wobble financially Ibid., 102.

"a low-calorie brew" Acitelli, "Turning on the Lite: The Origins of Miller Lite and Light Beer," *All About Beer*, June 9, 2014, http://allaboutbeer.com/turning-lite-origins -miller-lite-light-beer/2/.

in August 1973 Dave Herrewig, "The Creation of Miller Lite," *Behind the Beer* (a Miller-Coors blog), August 22, 2013, https://www.millercoorsblog.com/history/the-creation -of-miller-lite/.

"the champagne of beers" Miller High Life had also gone by the tag "the champagne of bottled beers."

hundreds of exercise videos Noel Zavoral, "Rating the Exercise Videos: All the Views That Are Fit to Rent," *Minneapolis Star Tribune*, February 23, 1992.

a boom in Cathy Hindaugh, "Home Bodies Bumping up Sales of Fitness Equipment Retailers," *Warfield's Business Journal*, January 31, 1992.

nearly $250 million ad budget Paul Gibson, "The George Weissman Road Show," *Forbes*, November 10, 1980, 179. The quarter-billion figure was adjusted for inflation from 1978 dollars.

went from the eighth largest; "a meteoric"; could capture half Crittenden, "It's Miller vs. Bud."

"We're looking for consistency"; "It's hard work" Lloyd Schwed, "What Makes a Good Beer?," UPI, October 21, 1983.

"took on a life"; "diminishing substance"; "Murphy was right" Walker, "Let There Be Lite."

36. A Final Twist

For five hours Acitelli, *Audacity of Hops*, 94–96.

Eckhardt had visited Maytag Ibid., 19–20.

Papazian had studied nuclear Ibid., 58.

"illegal possession"; "Nobody wanted to be" Greg Beato, "Draft Dodgers," *Reason*, March 2009.

a former navy mechanic Acitelli, *Audacity of Hops*, 14–16, 41–46.

"The people who sit" Merrill Sheils, "The Battle of the Beers," *Newsweek*, September 4, 1978, 59.

"produces a greater volume" Jackson, *New World Guide*, 203. The text in this is identical to what was in the 1977 original, *World Guide to Beer*.

"That's a great idea" Bilger, "Better Brew."

formed one day in a pub George Philliskirk, "Campaign for Real Ale (CAMRA)," *Oxford Companion to Beer*, ed. Oliver, 208–210.

a lower-alcohol version; "In the early 1970s" Jonathan Thompson, "British Thirst for Strong Alcohol Forces Heineken to Call Time for Weak Lager," *Independent* (UK), February 23, 2003.

"middle-aged men" Philliskirk, "Compaign for Real Ale," 209.

"No other nation" Jackson, *New World Guide*, 105.

was aggressively positioning Stella; through print advertisements Dan Bilefsky, "Interbrew Aims to Boost Its Profits by Elevating Stella to Top Shelf," *Wall Street Journal*, April 12, 2002.

was considered an everyday Ibid.

was on a shopping spree "Heineken, 1900–2000," *Van Der Meer* (blog), accessed June 6, 2019, http://famvandermeer.com/green-room/heineken-1900-2000/.

special Christmastime beer Bilefsky, "Interbrew Aims."

37. Snow and Reign

were working on the production "Interview with Bill Covaleski, Co-founder of Victory Brewing," Union Beer Distributors, June 14, 2017, https://www.unionbeerdist.com/news/interview-bill-covaleski-co-founder-victory-brewing.

number of US breweries "National Beer Sales," Brewers Association official website.

over bottles of the Belgian "Interview with Bill Covaleski," Union Beer Distributors.

"The housewife doing" Joseph F. Sullivan, "Ballantine Closing Ends Newark Era," *New York Times*, March 12, 1972.

Ballantine IPA essentially died McLeod, "Articles—B."

"Anheuser-Busch's quality"; an annual summer event Bilger, "Better Brew."

"Miller Lite was parading"; "You're walking into the biggest" Author's interview with Bill Covaleski for Tom Acitelli, "Why Some Craft Brewers Are Embracing Pilsner," *SevenFifty Daily*, March 7, 2019, https://daily.sevenfifty.com/why-some-craft-brewers-are-embracing-pilsner/. In addition to its IPA, called HopDevil, Victory had also released packaged and on draft Victory Festbier and Brandywine Valley Lager before it packaged Prima Pils.

Prima Pils topped Eric Asimov, "Finding Gold in a Glass of Pilsner," *New York Times*, March 30, 2005; Eric Asimov, "Take These Out to a Ballgame," *New York Times*, April 27, 2009.

"Our top beer"; "alive in the mouth" Asimov, "Finding Gold."

"It's a beer of great finesse" Oliver, *Brewmaster's Table*, 241.

both astounded and titillated; "When you travel" Smit, *Heineken Story*, 244.

"more toward the bland" Asimov, "Finding Gold."

boosted production; despite its unavailability "SAB Miller Buys Chinese Brewery," BBC News, January 4, 2007, http://news.bbc.co.uk/2/hi/business/6230107.stm.

5 percent of beer; it overtook America Lily Kuo, "The World's Top-Selling Beer Is a Watery Lager Sold Only in China for $1 a Liter," Quartz, May 22, 2015, https://qz.com/410413/the-worlds-top-selling-beer-is-a-watery-lager-sold-only-in-china-for-1-a-liter/.

would make up 75 percent Douglas Yu, "Chinese Consumers Demand Premium Beer Products," BeverageDaily.com, April 11, 2016, https://www.beveragedaily.com/Article/2016/04/12/Chinese-consumers-demand-more-premium-beer-products.

"each of his predecessors" Knoedelseder, *Bitter Brew*, 2.

"on my watch" Tom Daykin, "Anheuser-Busch Gets Buyout Bid," *Milwaukee Journal Sentinel*, June 12, 2008.

it faced investigations Knoedelseder, *Bitter Brew*, 321.

the largest cash acquisition Ibid., 6.

which was created out of a 2002 In a further sign of the confusion that could surround all this consolidation in the brewing industry, SABMiller operated with Molson Coors as Miller Coors in the United States. Miller Coors was born of a merger between Coors and Canada's Molson.

approved Anheuser-Busch InBev's; third-largest business acquisition Scheherazade Danesh-khu, "Shareholders Back AB InBev and SABMiller L79bn 'Megabrew' Deal," *Financial Times*, September 28, 2016.

was the bestselling beer in Brazil AB InBev brews Skol for the South American market. Denmark's Carlsberg owns the worldwide rights outside South America and Africa. Per Carlsberg Group, "Skol," accessed June 21, 2019, https://carlsberggroup.com /products/skol/skol/.

had acquired the company Ernest Beck and John Reed, "South African Breweries Acquires Pilsner Urquell for $630.6 Million," *Wall Street Journal*, October 8, 1999.

for $7.8 billion "Announcement Regarding the Acquisition of the Beer Business in Central and Eastern Europe," Asahi Group Holdings Ltd. corporate release, December 13, 2016, https://www.asahigroup-holdings.com/en/ir/pdf/16pdf/161213.pdf; Scheherazade Daneshkhu and Kana Inagaki, "Asahi to Buy SABMiller Beer Brands in €7.3bn Deal," *Financial Times*, December 13, 2016.

"The jewel in the sale" Daneshkhu and Kana Inagaki, "Asahi to Buy".

"Loosely, any golden" Michael Jackson, *The Simon and Schuster Pocket Guide to Beer* (New York: Simon & Schuster, 1988), 15.

"the most imitated" Stuart A. Kallen, *The Complete Idiot's Guide to Beer* (New York: Alpha Books, 1997), 82.

Pilsner Urquell underwrote Chris Fuhrmeister, "Watch a Clip from 'Brewmaster,' the New Doc That Claims to Be 'a Love Letter to Beer,'" Eater, November 13, 2017, https:// www.eater.com/2017/11/13/16634558/brewmaster-documentary-trailer-preview.

"Pilsner was the killer app" *Brewmaster* is available for streaming through Amazon Prime.

Epilogue: History Repeated

more than sixty-two thousand "FAQ: Attendees," Great American Beer Festival, accessed June 21, 2019, https://www.greatamericanbeerfestival.com/info/faq/. The author visited both the GABF and the Coors brewery on the Saturday of the 2018 GABF.

the world's largest brewery "Brewing Locations," MillerCoors website, accessed June 21, 2019, https://www.millercoors.com/breweries/brewing-locations (page discontinued).

a pilsner that had its origins "Coors Brewery Tour: History," Visit Golden, via the Wayback Machine, accessed June 21, 2019, https://web.archive.org/web/20150710111503 /http://visitgolden.com/coors-brewery-beer-tours/coors-brewery-tours-history. The best account of the founding and rise of Coors is Daniel Baum's *Citizen Coors*.

"a prize to be smuggled"; Kissinger was a fan Lichtenstein, "Sold Only in the West".

President Gerald Ford David Blend, "15 Things You Didn't Know About Coors Banquet," Thrillist, April 29, 2014, https://www.thrillist.com/drink/nation/15-things-you-didnt -know-about-coors-banquet.

ten million barrels annually "Brewing Locations," MillerCoors website.

about twenty-six million "Brewers Association Releases Annual Growth Report," Brewers Association official website, April 2, 2019, https://www.brewersassociation.org/press-releases/brewers-association-releases-annual-growth-report/.

The beer style guidelines "Brewers Association 2019 Beer Style Guidelines," April 15, 2019, https://s3-us-west-2.amazonaws.com/brewersassoc/wp-content/uploads/2019/04/BA-style-guidelines-2019.pdf.

consistently the bestselling style "Early 2018 Beer Style Trends," Brewers Association official website, May 30, 2018, https://www.brewersassociation.org/insights/early-2018-beer-style-trends/.

perhaps one in three beers Aamna Mohdin, "These Are the 224 Beer Brands That Will Soon Be Owned by Just One Company," Quartz, October 13, 2015, https://qz.com/522694/these-are-the-224-beer-brands-now-owned-by-just-one-company/.

maybe only 15 percent "Brewers Association Releases Annual," Brewers Association official website.

was the most talked-about "Anheuser-Busch InBev Reports Fourth Quarter and Full Year 2018 Results," Anheuser-Busch InBev, press release, February 28, 2019, https://www.ab-inbev.com/content/dam/universaltemplate/ab-inbev/investors/reports-and-filings/quaterly-reports/2019/FY18-Press-Release-Final-EN.pdf.

was a hoppier iteration Pamela Silvestri, "Pizza Rats Pilsner: A Brew Designed for the Staten Island Yankees," *Staten Island Advance*, June 5, 2019. The team is normally known as the Staten Island Yankees, but occasionally goes by the Pizza Rats per a name-changing contest to drum up fan interest.

BIBLIOGRAPHY

T*his is not meant to be an exhaustive bibliography of pilsner, but one of works consulted while writing this book, including those detailing the times during which pilsner evolved.*

Acitelli, Tom. *American Wine: A Coming of Age Story*. Chicago: Chicago Review Press, 2015.

———. *The Audacity of Hops: The History of America's Craft Beer Revolution*. Chicago: Chicago Review Press, 2017.

———. *Whiskey Business: How America's Small-Batch Distillers Are Transforming American Spirits*. Chicago: Chicago Review Press, 2017.

Alworth, Jeff. *The Beer Bible*. New York: Workman Publishing, 2015.

Baron, Stanley. *Brewed in America: A History of Beer and Ale in the United States*. New York: Arno Press, 1972.

Barr, Andrew. *Drink: A Social History of America*. New York: Carroll & Graf, 1999.

Baum, Daniel. *Citizen Coors: A Grand Family Saga of Business, Politics, and Beer*. New York: Harper Paperbacks, 2001.

Bernstein, Joshua M. *Brewed Awakening: Behind the Beers and Brewers Leading the World's Craft Brewing Revolution*. New York: Sterling Epicure, 2011.

Bilger, Burkhard. "A Better Brew." *New Yorker*, November 24, 2008, 88.

Blum, Jerome. *In the Beginning: The Advent of the Modern Age, Europe in the 1840s*. New York: Charles Scribner's Sons, 1994.

Bull, Donald, Manfred Friedrich, and Robert Gottschalk. *American Breweries*. Trumbull, CT: Bullworks, 1984.

Burch, Byron. *Brewing Quality Beers: The Home Brewer's Essential Guidebook*. Fulton, CA: Joby Books, 1986.

———. *Brewing Quality Beers: The Home Brewer's Essential Guidebook*. 2nd ed. Fulton, CA: Joby Books, 1993.

Bryson, Lew. *New York Breweries*. Mechanicsburg, PA: Stackpole Books, 2003.

Burton, Rob. *Hops and Dreams: The Story of Sierra Nevada Brewing Company*. Chico, CA: Stansbury Publishing, 2010.

Calagione, Sam. *Brewing Up a Business: Adventures in Beer from the Founder of Dogfish Head Craft Brewery*. 2nd ed. Hoboken, NJ: Wiley, 2011.

Campbell, Seamus, and Robin Goldstein. *The Beer Trials: The Essential Guide to the World's Most Popular Beers*. New York: Fearless Critic Media, 2010.

Cochran, Thomas C., ed. *The Pabst Brewing Company: The History of an American Business*. Westport, CT: Greenwood Press, 1975; orig. publ. New York: New York University Press, 1948.

Curtis, Wayne. *And a Bottle of Rum: A History of the New World in Ten Cocktails*. New York: Crown Publishers, 2006.

Daniels, Ray. *Designing Great Beers: The Ultimate Guide to Brewing Classic Beer Styles*. Boulder, CO: Brewers Association, 1996.

Debré, Patrice. *Louis Pasteur*. Translated by Elborg Forster. Baltimore: Johns Hopkins University Press, 1998.

Dornbusch, Horst D. *Prost! The Story of German Beer*. Boulder, CO: Brewers Publications, 1998.

Downard, William L. *Dictionary of the History of the American Brewing and Distilling Industries*. Westport, CT: Greenwood Press, 1980.

Eckhardt, Fred. *A Treatise on Lager Beers: A Handbook for Americans and Canadians on Lager Beer*. Portland, OR: Hobby Winemaker, 1970.

Erickson, Jack. *California Brewin': The Exciting Story of California's Microbrewery Revolution*. Reston, VA: Red Brick Press, 1993.

———. *Great Cooking with Beer*. Reston, VA: Red Brick Press, 1989.

———. *Star Spangled Beer: A Guide to America's New Microbreweries and Brewpubs*. Reston, VA: Red Brick Press, 1987.

Gourvish, Terry, and Richard G. Wilson. *The Dynamics of the Modern Brewing Industry*. Abingdon, UK: Routledge, 1998.

Griesedieck, Alvin. *The Falstaff Story*. Publisher unidentified, 1955.

Grossman, Ken. *Beyond the Pale: The Story of Sierra Nevada Brewing Co.* Hoboken, NJ: Wiley, unpublished first part of manuscript.

Heat-Moon, William Least. "A Glass of Handmade." *Atlantic Monthly*, November 1987.

Hernon, Peter, and Terry Ganey. *Under the Influence: The Unauthorized Story of the Anheuser-Busch Dynasty*. New York: Simon & Schuster, 1991.

Hieronymus, Stan. *Brew Like a Monk: Trappist, Abbey, and Strong Belgian Ales and How to Brew Them*. Boulder, CO: Brewers Publications, 2005.

Hillman, Howard. *The Gourmet Guide to Beer*. New York: Facts on File Publications, 1987.

Hindy, Steve, and Tom Potter. *Beer School: Bottling Success at the Brooklyn Brewery*. Hoboken, NJ: Wiley, 2005.

Holl, John. *Drink Beer, Think Beer: Getting to the Bottom of Every Pint*. New York: Basic Books, 2018.

Holland, Lee W. "The Evolution of the Brewers Association of America." Pamphlet. Colorado: Brewers Association of America, 1994.

Hornsey, Ian S. *A History of Beer and Brewing*. London: Royal Society of Chemistry, 2004.

Jackson, Michael. *The English Pub*. New York: HarperCollins, 1987.

———. *Great Beers of Belgium*. 4th ed. London: Prion, 2001.

———. *The New World Guide to Beer*. Philadelphia: Running Press, 1988.

———. *Ultimate Beer*. New York: DK Publishing, 1998.

———. *The World Guide to Beer: The Brewing Styles, the Brands, the Countries*. Englewood Cliffs, NJ: Prentice Hall, 1977.

John, Tim. *The Miller Beer Barons: The Frederick J. Miller Family and Its Brewery*. Oregon, WI: Badger Books, 2005.

Knoedelseder, William. *Bitter Brew: The Rise and Fall of Anheuser-Busch and America's Kings of Beer*. New York: HarperBusiness, 2012.

Lewis, Michael L., and Tom W. Young. *Brewing*. New York: Springer-Verlag, 2001.

Line, Dave. *The Big Book of Brewing.* Andover, MA: Amateur Winemaker, 1974.

MacIntosh, Julie. *Dethroning the King: The Hostile Takeover of Anheuser-Busch, an American Icon.* Hoboken, NJ: Wiley, 2011.

Magee, Tony. *So You Want to Start a Brewery? The Lagunitas Story.* Chicago: Chicago Review Press, 2014.

McCoy, Alfred W. *Beer of Broadway Fame: The Piel Family and Their Brooklyn Brewery.* Albany: State University of New York Press, 2016.

Mittelman, Amy. *Brewing Battles: A History of American Beer.* New York: Algora Publishing, 2008.

Mosher, Randy. *Radical Brewing: Recipes, Tales and World-Altering Meditations in a Glass.* Boulder, CO: Brewers Publications, 2004.

———. *Tasting Beer: An Insider's Guide to the World's Greatest Drink.* North Adams, MA: Storey Publishing, 2009.

Noel, Josh. *Barrel-Aged Stout and Selling Out: Goose Island, Anheuser-Busch, and How Craft Beer Became Big Business.* Chicago: Chicago Review Press, 2018.

Oakes, Josh, ed. *The Beer Guide.* Fort Worth: Savory House Press, 2006.

Ogle, Maureen. *Ambitious Brew: The Story of American Beer.* Orlando: Harcourt, 2006.

Okrent, Daniel. *Last Call: The Rise and Fall of Prohibition.* New York: Scribner, 2011.

Oliver, Garrett. *The Brewmaster's Table: Discovering the Pleasures of Real Beer with Real Food.* New York: HarperCollins, 2003.

———, ed. *The Oxford Companion to Beer.* New York: Oxford University Press, 2012.

Owens, Bill. *How to Build a Small Brewery: Draft Beer in Ten Days.* 3rd ed. Hayward, CA: Bill Owens, 1992.

Papazian, Charlie. *The New Complete Joy of Homebrewing.* 2nd ed. New York: Avon, 1991.

Plavchan, Ronald Jan. *A History of Anheuser-Busch, 1852–1933.* New York: Arno Press, 1976.

Purinton, Malcolm. "Empire in a Bottle: How the Pilsner Lager Became the Imperial Beer, 1842–1930." Northeastern University Department of History Ph.D. dissertation, 2016.

Rail, Evan. *Good Beer Guide Prague & the Czech Republic.* St. Albans, UK: CAMRA Books, 2008.

———. "On the Founding of Pilsner Urquell, Part I." *Beer Culture* (blog), August 29, 2012. http://www.beerculture.org/2012/08/29/on-the-founding-of-pilsner-urquell-part-i/.

———. "On the Founding of Pilsner Urquell, Part II: The Request of the Burghers with Brewing Rights for the Construction of Their Own Malt- and Brewhouse." *Beer Culture* (blog), August 29, 2012. http://www.beerculture.org/2012/08/29/pilsner-urquell -founding-document-of-1839/.

———. "On the Founding of Pilsner Urquell, Part III: Mistakes and Misunderstandings." *Beer Culture* (blog), September 19, 2012. http://www.beerculture.org/2012/09/19/on-the -founding-of-pilsner-urquell-mistakes/.

Schlüter, Hermann. *The Brewing Industry and the Brewery Workers' Movement in America.* New York: Burt Franklin, 1910.

Sismondo, Christine. *America Walks into a Bar: A Spirited History of Taverns and Saloons, Speakeasies and Grog Shops.* New York: Oxford University Press, 2011.

Slosberg, Pete. *Beer for Pete's Sake: The Wicked Adventures of a Brewing Maverick.* Boulder, CO: Brewers Publications, 1998.

Smit, Barbara. *The Heineken Story: The Remarkably Refreshing Tale of the Beer That Conquered the World.* London: Profile Books, 2014.

Smith, Gregg. *Beer in America: The Early Years—1587–1840: Beer's Role in the Settling of America and the Birth of a Nation.* Boulder, CO: Brewers Publication, 1998.

Steele, Mitch. *IPA: Brewing Techniques, Recipes and the Evolution of India Pale Ale.* Boulder, CO: Brewers Publications, 2012.

Unger, Richard W. *Beer in the Middle Ages and the Renaissance.* Philadelphia: University of Pennsylvania Press, 2004.

Van Munching, Philip. *Beer Blast: The Inside Story of the Brewing Industry's Bizarre Battles for Your Money.* New York: Times Business, 1997.

Yaeger, Brian. *Red, White and Brew: An American Beer Odyssey.* New York: St. Martin's Griffin, 2008.

INDEX